vdp

Schriftenreihe
des Verbandes deutscher
Pfandbriefbanken

Band 44

This book is a translation of vdp's publication series, Volume 43:
Flexibilität, Sicherheit und Effizienz der Grundpfandrechte in Europa Band III,
2. erweiterte Auflage
by Otmar M. Stöcker and Rolf Stürner

Translation based on a professional translation service

Berlin 2010

Table of Contents

Foreword

In 1989 the Association of German Pfandbrief Banks (vdp) – at that time under the
name of the Association of German Mortgage Banks (VdH) – began to examine the
legal framework for real estate financing in the individual European legal systems.
Its groups of experts devised lists of questions that dealt both with the topics of
mortgage and land register law, and with the issue of what happens to mortgages in
enforcement and insolvency proceedings. The studies prepared related in each case
to one legal system and contained only occasional comparative law references.

In recent years the need for reports on the law of mortgages covering several countries or even covering all of Europe has sharply increased. The reasons for this lie
partly in the increasing cross-border mortgage business in Europe. The result of this
is that a growing number of people is having to deal with the associated legal questions and the need for getting up to speed quickly with a different legal system is
growing. Comparative reports and overviews make this easier. In addition, the involvement of foreign legal systems in the credit process and, moreover, particularly
in risk management, inevitably results in individual credit institutions having to
develop assessment procedures in order to evaluate the different regulations.

Procedures for assessing legal structures require, in the first place, a detailed description of the different legal systems in accordance with a standard base model. To
develop this is a major challenge. On the one hand, the questions asked must be
worded so generally that they are meaningful for all the legal systems involved. On
the other hand, the degree of detailed analysis must be as high as possible in order
that the strengths and weaknesses of the individual legal systems can be truly understood – and all while taking careful account of the framework conditions of individual business models or types of business. Thus, different legal questions are to
some extent relevant in the case of private housing finance than is the case in relation to commercial property loans.

The vdp has therefore set itself the goal of contributing to transparency in the law
on mortgages in Europe not only in the form of publications relating to specific
countries but also by developing transnational slides that facilitate rapid access to
detailed information and legal facts. It was for this purpose that the so-called "Round
Table: Flexibility of security rights over real property in Europe" was established, in
which mortgage collateral specialists from 24 countries are now involved. 13 national
reports and a series of comparative law slides by authors from this expert group
have already been published in volumes 23 and 32 of the vdp's publication series.
The Round Table is also reflecting the need for a form of neutral appraisal of legal
facts.

Since the crisis in financial markets triggered by the subprime mortgage crisis, if
not earlier, the degree of transparency required of structures within the capital and
banking markets has generally increased. Professionals who deal with several legal
systems in the course of their international mortgage business have, time and again,
articulated their need for clearly set out descriptions of the law of property. Alongside
their function as an information source, publications also have important significance

for the credibility of an assertion or an analysis because they are open to review by a specialist audience, unlike secret legal opinions about complex capital market instruments which cannot be the subject of broad, academic review.

Volume 39 contained a substantial series of slides, displaying a comparative description of the law of security rights over real property for 22 jurisdictions with explanations to the individual questions and answers. On this basis, in two additional workshops of the Round Table on 26/27 March and 5/6 November 2009 in Berlin, an assessment process could be developed, generally and for specific business perspectives. This process and its results are published here in this volume. In addition, with France and Greece 2 more countries could be integrated into the system of slides. As a consequence, in this second edition presented now the number of analysed jurisdictions increases to 24. Vdp is prepared to foster materially scholarly-based development of such evaluation procedures also in future. For this, cooperations with scholars in Sweden and other European countries were initiated with the objective to integrate more jurisdictions into the work of the Round Table.

The authors and the vdp thank all of the Round Table experts who have contributed to the progress of the project by dedicated contributions in the workshops and to the present publication. Particular thanks go to Mr Andreas Luckow for his valuable suggestions for consideration of mortgages and their problems from the distinctive perspective of credit institutions and also to Mrs Rosemarie Hafner for her untiring preparation and updating of the very technically demanding slides. Only through all these contributions has it been possible for the slides to attain the desired degree of transparency and clarity. The authors would like to express their gratitude to HypRating for their transposition of the results of the Round Table into the various spread sheets of the weighting ratios and the tabulation in form of bar graphs.

Berlin, March 2010

Dr. Otmar M. Stöcker   Prof. Dr. Rolf Stürner

A. Introduction and how the slides are arranged

Comparative law accounts of the law on security rights over real property in Europe are rare. Some detailed investigations are targeted at dealing with considerations concerning a Eurohypothec and for this purpose describe only a few mortgage law systems.[1] The studies by the European Mortgage Federation overwhelmingly offer[2] only a superficial overview[3] or merely address some individual aspects in more detailed form.[4] Other works apply only to individual countries[5] or provide a broad picture in the context of a description of the law of property in the form of national reports.[6]

1. Comparative law information requirement

The need for studies into mortgage law is, however, more urgent than ever. This applies not only in respect of the many individual credit institutions that have cross-border operations. Banking groups that operate on a pan-European basis also have to deal with the legal systems of several countries in relation to risk management and group-wide risk weighting rules. Not least, however, for several years in many countries, primarily in Central and Eastern Europe, the civil law systems as a whole have been subjected to scrutiny and have undergone far-reaching modernisation;

---

1   *Kiesgen,* Ein Binnenmarkt für den Hypothekarkredit – Der Vorschlag zur Einführung einer Eurohypothek unter besonderer Berücksichtigung des Sicherungsvertrages [*A single market for mortgage lending – a proposal for the introduction of a Eurohypothec having special regard to the security agreement*], Cologne 2004 – with a description of German, French and Italian mortgage law; Kircher, Grundpfandrechte in Europa – Überlegungen zur Harmonisierung der Grundpfandrechte unter besonderer Berücksichtigung der deutschen, französischen und englischen Rechtsordnung [*Mortgages in Europe – Reflections on the harmonisation of mortgages taking particular account of the German, French and English legal systems*], Berlin 2004; *Stöcker,* Die Eurohypothek – Zur Bedeutung eines einheitlichen nicht-akzessorischen Grundpfandrechts für den Aufbau eines "Europäischen Binnenmarktes für den Hypothekarkredit" mit einer Darstellung der Verwendung der Grundschuld durch die deutsche Hypothekarkreditpraxis sowie des französischen, spanischen und schweizerischen Hypothekenrechts [*The Eurohypothek – on the significance of a uniform non-accessory mortgage for the creation of a "European single mortgage market" with a description of the use of the Grundschuld in German mortgage practice and of French, Spanish and Swiss mortgage law*], Berlin 1992.
2   The study on the efficiency of mortgage collateral in the European Union, Brussels 2002/2007 is a special case.
3   Hypothekenverband bei der EG, Mortgage credit in the European Union, Bonn 1990.
4   Hypothekenverband bei der EG, Vergleichende Studie der Grundstückspfändungsverfahren [*Comparative study of property mortgaging procedures*], Brussels 1979.
5   E.g. *Jaschinska,* Polnische und deutsche Grundpfandrechte [*Polish and German mortgages*], 2004; *Hofmann,* Mortgage and Change. Gestaltungsmöglichkeiten im englischen Kreditsicherungsrecht [*Credit structure options in English security law*], 2002; *Rink,* Die Sicherheit von Grundpfandrechten in Deutschland und England [*The security of mortgages in Germany and England*], 2006; *Schulz-Trieglaff,* Grundschuld und Floating Charge, 1997; *Steven,* Immobiliarsicherheiten im englischen und deutschen Recht [*Real securities in English and German law*], 2002; *Jungmann,* Grundpfandgläubiger und Unternehmensinsolvenz (Deutschland – England – Schottland) [*The mortgagee and company insolvency (Germany – England – Scotland)*], 2004; *Städtler,* Grundpfandrechte in der Insolvenz [*Mortgages in an insolvency*]; *Stürner/Kern,* Grundsatzfragen des US-Hypothekenrechts [*General policy matters in US mortgage law*], Festschrift Schlechtriem, 2003.
6   E.g. *Frank/Wachter,* Handbuch Immobilienrecht in Europa [*Handbook of property law in Europe*], 2004; v. Bar (publisher), Sachenrecht in Europa [*Law of Property in Europe*], Vol. 1, 2000; Vol. 4, 2002; *Baur/Stürner,* Sachenrecht [*Law of Property*], 18th ed. 2009, section 64 B, marginal note 7 et seq. (France, Italy, Spain, England, USA, Switzerland, Austria, etc.); *Sparkes,* European Land Law, 2007.

mortgages figure highly here and the experts involved are very interested in transnational exchanges of opinion and experience. But in Western Europe too the law of security rights over real property has been amended and supplemented in many countries, e.g. by the introduction of the "hypothèque pour toutes sommes" in Belgium (1996), the "hypothèque rechargeable" in France (2007) and by expansion of the scope of application of the "hipoteca de máximo" in Spain (2007). All three changes have been in the direction of greater flexibility in countries in which mortgages had hitherto been among the least flexible.[7]

The vdp therefore ventured at an early stage to initiate and support the exchange of knowledge and practice-related know-how transfer. Motivated by numerous requests, it has been involved since 1993 in the modernisation of the mortgage and land register law in many countries. The proposal initiated by it for a non-accessory security right over real property for Central Europe[8] laid the foundation stone not only for a series of legislative instruments on security rights in Central Europe[9], but also for the realisation of efforts towards a Eurohypothec[10]; the most important element of these efforts are the guidelines for a Eurohypothec.[11]

2.   Round Table on flexibility of mortgages

In order to put further investigations on a broader footing the vdp initiated and organised a "Round Table: Flexibility of security rights over real property in Europe". In three two-day discussion sessions based on selected questions contained in the "Basic Guidelines for a Eurohypothec", renowned experts from Bosnia-Herzegovina, Germany, Estonia, Croatia, Austria, Poland, Slovenia and Hungary discussed the doctrinal principles and the practical applicability of the mortgages that exist in their countries and drew up detailed national reports. The results of this Round Table have been published.[12] The detailed national reports on the eight participating countries were compiled at three workshops between June 2005 and May 2006 at which the legal structure of the mortgages, experiences upon the introduction of new types of mortgage, and the utilisation in practice of the most flexible mortgage types were the subject of detailed exchanges of opinion. The most important results of the

---

7   On the fundamental trend towards non-accessoriness cf. previously *Stürner,* Das Grundpfandrecht zwischen Akzessorietät und Abstraktheit und die europäische Zukunft [*The mortgage between accessoriness and abstractness and the European future*], Festschrift for Rolf Serick, Heidelberg 1992, p. 377 et seq.

8   *Wolfsteiner/Stöcker,* Nicht-akzessorisches Grundpfand für Mitteleuropa, ZBB 1998, 264 – 270, and DNotZ 1999, 451 – 467 (the English translation – A non-accessory Security Right over Real Property for Central Europe – appeared in Notarius International 2003, 116 – 124). The text is also reproduced in *Staudinger/Wolfsteiner* (2002), preliminary note 241 et seq. on section 1191 et seq.

9   This applies in particular for the further development of the independent lien (önálló zálogjog) in Hungary and the development of a new benchmark-setting draft law for a property charge (dług gruntowy) in Poland; both types of security rights over real property reflect on the German land charge created to secure a claim.

10   For the development of the various proposals cf. *Stöcker,* Die grundpfandrechtliche Sicherung grenzüberschreitender Immobilienfinanzierungen, Die Eurohypothek – ein Sicherungsinstrument mit Realisierungschancen, WM 2006, p. 1941 et seq. (p. 1945 et seq.); this contribution was published in English translation: *Stöcker,* Real estate liens as security for cross-border property finance, The Eurohypothec – a security instrument with real prospects, Revista Crítica de Derecho Inmobiliario, Madrid 2007, p. 2255 et seq.; *Baur/Stürner,* Sachenrecht [*Law of Property*], 18th ed. 2009, section 64 marginal note 76 et seq.

11   Cf. in more detail D.III.

12   *Stöcker* (ed.), Flexibilität der Grundpfandrechte in Europa [*Flexibility of mortgages in Europe*], Volume I, Berlin 2006 (vdp's publication series, Volume 23).

workshop were included in the appendix in the form of slides; four additional countries were taken into consideration in the process.

These discussion sessions were continued with the inclusion of additional countries. Workshop IV took place in September 2007. The number of legal systems represented there increased from 12 to 15. New national reports relating to Norway, Romania, Russia, Serbia and the Ukraine were compiled and these were published in Volume II, the articles on Norway and Serbia in English.[13] Using the list of questions used for Volume I, the workshop again addressed fundamental topics such as the structure and scope of accessoriness or non-accessoriness and protection of the owner, and also issues of relevance in practice, e.g. the extent to which modern forms of credit can be secured by the relevant mortgages and how mortgages can be adapted to constant changes in economic circumstances.

The results obtained to date have shown that in many countries where mortgages have an accessory structure, the type of security right primarily used is the maximum amount hypothec. This has, to some extent, a very high level of flexibility, but only as long as the owner and creditor do not change. An in-depth academic reappraisal of mortgages in Europe from a comparative law perspective will not be completed for a long time yet. There is a great need for comparative law investigations into the structural linking of loan agreement and creation of the mortgage, the issue of allocation of the burden of proof, as well as acquisition in good faith and the use of unconditional promises of payment.

One of the issues focussed on at Workshop IV was the further development of detailed slides. Separate new chapters were added covering enforcement law and insolvency law. Copies of these slides were not included in Volume II as they had already become very voluminous and they were, moreover, to be the subject of a separate analysis which has been published in German as Volume III.[14] This volume has also been translated into English.[15]

Workshop V on 4/5 September 2008 in Berlin saw the participation of experts from additional countries to work on the further development and revision of the slides, the central subject matter of Volume III, so that the number of legal systems represented in the slides has grown to 22.

Workshop VI on 26/27 March 2009 developed an assessment system.[16]

The central issues of workshop VII on 5/6 November 2009 were the evaluation of the results of this assessment system, the updating and integration of the information on particular jurisdictions into the slides and the integration of two more countries (France and Greece) into the system of questions and answers of the Round Table.

---

13 *Stöcker* (ed.), Flexibilität der Grundpfandrechte in Europa [*Flexibility of mortgages in Europe*], Volume II, Berlin 2007 (vdp's publication series, Volume 32).
14 *Stöcker/Stürner* (ed.), Flexibilität, Sicherheit und Effizienz der Grundpfandrechte in Europa. Volume III, Berlin 2008 (vdp's publication series, Volume 37).
15 *Stöcker/Stürner* (ed.), Flexibility, Security and Efficiency of Security Rights Over Real Property in Europe, Volume III, Berlin 2009 (vdp's publication series, Volume 39).
16 More about this outrightly under 3. and in more detail under D.II.

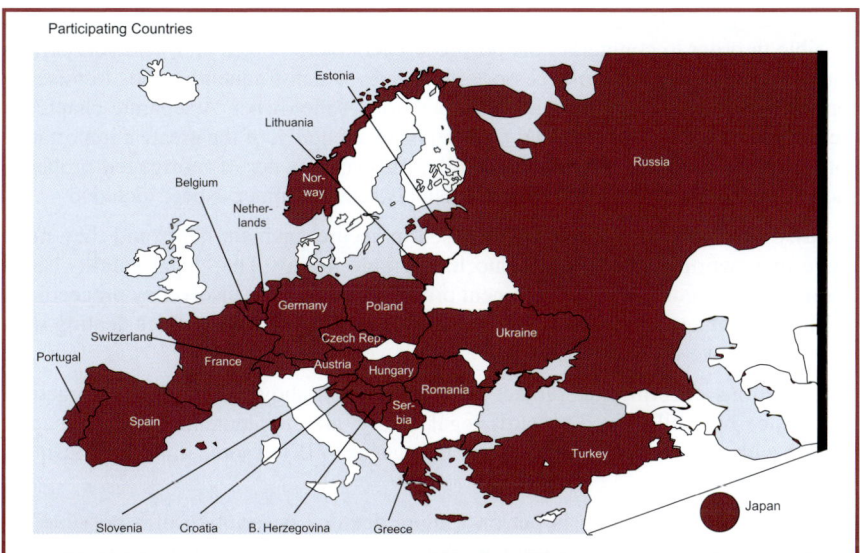

When these slides were being discussed there was constant cross referencing to the proposals in the "Basic Guidelines for a Eurohypothec". The present text thus also makes reference to this future model insofar as this appears useful and informative.

3.   Assessment system for mortgages

The scope of the topics covered in the slides not only increases the value of the slides for an exchange of knowledge in the context of the impending modernisation of the law of mortgages on a national level and across Europe. It also offers credit institutions that operate across borders the opportunity to obtain important information on a multiplicity of legal systems in an easily comprehensible format which they can take into account in the context of an internal rating system in accordance with Basel II for assessing the loan securities used by them.[17] This topic will be gone into in more depth in D.II. This has given a new dimension to the work of the Round Table, to which workshops VI and VII were designated.

The present 2nd edition of volume III does not only document the approach to the development of the assessment system, but also the details of the weighting and assessment ratios as well as the results of the assessment in form of bar graphs.[18]

4.   How the slides are arranged

The commentary on the slides about the law of mortgages is divided up into seven subject areas.

Following some basic remarks on types of mortgages (I.), central issues regarding register systems, and how they bring about the requirements of public disclosure for mortgages, are addressed (II.).

---

17   On the subject of an internal rating procedure for the purposes of capital backing of credit risks cf. the website www.hyprating.de; on the legal monitoring required for this, vdp, Annual Report 2007, p. 32.

18   These bar graphs are published in chapter E.

The discussion of the effects of accessoriness (III.) draws as many distinctions as possible in order to counteract the normally encountered black and white classification into accessory and non-accessory mortgages which frequently leads to misconceptions, in particular with regard to protection of the owner. A separate chapter is therefore devoted to this issue (IV.), which is, incidentally, of the greatest importance not only for consumers but also generally, for every owner of mortgaged property, and it is therefore dealt with comprehensively, the consumer aspect included.

Security rights over real property are used to secure payment debts and they must prove their worth if the debtor is no longer able to pay. The "legal solidity" of a mortgage in the context of enforcement proceedings (V.) and insolvency proceedings (VI.) is thus of key importance for credit practice. The numerous slides dealing with these issues take account of this.

The questions covering the subject areas mentioned above, which are of practical importance but still geared towards legal theory, are supplemented with a chapter dealing with the practical application of mortgages (VII.) in some important business cases.

Another focus of the study is put on a more detailed description of a possible assessment system for the legal framework for mortgages in Continental Europe (D.). It is intended to offer an initial overview as to how the "legal soundness" of security rights over real property could be comparatively "measured" in a general or a bank-specific manner, or in accordance with the particular type of business. It does, however, not demand to be a fully developed econometric international comparison.

The works of the Round Table even at their actual development already attracted the attention of banking practice, as documented by the use of the results by Hyp-Rating.[19] Also academics begin to discuss the issues of the Round Table.[20]

---

19 See D.II.4.
20 See *Dürr*, Schweizerisches Zivilgesetzbuch, Teilband IV 2b, Das Grundpfand, Rdnr. 444 ff.

B. List of participating experts

The quality of the information offered in the slides would not be possible without the excellent technical knowledge and great commitment of the individual country experts. They are also due special appreciation for the fact that, both in the workshops and in their contributions towards development of the slides, they mastered German. By virtue of the joint historical roots of the Roman civil and continental common law traditions, the concepts relating to the law of mortgages in Continental Europe can be expressed more precisely in German than in English.

A brief introduction to the experts who contributed to the development of the slides is given below.

Sibylle Barent, lawyer, licenciée en droit, has worked since 2007 for the Association of German Pfandbrief Banks in the area of "Covered Bond Law and International Business". She completed a banking training with Deutsche Bank AG and studied law in Berlin and Paris. After an internship at the Oberlandesgericht [Higher Regional Court] Bamberg, she worked for three years as a lawyer in a civil law notaries' practice in Berlin.

Dr. Jens Bormann, LL.M. (Harvard), is Chief Executive of the Federal Chamber of Notaries in Berlin. After studying in Constance, Geneva and Harvard and internship in Freiburg he worked for several years as a research assistant at the University of Freiburg and since 2002 he has been a candidate notary with the Chamber of Notaries of the Rhineland. Appointed in 2005 as division head for commercial and company law at the Federal Chamber of Notaries, he has been in charge of their office since 2006. Dr. Bormann lectures at the Jurisprudence Faculties in Freiburg, Göttingen and Hanover.

Dr. András Gábor Botos, Secretary General, Association of Hungarian Mortgage Banks (Magyar Jelzálogbank Egyesület), Budapest, graduated from the Faculty of Law at Pázmány Péter Catholic University in 2001 and studied commercial law at the Institute of Post-Graduate Legal Studies at the Faculty of State Law and Jurisprudence, Eötvös-Loránd University of Sciences in Budapest. Since 2004 he has been Director of the Association of Hungarian Mortgage Banks.

Dr. Agnieszka Drewicz-Tułodziecka has been President of the Polish Mortgage Credit Association (Association of mortgage lenders) (Fundacja na Rzecz Kredytu Hipotecznego) in Warsaw since 1995. Along with the largest mortgage institutions she oversees legal reforms to improve the flexibility and efficiency of mortgage financing in Poland. Polish Parliament expert and adviser to the government expert committee, she is also a member of the executive committee and of several committees of the European Mortgage Federation in Brussels. She is the author of numerous publications on the Polish system of real estate financing and has conducted more than 80 specialist seminars and conferences on the subject of mortgage financing in Poland. She is a lecturer at the University of Warsaw.

Dr. Petr Dušek is a banking lawyer with GE Money Bank in Prague, Czech Republic. After his studies at the Law Faculty at Charles University in Prague and at the Institute of Foreign Relations in Moscow, he worked for five years in the Czech

Foreign Ministry and thereafter for 9 years as legal counsel with the HypoVereinsbank Czech Republic. Since 2003 he has also had special responsibility for debt recovery and also for banking law at GE Money Bank. In 2008 he became legal adviser to the Mortgage Commission of the Association of Czech Banks.

Ieva Lukrecija Erstikyté is a lawyer with the firm of Raidla, Lejins & Norcous in Vilnius, Lithuania. Her main areas of practice are property and construction law, with an emphasis on project development and financing. She completed a two-year post-graduate course on German and European Union law at the Centre for German Law (Lithuania). She gained further experience in the area of real estate financing during her time as a visiting lawyer with the international law firm Allen & Overy in Frankfurt am Main.

Dr. Klaus-Peter Follak is director with a major international real estate finance institution. In various roles he was, among other things, head of funding transactions, head of legal and regulatory affairs and joint project manager for the implementation of Basel II group-wide. He has many years of experience in the international real estate finance business, in particular in the business areas of covered bond issue and in international banking supervisory law. He is a member of various committees in the banking industry and of the committee on International Monetary Law of the International Law Association and has advised various Central and Eastern European states in relation to the development of their banking and real estate financing sectors.

Aleksandra Gregorowicz has worked since 2000 as a legal adviser with the Mortgage Credit Foundation (Fundacja na Rzecz Kredytu Hipotecznego) in Warsaw. She is responsible for legal issues relating to mortgage credit and the harmonisation of registration practice at the land registry courts. She assists in the legislative process in the area of mortgage financing.

Kurt Haefeli, lic. iur., lawyer, is legal counsel with UBS AG and has many years of experience as a banking lawyer with special emphasis on the areas of loans, securities and enforcement.

Laurent Hosana, LL.M. (University of Munich), is a notary in Paris. After studying economics (1996) he graduated in law in Paris (2000) and in Munich (LL.M.). Laurent Hosana lectured French law at the University of Jena (2000). During his studies in Munich he worked with a notary there during one year.

Prof. Tatjana Josipović, University of Zagreb, Faculty of Law, is a fully tenured professor in the Chair of Civil Law in the Faculty of Law at the University of Zagreb. She is involved in particular with property and land register law. She was a member of the Justice Ministry Commission for the preparation of numerous laws in the area of civil law, such as the law of ownership and other real rights, land register law, regulations for land register transactions, the new succession law etc. She is a member of the Justice Ministry Commission that is preparing regulations for transactions on the electronic land register. She is the author of several books and numerous academic works in the area of civil law and co-author of several monographs.

Y. S. Kaan Kalkan is a lawyer with the law practice of Diem & Partner in Stuttgart, which also has a branch in Istanbul. His main area of practice is construction and property law, including Turkish property and public procurement law, in addition to consultancy work and providing general and legal representation for medium-sized and large companies from the construction and property industries in Germany.

Konstantin Kaysers, M.E.S. (La Coruña), worked as a lawyer with the firm of Dr. Reichmann Rechtsanwälte in Frankfurt am Main until end of 2009. He advised in the area of German-Spanish financial law, commercial and corporate law, and German-Portuguese property and mortgage law. Alongside this he supported clients in relation to the implementation of financing projects in Spain, Portugal and Germany. Now he is head of the International Contract Management at ThyssenKrupp Fördertechnik GmbH.

mr. Hans Kemper, LL.M. (University of Groningen), is a notary and partner with the firm of Schaap & Partners, Lawyers and Notaries, in Rotterdam. His main areas of practice are property law and corporate law. Within property law he specialises in advising on, supervising and completing property transactions, establishing property funds and project development. In the area of domestic and foreign financing and securities, including mortgages, he regularly advises financial and other institutions.

Konstantin Kucherenko completed his studies in private international law at the Taras-Shevchenko University in Kiev in 2005. Since February 2006 he has been employed as legal adviser to the Ukrainian National Mortgage Association (UNIA) in Kiev and is there responsible in particular for the development of legislative initiatives. In addition Mr Kucherenko works as legal adviser to a Ukrainian investment bank. He deals primarily with the law relating to securities, banking, property and covered bonds.

Dr. Tim Lassen, lawyer, Frankfurt am Main/Berlin/Moscow, was employed from March 1998 to September 2005 by the Association of German Pfandbrief Banks (vdp, formerly VdH), Berlin, as legal counsel in the area of "Mortgage Bank Law, International Business and System Marketing". He was, among other things, responsible for the activities of the Association in Central and Eastern European in relation to the introduction of mortgage bank and covered bond systems and improvement of the legal framework for real estate financing. In October 2005 he moved to Eurohypo AG, Eschborn in the "Corporate and Investment Banking" department. Since September 2007 he has been working in the representative office of Eurohypo AG in Moscow and is there responsible for real estate financing in Russia and partly in the Ukraine. He has published several specialist papers on mortgage bank and covered bond law and on real estate financing in Europe. In 2008 he was awarded a doctorate with the thesis "The Mortgage under Russian Law as Loan Collateral" at the Christian-Albrechts University in Kiel.

Andreas Luckow, lawyer, has been Head of International Real Estate Finance at the Association of German Pfandbrief Banks since 2007. From 2002 he worked for the vdp in the area of "Covered Bond Law and International Business" and dealt with transnational issues of real estate finance and mortgage collateralisation. From 1988 he worked for the Berlin Pfandbriefbank, and thereafter for the Berlin-Hannoversche Hypothekenbank, a real estate finance bank in Berlin, in various roles. From 1998 to 2002 he was Department Head International Finance and responsible for cross-border real estate financing. From 1995 to 1998 he was Head of the Central Department with responsibility for legal issues.

Reiner Lux received his degree in Business Administration at the University of Cologne where he majored in banking management, financing and tax law. He began his career in financial controlling at the Bayerische Landesbank Girozentrale in Munich. After various phases in industry he took over the management of HypZert GmbH in 1996. Since 2002 he has, in addition, been Managing Director of Hyp Real Estate Rating Services GmbH (HypRating for short), a 100% owned subsidiary of the Association of German Pfandbrief Banks (vdp). The main focus of HypRating is the continued development of the LGD gradings for the real property asset category (methodology and data pool) and public sector and country rating.

Prof. Dr. Hans Fredrik Marthinussen is associate professor in the Faculty of Law at the University of Bergen where he lectures in property law and insolvency law. He also gives lectures on the right of lien as visiting lecturer at the University of Tromsø. He is particularly involved in researching the relationship between security rights and the secured claim, as well as with credit law development. He wrote his doctorate on the relationship (accessoriness) between the right of lien and the secured claim. In addition he has published several works on property law.

Prof. Tomomi Nakayama has been tenured professor at the Law School of the University of Meiji in Tokyo since 2007. After studying in Kyoto, from 1986 to 1987 he was at the LMU in Munich on a DAAD scholarship under the tutelage of Prof. Medicus. From 1987 he was employed as lecturer, associate professor and tenured professor at the State University of Yamaguchi. From 1999 to 2007 he taught as tenured professor at the University of Toin in Kanagawa.

Prof. Dr. Sergio Nasarre Aznar is an Associate Professor (habil. Professor) in Civil Law at University Rovira i Virgili (Spain). He is the author of 3 books (2 about mortgage market in comparative perspective) and of more than 50 research articles published in 9 countries. He has been visiting researcher and visiting professor in several Universities and research centers around Europe, such as University of Cambridge, University of Oxford, University of Bremen and National University of Ireland. He is engaged in several international research projects about the eurohypothec, international mortgage market and housing.

Dr. Radka Opltová, Ph.D., is legal counsel at the Czech Banking Association (Ceská bankovní asociace) in Prague and member of the Legal Committee of European Banking Federation. After completing her studies at Charles University in Prague she has worked since 1992 with the Ceská obchodní banka in the Strategy and Marketing department. From 1994 to 2008 she was employed as legal adviser by the Hypoteční banka and GE Money Bank; she dealt there with legal issues relating to the mortgage credit business.

Prof. Dr. Meliha Povlakić is assistant professor at the Institute of Civil Law at the Law Faculty of the University of Sarajevo. Her main research interest lies in property and land register law but particularly in the law of collateral security. Her doctorate thesis and other works dealt with the law of collateral security, and in particular with the reform of the law of collateral security in South East European countries from a comparative law perspective. As a member of the expert group that drafted the new law on property rights for Bosnia and Herzegovina, she supported the introduction of the land charge into Bosnian law.

Dr. Armin Reichmann is the founder of the law practice Dr. Reichmann, Lawyers, with offices in Frankfurt am Main and Palma de Mallorca, which he has now headed for more than 20 years. He provides advice in the area of German-Spanish commercial law and in international property and mortgage law. Dr. Reichmann, who is also a sworn interpreter of Spanish, advises clients in relation to financing projects in Spain, Mexico, Brazil and Germany, among others.

Adrian-Stefan Sacalschi, LL.M. (University of Constance), FHB Kereskedelmi Bank Niederlassung Frankfurt, is a Romanian lawyer and studied law and economics in Romania. Thereafter he completed his LL.M. studies at the University of Constance with a master's thesis on a comparison of the German law on covered bonds and the Romanian Covered Bond Act. At present he is deputy head of the FHB Kereskedelmi Bank Frankfurt branch and doing a doctorate at the University of Constance in the area of property and covered bond law.

Ninel Jasmine Sadjadi, LL.M. (University of London), completed law studies in Vienna and a post-graduate course in London and since 2000 has been Project Manager at the Center of Legal Competence (CLC) dealing primarily with consultancy and research projects in the area of land management. From 2004 to 2005 she was employed as a long-term expert in a cadastre and land register project in Romania and ran a project to develop corporate strategic plans and business plans for the Bulgarian land register authority, as well as a transministerial project on restitution, privatisation and construction and planning law in Serbia. In addition Ms Sadjadi is responsible for coordinating all publications by the CLC on the topic of land register and mortgage law.

Dr. Otmar Stöcker has been Managing Director since 2001 of the Association of German Pfandbrief Banks. He has worked for the Association since 1989, heading up the "Covered Bond law and International Business" section from 1997 – 2007. He has dealt extensively with mortgage law and the law of covered bonds in Europe in several monographs (including "Die Eurohypothek") and numerous academic papers. Since 1993 he has acted as a consultant in Central and Eastern Europe in relation to the modernisation of the legal structures for real estate financing. He lectures at the University of Warsaw.

Prof. Dr. Rolf Stürner is Director of the Institute for German and Comparative Civil Procedure at the University of Freiburg, Visiting Professor Harvard Law School 2001, 2003, 2005, co-author of the text book Baur/Stürner, Sachenrecht [Law of Property], 18th edition, 2009 and author of numerous articles and opinions on covered bond law, real property law, and international enforcement and insolvency law. For many years he was President of the Association of German, Swiss and Austrian Proceduralists and member of the Permanent Deputation of the German Lawyers' Council. He is a member of the American Law Institute, Philadelphia, and corresponding member of Unidroit, Rome.

Mario Thurner after working for many years at the Institute for Central and Eastern European Business Law (FOWI) in Vienna, since 1999 has been Project Director of the Center of Legal Competence (CLC), a consulting and research association set up by order of the Federal Council of Ministers in 1998 that predominantly undertakes EU-funded projects in the areas of land law and collateral security law, civil procedure, enforcement and insolvency law, as well as administration of justice in the transition states of Central and Eastern Europe. He has written many publications and presented many lectures at home and abroad, predominantly on insolvency law in the states of Central and Eastern Europe undergoing reform and is a member of the Editorial Board of the Insolvency Law Journal (ZInsO).

Prof. Dr. Rein Tiivel held the Chair of Administration of Justice from 2000 and since July 2006 has been associate professor in the Department for Private Law at the Public Administration College (Sisekaitseakadeemia) in Tallinn. He was involved in drafting the Estonian statute on real property law (1992 – 1993), headed the department in the Justice Ministry for notaryship, the land register and the commercial register (1993 – 2000) and published the text book "Asjaõigus" (Real Property Law, 2003, 2007) and "Kinnistusraamatuõigus" (Land Register Law, 2005), as well as various academic articles in "Juridica", the journal of the Law Faculty at Tartu University on real property and land register law (since 2004).

Jozef T'Jampens has been Legal Counsel Mortgage Credit with the Union Professionnelle du Crédit in Brussells since 1982, member of the Belgian working group "Credit institutions-Notaries-Administration of the Patrimonial Documentation-Mortgage Registrars", member of the Legal Affairs Committee of the European Mortgage Association and of the Mortgage Credit Working Group of the European Banking Association.

Prof. Dr. Matjaž Tratnik is Professor in the Law Faculty at the University of Maribor. He is co-author of the new Slovenian property law code and author of several publications in the area of real property law, in particular the law of mortgages and land register law.

Dimitrios-Panagiotis Tzakas, LL.M. (Hamburg), graduated at the Faculty of Law at the University of Athens and is licensed to the bars of the Athens Courts of first and second instance as a barrister (Dikogoros). Since 2009 he is Research Fellow at the Department of European Law at the Université Catholique de Louvain. He is doing a doctorate at the University of Hamburg (Prof. Dr. Jürgen Basedow) in the sector of International Antitrust Torts Law. During his studies he was awarded a scholarship of DAAD (Deutscher Akademischer Austausch Dienst) and the University of Hamburg.

Dr. Miloš Živković is assistant professor at the Belgrade University Law School and consultant in the law practice Živković & Samardžić. He is co-author of the draft Serbian property law code and is responsible in particular for security rights. He was involved in preparing the draft of a new cadastral register law for Serbia that includes the material on land register law. He is the author of several articles about mortgage law and property register law and wrote his doctoral thesis (in Serbia post-doctoral thesis) about the accessoriness of mortgages.

C. Commentary on the slides

The difficulty with any overview is that it must simplify matters in order for it to achieve any sort of efficiency gain in relation to a collection of detailed information at all. However, any simplification inevitably results in a greater or lesser degree of standardisation and consequently slight falsification of details, which does not sit easily with an academic claim as to the quality of the work. This already applies in respect of comprehensive summaries in table form and all the more so in the case of slides where the information content that can be introduced is even more limited.

Nevertheless, after extensive discussions at the workshops, in view of the abundance of distinctions, this structure was chosen in order to facilitate rapid access and increased clarity by means of the visual format. Academics must note that it is sometimes better to put forward not entirely correct information to the target public than run the risk that the central message fails to get across at all. What is important is that through a balanced choice of topics and questions the possible "error rate" is made transparent in the detailed area, so that it can be left to experts and to further studies to present the requisite refined analysis in specialist works.

In order to tackle this extremely complex task it is first necessary to identify the central questions for assessing security rights over real property and to phrase them in such a way that they are meaningful for each of the legal systems covered here. On the other hand the questions must be asked in such a way that one answer can be given for each legal system, which is correct at least in principle, even if exceptions and anomalies should be disclosed in detail. These are shown in the detailed descriptions of individual countries in the preceding volumes and can only be taken into account in the commentary in important special cases in order not to go beyond the scope of an overview.

The choice of legal systems covered was not made on the basis of academic criteria or according to legal policy objectives, e.g. with the intention of covering the legal systems of all EU states. Instead the content of the slides is the result of an academic and practice-orientated exchange that has grown over many years, which the vdp organised in the context of research, and of the associated build up of a network of contacts with experts from many countries. The participating experts must not only be acknowledged specialists in their national mortgages, they must also have had extensive involvement with at least one and usually several other legal systems so that they bring with them a profound understanding of comparative law and accordingly of transnational issues. The original core of the group of experts is made up of members who are or have been actively involved and play or have played a leading role in legal development in their countries and in the course of this contribute or have contributed to the deliberations concerning a Eurohypothec, at least in the sense of a benchmark for analysing the current position of their own national mortgages. Along with the good knowledge of German that has already been mentioned, a considerable commitment of time was necessary that not all the experts suitable in principle were able or willing to make.

The participating legal systems cover the largest legal families in Continental Europe, albeit with some gaps. The English legal system is missing at present. It has been intentionally omitted for the time being because, for historic legal reasons, the English "mortgage" (or better "land charge") exhibits particular features both from a legal doctrine perspective and in its practical application compared to Continental European mortgages. To have included it, the degree of abstraction in the slides would have had to be sharply increased with the consequence of a far less detailed depth of description.

By contrast, Japanese mortgage law, which is closely related to German and French law, could be included. Prof. Nakayama is an academic with whom the vdp has conducted academic exchanges for many years and who has provided significant support in relation to the vdp's research that began in 2007 into Japanese mortgage and land register law.[21] The example of Japan also shows that some legal systems outside Europe that are strongly continentally influenced can be incorporated without difficulty into comparative law descriptions and assessment systems created for Europe. The fact that the title of the work only mentions Europe and not also Japan is intended to emphasise the focus of the work so that people are not misled into expecting a worldwide investigative analysis.

The commentary on the slides has the following format:

- The meaning of the question labelling the slide is firstly described in the overall context.

- The varied responses are then explained without reference to the individual legal systems.

- Thereafter some of particular features of individual legal systems are mentioned insofar as these may lead to important deviations from the information contained in the slides.

- Each section chapter is supplemented by a coloured slide that shows the legal position in the individual countries.

---

21   The most important results of this research were published by *Stöcker*, Immobilienfinanzierung
     in Japan und deutsche Pfandbriefe, ZJapanR 2009, p. 205 ff.

I.   Types of security rights over real property

1.   How many types of security rights over real property are there?

If one is going to talk about the mortgage law of a country, the first question that arises is whether this legal system only knows one type or kind of security right over real property or whether there are several types or forms, as is the case in most countries. Whether a security right over real property qualifies as an independent type of security right over real property, that is dealt with separately in literature and case law, or as a form differing in detail either as a result of statutory provisions or credit practice, is not to be determined on the basis of strictly applied standardised criteria. Instead this decision has been left to the respective national experts.

In relation to many subsequent questions on other slides, the answer then depends on whether the question and the answer variants are formulated in a sufficiently abstract and general manner that they apply in respect of all types of security right over real property. Where this is not the case then the answer applies in respect of the security right over real property on which slide I.4 is based as the most important type of mortgage and which, in accordance with the aim of the work of the Round Table, is the one with the greatest flexibility.

The maximum amount hypothec, so important in credit practice, can be understood in most cases as a special form of the intrinsically accessory hypothec. On account of its structure, which in many countries is far removed from strict accessoriness, it is, however, in most cases classified by the participating experts as a separate type of security right over real property.

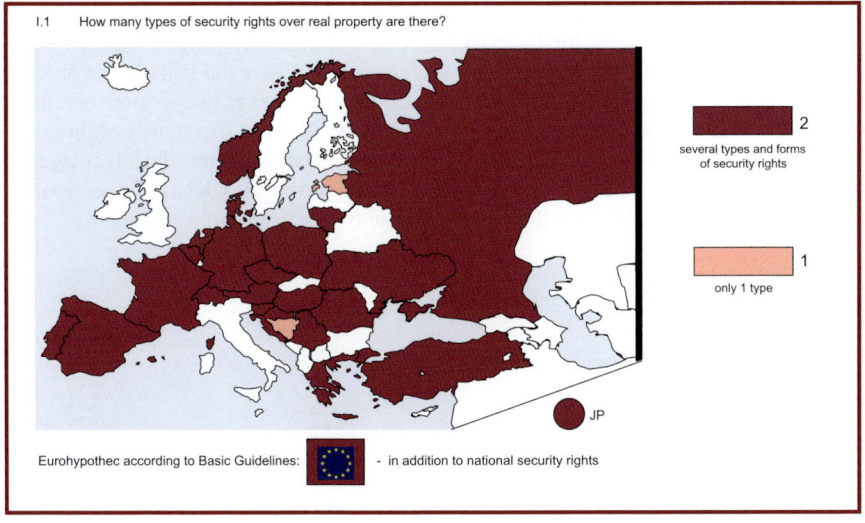

2.   Are mortgages embodied in a security paper (certificated rights) or are they only entered in the register?

The question as to whether a mortgage is only recorded in a register or whether it may (also) be embodied in a deed is of fundamental importance for many reasons.

It is true that the creation of a certificated mortgage is associated with somewhat greater expense, but as a rule registration costs can be avoided on its transfer and transactions can be carried out more quickly. The speed of transactions can, however, also be very rapid with electronic registration systems so that in countries with largely computerised registration systems this difference loses significance in this respect.

It can be observed particularly in Sweden that the well advanced computerisation of the land register is displacing certificated rights which are, in principle, widely used. Sometimes certificated rights survive in theoretical form, but are generally no longer issued as paper documents, being instead only recorded in registers ("virtual certificated rights").[22] The difference between the certificated right and the register right thus begins to become blurred. The legal situation in Denmark is similar, but the issue of certificates there has, in the meantime, actually been prohibited.[23]

Constructive possession under the law of property is, however, possible with certificated rights that are paper-based (issued in document form).[24] This facilitates partial assignments that are effective in rem, making efficient syndication easier. In addition certificated rights may permit insolvency-proof fiduciary arrangements.

The embodiment of a mortgage in a security paper does not necessarily mean that the transfer principles under the law relating to securities are applicable, quite irrespective of the question as to the type of security paper in which a mortgage is embodied. Ultimately it can be seen that the form of the mortgage may indeed have consequences, particularly for its marketability, but this only plays a minor role in countries where an efficient land register system exists. Where the registration process is still time-consuming the circumstances are different, however, and in these countries certificated rights can certainly contribute to an efficient use of security rights over real property, particularly in the area of syndication.[25] Basically it may be advantageous with the current state of computerisation of register systems if a legal system permits both forms so that in practice the best option may be chosen in a given case.

---

22   So-called datapantbrev, regulated in lag (1994:448) om pantbrevsregister. *Marthinussen,* Forholdet mellom panterett og pantekrav (The relationship between right of lien and mortgage claim), Bergen 2009, 12.2.3.1., p. 218, footnote 898 with further references to Swedish law.

23   *Marthinussen,* Forholdet mellom panterett og pantekrav, 11.5., p. 197, footnote 895 with further references to Danish law.

24   On the partial assignment of certificated land charges without partial certificate issue under German law cf. *Picherer,* Sicherungsinstrumente bei Konsortialfinanzierungen von Hypotheken-banken [*Security instruments for consortium financing by mortgage banks*], Frankfurt a.M. 2002 (vdp's publication series, Volume 14), p. 256 et seq.

25   Cf. VII.11.

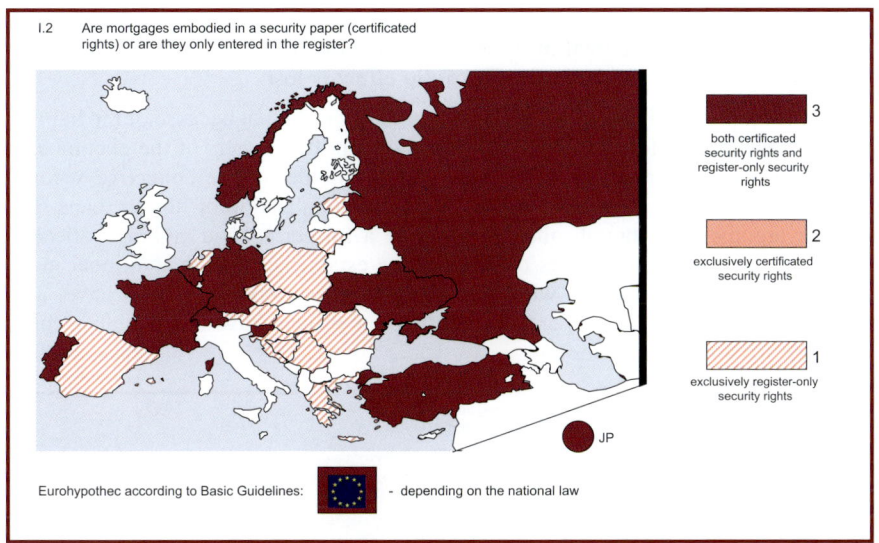

I.2   Are mortgages embodied in a security paper (certificated rights) or are they only entered in the register?

3 — both certificated security rights and register-only security rights

2 — exclusively certificated security rights

1 — exclusively register-only security rights

JP

Eurohypothec according to Basic Guidelines: — depending on the national law

3.   Can mortgages be established on several properties in such a way that the mortgagee can choose from which property to be satisfied?

It happens frequently in practice that the level of a loan far exceeds the value of an individual plot of land. It is then very beneficial as regards the loan accommodation if additional plots of land are also available that can be used to secure the loan. The inclusion of several plots of land in one investment is the rule, when larger properties are built that extend simultaneously over several plots of land.

In many countries the statutory solution is for various mortgages to be established on several plots of land in respect of the same claim. This does usually have the consequence, however, that costs and expenses are incurred for each mortgage separately.

The normal case in Europe is for a single mortgage to be created over several plots of land, in other words a collective security right. A marked reduction in costs and charges can be achieved in this way. For the individual landowner the collective security charge has the positive effect that his in rem liability is reduced to the extent that the mortgagee is satisfied from another plot of land.

For the mortgagee the collective security right has the advantage that the reduction in value of one plot of land may be balanced by the increase in value of another plot of land. The joint in rem liability of the collective security right thus achieves a portfolio effect that can play a significant role precisely in relation to the financing of property portfolios. This is also very useful for the property investor who possibly could not implement his whole project without this balancing and risk-reducing portfolio effect, because one or more of the plots of land could not have been included in the project or could not have been included on the same loan terms without this balancing effect.

Spanish law has a distinctive feature. In principle it does permit the collective security right but the amount of the claim must be divided up among the plots of land so that in each case a calculable share of the loan amount is apportioned on the individual plots of land. The total of these shares is not permitted to exceed the amount of the loan. Accordingly the in rem portfolio effect is lost.

It is frequently argued against the collective security right that because of the liability of each plot of land for the full amount of the loan, the owners of the encumbered plots of land are completely at the mercy of the holder of the collective security charge because there is no more room for the collateralisation of further loans. The counter argument is, though, that in principle a further second-ranking collective security right on the same plots of land can be established for an additional mortgagee. However, particularly with portfolio financing, property values have, as a rule, been used up to such an extent that the plots of land have no suitable security coverage for any further lending.

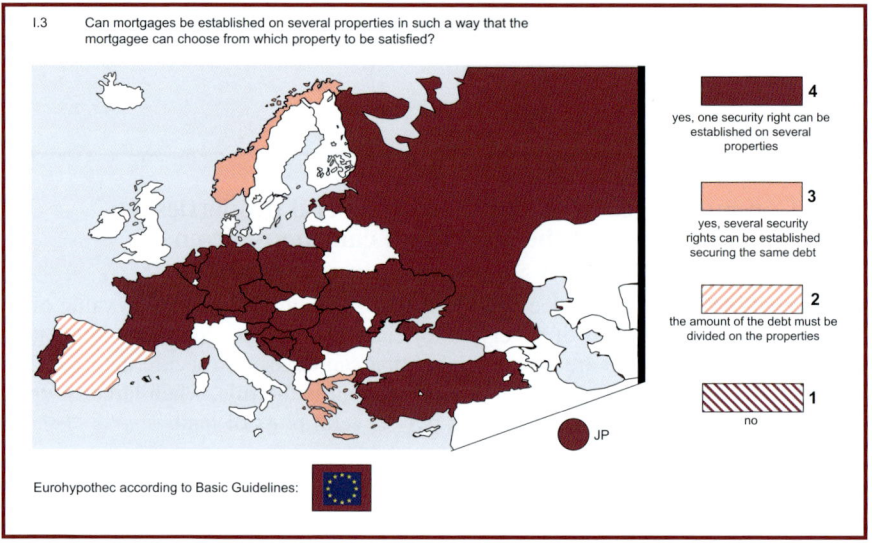

4.   Table of security rights over real property

The chart specifies in alphabetical order of the countries covered the type of security right over real property primarily taken as a basis in this paper and its name in the national language.

In accordance with the objective of the work of the "Round Table", in each case the most flexible type of security right over real property from each legal system is included, even if this is not the most frequently chosen variant in practice, but if it is still at least used with representative frequency.

By way of example, in Turkey the most flexible option would in principle be the mortgage certificate modelled on the Swiss Schuldbrief (debt certificate – cédule hypothécaire) but it is not used in practice in Turkey. The reason for this is that in accordance with section 899 of the Turkish Civil Code the competent land registry would have to issue a valuation of the property to be encumbered, and the state would be liable for any error in connection with this valuation in terms of section 905 Civil Code.[26]

---

26   On the parallel in French law at the end of the 18th Century cf. *Stöcker*, Die Eurohypothek [*The Eurohypothec*], p. 90.

This is similar to French law, where in 2006 the legislator introduced the "hypothèque rechargeable", this being a flexible security right over real property, but so far not commonly used in practice. This edition, therefore, takes the normal contractual "hypothèque" as a basis of the answers regarding France.[27] To finance the acquisition of real property French practitioners regularly refer to the more cost efficient "privilège du prêteur de denier", which, however, employs almost the same legal theory as the contractual "hypothèque".[28]

The following slides show the legal situation of the types of security right over real property mentioned here, which are the most flexible types in their respective legal systems:

Austria	maximum amount hypothec	*Höchstbetragshypothek*
Belgium	maximum amount hypothec	*hypothèque pour toutes sommes*
Bosnia – H.	hypothec	*hipoteka*
Croatia	maximum amount hypothec	*hipoteka do najvišeg iznosa kreditna hipoteka kauciona hipoteka*
Czech Republic	lien on real estate	*zástavní právo k nemovitostem*
Estonia	hypothec	*hüpoteek*
France	hypothec	*hypothèque*
Germany	securing land charge	*Sicherungsgrundschuld*
Greece	hypothec	*υποθήκη (ipothiki)*
Hungary	independent mortgage	*önálló zálogjog*
Japan	maximum amount hypothec	*neteito*
Lithuania	maximum amount hypothec	*maksimalioji hipoteka*

Netherlands	bank hypothec	*Bankhypotheek*
Norway	abstract mortgage certificate	*gjort pantobligasjon* [1)]
Poland	maximum amount hypothec	*hipoteka kaucyjna*
Portugal	hypothec	*hipoteca*
Romania	hypothec	*ipoteca*
Russia	hypothec	*ипотека (ipoteka)*
Serbia	out of court enforceable maximum amount hypothec	*vansudska izvršna hipoteka na najviši iznos*
Slovenia	securing land charge	*zavarovalni zemljiški dolg*
Spain	maximum amount hypothec	*hipoteca demáximo*
Switzerland	debt certificate conveyed as security	*Sicherungsübereigneter Inhaberschuldbrief*
Turkey	maximum amount hypothec	*üst sınır ipoteği*
Ukraine	hypothec	*іпотека (ipoteka)*

1) Since 1999 forbidden to use if the the owner is a consumer according to the Financial Contracts Act

---

27 Regarding "hypothèque rechargeable" see *Aynès/Crocq,* Les sûretés – La publicité foncière, 4th edition 2009, p. 303 et seq.; *Legeais,* Sûretés et garanties du crédit, 7th edition 2009, p. 416 et seq.; *Dagot,* L'hypothèque rechargeable, 2006; *Gourio,* L'hypothèque rechargeable, RD bancaire et fin. No 9/10 2006, p. 39 et seq.

28 See *Aynès/Crocq,* Les sûretés – La publicité foncière, 4th edition 2009, p. 330 et seq.

5.   Is the duration of the security right over real property limited by law?

Security rights over real property are, as a rule, used to secure long term loans. Therefore by far the majority of European legal systems do not provide for any kind of time limit, but instead provide, in principle, for security rights over real property to have unlimited validity.

An absolute time limit imposed by statute on a security right over real property[29] carries the risk that the mortgagee of the claim to be secured loses his security right. The outcome of this is that legal transactions using the mortgage for long-term financing are impeded. This applies in effect also where a time limit is agreed contractually, unless it is able to extend well beyond the duration of the loan. In this case, however, the question in turn arises as to what purpose an optional time limit of this sort is supposed to serve. Sometimes it is provided that the mortgagee may have an extension of the mortgage recorded or registered, such as, for example, in Finland. Regulations of this type may have had at their base the efforts of the 19th Century reform movements to prevent new burdens on land with no time limitation after the abolition of feudal burdens. Today such restrictions appear if anything to be an impediment for legal transactions.

If a security right over real property ends as a result of the term expiring and if it can be extended, the question arises as to whether the same formal requirements have to be fulfilled as applied when it was initially arranged and to what extent reduced formal obligations with lower costs can make an extension easier.

A particular feature is found in Lithuania. There the maximum amount hypothec is automatically converted after 5 years into a normal hypothec without the possibility of this being excluded contractually or any subsequent agreement to the contrary. The consequence of this is that flexibility is then lost.

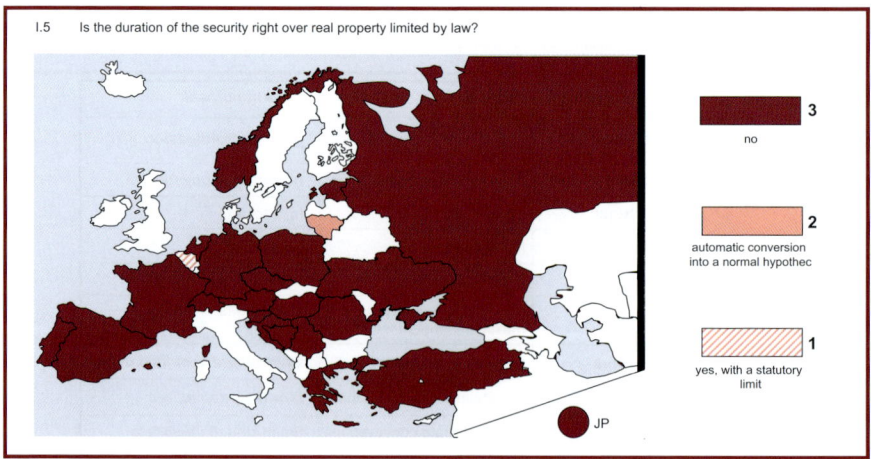

I.5   Is the duration of the security right over real property limited by law?

3 — no

2 — automatic conversion into a normal hypothec

1 — yes, with a statutory limit

JP

---

29   Such a limitation applies e.g. in Belgium and Luxembourg as regards the effect against third parties; by contrast the security right over real property is effective between the parties as long as the secured claim exists.

II. Public disclosure requirements and protection of trust

The security of rights in real property and accordingly also of mortgages is dependent to a very large extent on the reliability and effectiveness of the register system in which rights over land are registered. The reliability of such systems is an essential prerequisite for the security of property transactions in general and for protection of mortgagees in particular. Special importance thus attaches to the protection of reliance on the accuracy and completeness of registration.

Even though in many European legal systems the issuing of documents regarding rights in property was of fundamental importance for a long time, for many years a noticeable trend has been apparent across Europe towards strengthening the significance of registration. It has been supported not least by the development of the computerised register.[30]

1. Who keeps the land register?

Register systems for real property go under widely differing designations. The term land register is going to be used here as this form of register is common in many Continental European legal systems.[31]

In Central Europe the task of keeping the land register is primarily entrusted to land register authorities that are based at the courts. This is particularly the case in countries where, to a greater or lesser extent, legal inquiries are undertaken in the course of the registration.

The desire behind this tradition of court-based operation of the land register is to make legal dealings between private individuals independent of state authorities who could be subject to instructions from the government, and to incorporate the independent justiciary as an element of precautionary administration of justice. If the general guarantee of judicial review of official acts is implemented, as, for example, in Germany (Art 19 para. 4 of the Basic Law [Grundgesetz – GG]), this consideration should, however, have lost some of its original importance, even though the notion of judicially guaranteed independence still has something in it. In many Central and Eastern European countries importance is still attached to this notion, not without reason. It is precisely in these countries that the land register system can benefit from the legal know-how of judicial employees and judges.

In countries where traditionally some authorities exist, which are to a greater extent, not under a duty to comply with instructions, such as in Sweden and Great Britain, for instance, the land register is often run by a central national authority. Where, as in Sweden, quasi-judicial functions within the law relating to adjoining owners and the law of enforcement are allocated to this authority, a close relationship to the judicial system can be seen. In other countries, such as the Netherlands, for example, centralisation was introduced hand in hand with the modernisation of the register because reforms can be implemented more quickly within a centralised agency.

---

30 Cf. above in C.I.2.
31 Only if the purchaser can confine himself to inspection of the land register is the narrower sense of a Central European land register system (Grundbuch) being referred to. The other public disclosure systems are, by contrast, mostly described as property registers or mortgage registers. In this study this distinction is, however, not made as it does not permit sharp dividing lines to be drawn and in addition is not used uniformly in international usage.

It is primarily in parts of Central Europe and in Eastern Europe that the land register system sometimes lies within the jurisdiction of administrative authorities under a duty to comply with instructions. Quite commonly, in the Czech and Slovak Republics, for instance, this can be traced back to the fact that after the end of Communism the land registers were re-established on the basis of the land cadastre with the cadastral authorities playing an important role.

Further afield still, in some provinces of Canada (British Columbia and New Brunswick) and in parts of the Commonwealth, the authorities contract private companies to run the land register.

Nothing can be said about the reliability of the running of the register merely on the basis of how it is classified. What is important is to ensure that as the central source of confidence in the security of real estate transactions, the land register administration is reliable and not subject to interference.

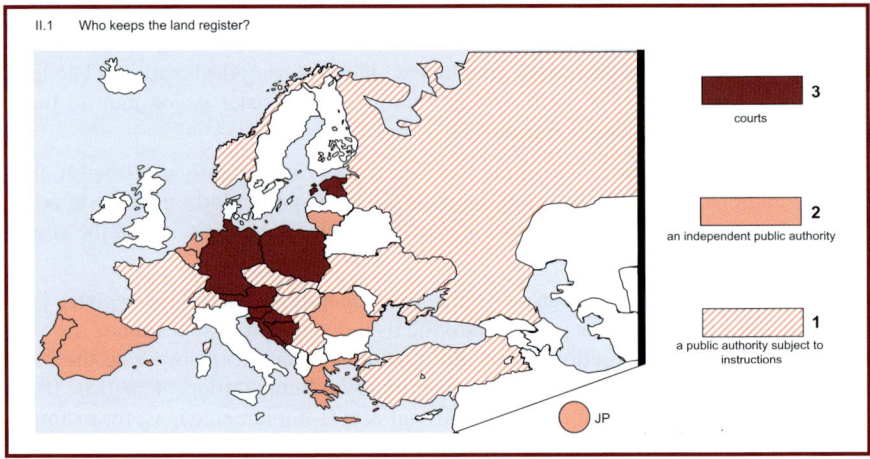

II.1   Who keeps the land register?

3 courts

2 an independent public authority

1 a public authority subject to instructions

JP

2.   Which rights are registered?

Nearly all the legal systems covered here agree that ownership, mortgages and other rights in rem can be registered in the land register. Only as an exception is a special register operated for mortgages.[32] This, however, can also be achieved by a common user surface for the different registers as exists in Lithuania. It is certainly preferable for all rights to be included in one single register so that quick and efficient access to information can be provided.

---

32   On the current situation and on the efforts to bring in reforms in Ukraine cf. *Kucherenko/Lassen*, p. 214 et seq.

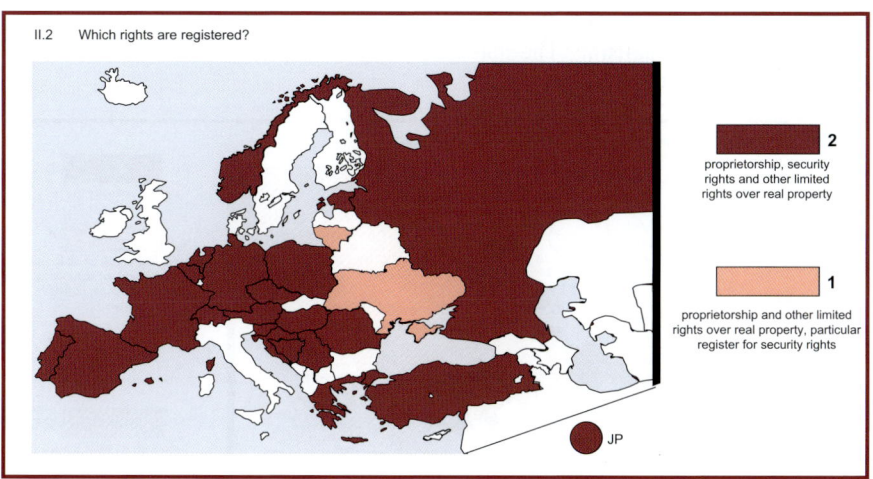

II.2   Which rights are registered?

2
proprietorship, security rights and other limited rights over real property

1
proprietorship and other limited rights over real property, particular register for security rights

JP

3.   Are contracts and disposals over real property concluded before a notary?

The legal situation in Europe is very diverse in relation to the question of what formal requirements apply in respect of contracts and disposals relating to real property. In countries with civil law notaries, notaries usually have a crucial part to play in real property transactions. In many countries involvement of a notary is even a mandatory stipulation of the law; in others it is at least a requirement for later registration and for this reason it is common in practice. In some countries real property transactions are mostly carried out by specialist advocates.

Many countries stipulate that an independent expert who conducts the transaction is consulted as a "neutral third party". The state wishes in this way to ensure the reliability of real estate dealings and the transparency of legal transactions in relation to plots of land. There is manifold public interest in this. Uncertainties and erroneous transactions represent a non-manageable risk for the parties involved, but they also represent a significant non-manageable risk for all third parties who are later involved with a property. If real estate transactions are unreliable, the whole real estate industry and accordingly a considerable part of the national economy may be adversely affected. Quite normal transactions such as the sale of a property with, as far as possible, the simultaneous cancellation of encumbrances and creation of new mortgages, attain a high degree of complexity that requires professional support. It is therefore not surprising that nearly all countries make such an intermediary role either mandatory or commonly refer such transactions to a particular group of persons who regularly handle real estate transactions such as, for example, the specialised advocates (or licensed conveyancers) in England or by estate agents, who are under special public supervision, or banks in Scandinavian countries. If the involvement of a notary is not generally mandatory but does normally happen, such as in Austria, this is a matter of a voluntarily accepted offer of neutral advice. The notary's involvement for recording purposes is often arranged in considerably different ways but the office of notary must certainly be allowed the highest degree of neutrality, intensity of service and professionalism.[33] The state frequently also combines fiscal interests with the involvement of third parties.

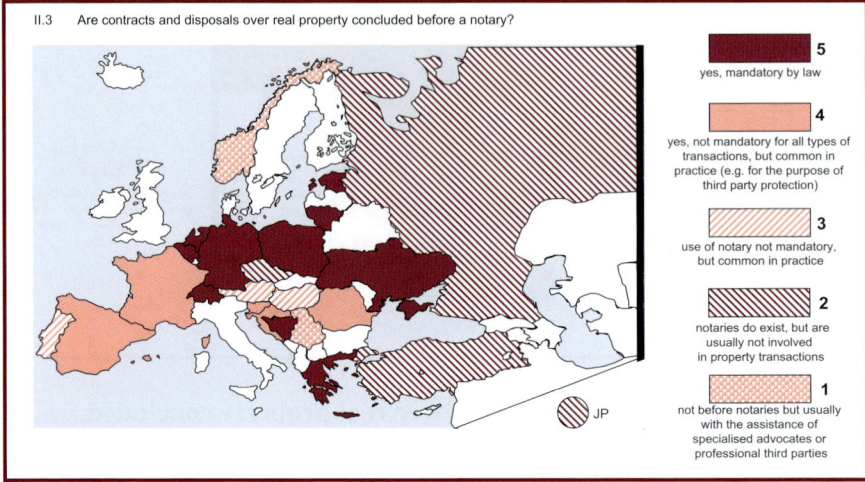

II.3 Are contracts and disposals over real property concluded before a notary?

5 yes, mandatory by law

4 yes, not mandatory for all types of transactions, but common in practice (e.g. for the purpose of third party protection)

3 use of notary not mandatory, but common in practice

2 notaries do exist, but are usually not involved in property transactions

1 not before notaries but usually with the assistance of specialised advocates or professional third parties

4. What is the connection between the land register and the cadastre?

The binding data concerning the location and dimensions of a property is usually recorded in a cadastre. By contrast the legal relationships in real property are published in the land register. It is thus of particular interest who administers these registers and how their legal relationship to one another is structured.

Where there is well-functioning, proper administration it can be an advantage for land register and cadastre to be jointly administered. Predominantly, however, both registers are run separately, with the land register then making reference to the cadastre in order to clarify where the property is situated. It is striking that all the countries investigated here have a cadastre. Reference is, however, made to the UK where there is no separate cadastre[34], but the register with its data on, e.g. boundaries and surface areas seems to this extent also to have no positive disclosure effect.

---

33 An interesting comparison on the significance of the office of notary in relation to real property transactions was produced by *Murray, Peter L.*: Real Estate Conveyancing in 5 European Union Member States: A Comparative Study, August 2007; on this see also *Murray,* There is no free lunch, notar 5/2008, p. 4 et seq. Along with a comparative account the study contains individual national reports on Germany, England/Wales, Estonia, France, Sweden and the USA (Maine und New York); the study describes the relevant legal rudiments of a real property purchase and creation of a mortgage, the course of the transaction and the costs.

34 Cf. *Peter Sparkes:* Real Property Law and Procedure in the European Union, Annotated Draft Questionnaire, Report from England and Wales, project is co-directed by the European University Institute (EUI) and the Deutsches Notarinstitut (DNotI), Würzburg/Germany, http://www.iue.it/LAW/ResearchTeaching/EuropeanPrivateLaw/Projects/Real%20Property%20 Law%20Project/England%20and%20Wales.PDF; LRA 2002 s 2 und s 68(1) (Land Registration Act 2002); *D. A. Hurndall:* England and Wales, 3.2.1 in: Property in Europe – Law and Practice, ed. Anthony Hurndall, London 1998, p. 113; *Robert M. Abbey, Mark B. Richards:* Blackstone's Guide to the Land Registration Act 2002, Oxford 2002, p. 71.

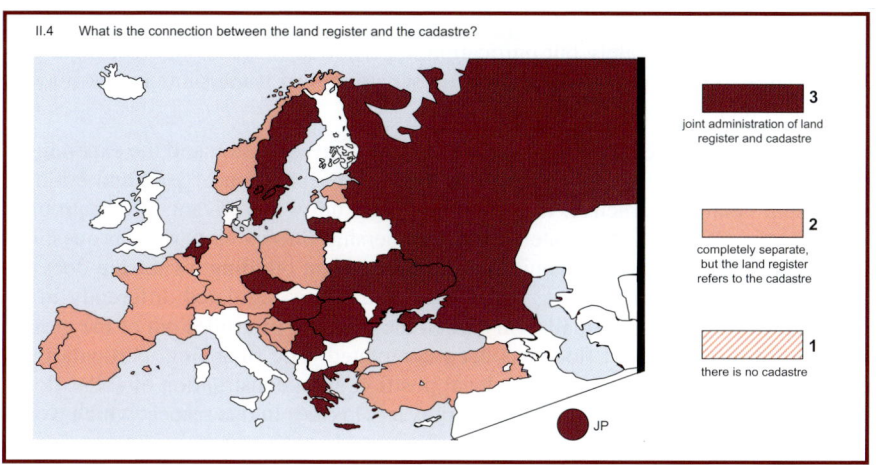

5. Are buildings part of real property (apart from rights equivalent to real property), or are they legally separate and registered separately?

The regulation of the legal relationship between the ground and land on the one hand and the buildings or structures situated on it on the other hand is an elementary component of every property law system with far-reaching consequences for legal clarity, legal certainty and the sequence of processes relating to the granting of a loan secured by a mortgage. Along with issues of the substantive law, the form of the duty of public disclosure under the law of property also plays an important role in this respect.

The principle that applies predominantly is that the buildings are legally an integral part of the plot of land and the transfer or encumbrance of the plot of land automatically applies also in respect of the building (superficies solo cedit). Another topic, not gone into in detail here, is the possibility under many laws of putting rights equivalent to real property as a charge on the property, as it were between the land ownership and the building so that the building then appertains legally to this right equivalent to real property and not to the plot of land.[35]

In Russian law the building is legally not part of the plot of land. However, the recent Russian law aims as far as possible to arrive at a synchronised legal destiny for the building ownership and the land ownership. Thus, the building and the right to the land can only be jointly encumbered with a mortgage.[36]

---

35   These rights equivalent to real property are, e.g. the German hereditary building right (Erbbaurecht), the Dutch hereditary tenancy (erfpacht) and the Polish perpetual usufruct (użytkowanie wieczyste). Rights of this type are basically found in practically all countries, though they are structured very differently in detail. Such rights are in principle unknown in the Czech and Slovak Republics, but the prevailing separation there of plot of land and building is used to achieve the same economic purpose; on the Czech law cf. *Ebner*, Grundeigentum und Sicherheiten in Tschechien [*Real Property and Securities in the Czech Republic*], Berlin 2006 (vdp's publication series, Volume 21), p. 6 et seq.

36   Cf. on this in detail *Lassen*, Die Hypothek nach russischem Recht als Kreditsicherungsmittel [*The Mortgage under Russian Law as Loan Collateral*], Berlin 2007 (vdp's publication series, Volume 30), p. 107; *Lassen*, Das neue russische Katastergesetz, BDVI Forum 3/2009, p. 146 et seq.

Under some legal systems in Europe the ownership of the land and the building are in principle held separately but unification is permitted, whereas in other legal systems both ownership rights always remain separate even if the same owner may be entitled to them.

If one considers the legal problems, the expense of investigation and the expenditure of time required for a real estate transaction that a separation of land and building ownership entails in practice, it is clear that legal unity has advantages on grounds of economic efficiency. Separate building ownership throws up particular questions in relation to the erection of a building, as independent building ownership does not arise with the foundation stone, but instead, and this is regulated differently in individual legal systems, normally only when the building protrudes out of the ground or even when the ground floor has been completed. The financing, particularly of the first construction phase, and the legal position upon construction of cellar floors and underground garages throws up complex legal issues in this respect which would not arise at all in the case of legal unity.

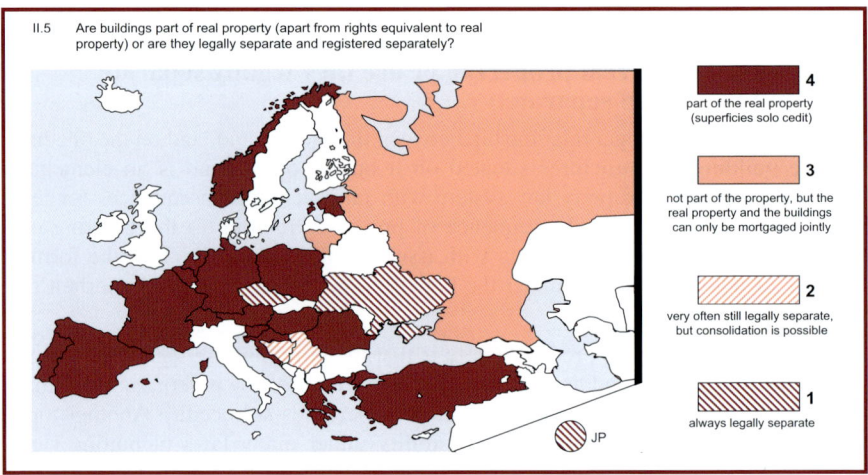

II.5   Are buildings part of real property (apart from rights equivalent to real property) or are they legally separate and registered separately?

4 — part of the real property (superficies solo cedit)

3 — not part of the property, but the real property and the buildings can only be mortgaged jointly

2 — very often still legally separate, but consolidation is possible

1 — always legally separate

6.   Can requests for registration be indicated even before registration of a mortgage?

For legal transactions not only is the reliability and the publicity effect of registration in the land register of importance, but also the issue of how quickly publication can bring about a legal effect. Full implementation of registration should not alone, however, be treated as the determining factor.[37] Instead the entire registration process with its possible antecedent effects must be taken into account. If one also wishes to evaluate the speed of a land registry or register system, account cannot only be taken of the legal consequences that can be achieved by registration but also what protective effects are achievable at certain preliminary stages. From the point of view of a credit institution, this distinction is of decisive importance, particularly for the time at which a mortgage provides effective security.

---

37   This insufficient view forms the basis, however, of the study Mortgages in Transition Economies by the European Bank for Reconstruction and Development (EBRD), London 2007. Cf. D.I.2.

If the matter is examined more closely it can readily be concluded that every legal system links the filing of the application for registration to certain legal consequences. In general, one important legal consequence is the securing of ranking which, particularly in compulsory enforcement proceedings, determines the order of satisfaction out of the proceeds. In addition, in many countries the application for registration also has a security and ranking effect in the insolvency of the owner of the property.[38]

The legal protection brought about in some countries upon the filing of the application for registration is more important than the legal consequences that some countries link to the registration as a whole. The speed of the entire registration process alone therefore says very little about the reliability and efficiency of a land register system. On the other hand it can be concluded that protective mechanisms such as the effect of the registration application, a priority notice or marginal note lose importance if it is possible for registration of the mortgage itself to take place quickly.

In many countries the same security effect can be brought about by a priority period such as exists in the UK.[39]

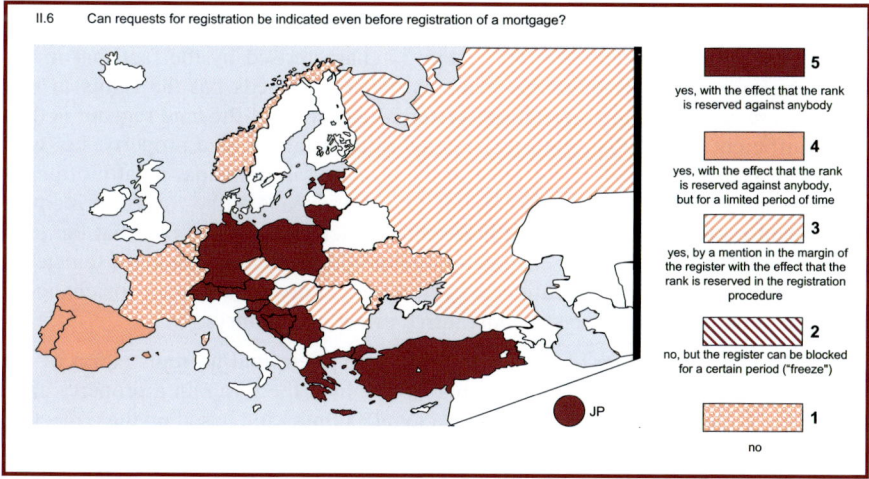

II.6 Can requests for registration be indicated even before registration of a mortgage?

5 yes, with the effect that the rank is reserved against anybody

4 yes, with the effect that the rank is reserved against anybody, but for a limited period of time

3 yes, by a mention in the margin of the register with the effect that the rank is reserved in the registration procedure

2 no, but the register can be blocked for a certain period ("freeze")

1 no

7. How is the grantor's consent to registration verified?

All the legal systems examined make the filing of an application for registration subject to formal requirements, the majority even stipulating the involvement of an expert such as a notary or advocate. A special case is that of Poland where the banks may draw up the formal documents necessary for a land register entry themselves, which is a relic from the time when the banks were state-run.[40]

---

38 Cf. C.VI.7.

39 Cf. LRA 2002 p. 72; *Robert M. Abbey, Mark B. Richards:* Blackstone's Guide to the Land Registration Act 2002, Oxford 2002, p. 72 et seq.

40 *Drewicz-Tułodziecka/Fundacja na Rzecz Kredytu Hipotecznego* (publisher), Nieruchomość jako przedmiot obrotu i zabezpieczenia w Polsce, Warsaw 2008, Part V, Chapter IV.5.5.1, p. 321 et seq. (in German translation: Immobilien, Grundeigentum und Sicherheiten in Polen, Berlin 2009 (vdp's publication series, Volume 42), Part V, Chapter IV.5.1, p. 319 et seq.).

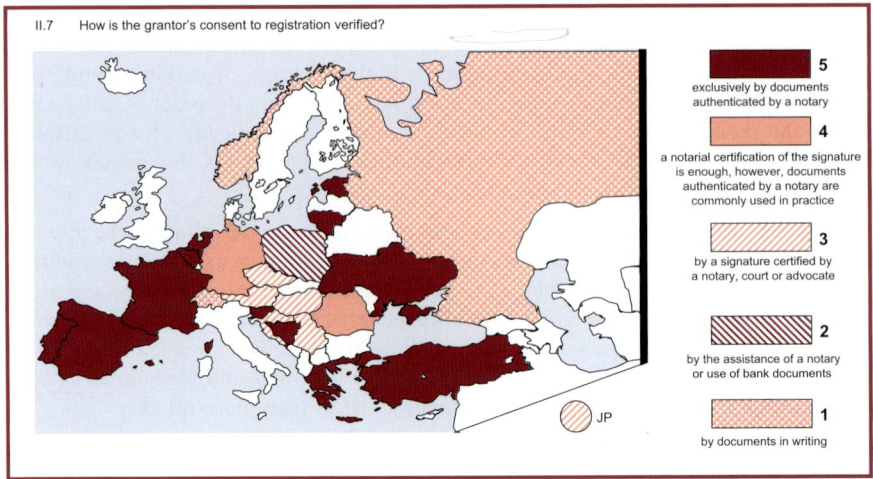

II.7   How is the grantor's consent to registration verified?

5 exclusively by documents authenticated by a notary

4 a notarial certification of the signature is enough, however, documents authenticated by a notary are commonly used in practice

3 by a signature certified by a notary, court or advocate

2 by the assistance of a notary or use of bank documents

1 by documents in writing

8.   What is the basic structure of the register?

The Central European land register system is characterised by the fact that in the land register not only is reference made to registered deeds but the rights in real property are registered in a formalised system. Inspection of the land register is thus often sufficient to establish the precise legal circumstances of a property, i.e. who the owner is and what real rights exist in the property, in particular what mortgages there are and for what (maximum) amount. One thus speaks of the "mirror principle" of the land register.[41] This function is essentially achieved by the fact that the land register maintains one page for each individual property and reliance in the registered content is protected, or registration is even a mandatory requirement for changing the legal situation of a property (constitutive effect of an entry).

By contrast, it is a feature of the French register system that no registration of the rights themselves takes place; documents from which the rights in a property arise are merely collected and registered. Here a legal examination based on the collected, registered documents is necessary in order to build up an accurate picture of the legal situation relating to a plot of land. The situation is similar in many US federal states.

The land register should engender and maintain transactional reliance in the legal circumstances of plots of land with its record keeping. This is naturally very much easier and better possible if the legal circumstances are clearly displayed; the more clearly the legal circumstances are shown, the quicker they can be inspected and consequently a closer relationship is created between registration and the legal situation. It is obvious that a reflection of the legal situation on one sheet of the land register, as in Central Europe, can achieve this more readily and more easily than a system that requires users to carry out their own research to establish the legal situation. It is a logical development, therefore, that countries in the French tradition of mere document collection have introduced the consolidation of the information on

---

41   *Zevenbergen,* Registration of property rights; a systems approach – Similar tasks, but different roles, Notarius International 2003, p. 125 (136 et seq.).

summary sheets.[42] These do not, it is true, contain any legally binding information or documents but, in the Netherlands, for example, they are relied upon in legal transactions on the basis of a process of double checking by notaries and land register experts.

As an exception, slides II.8. and II.11. cover also countries not represented at the Round Table, because information on these issues could be taken from the Eulis project.

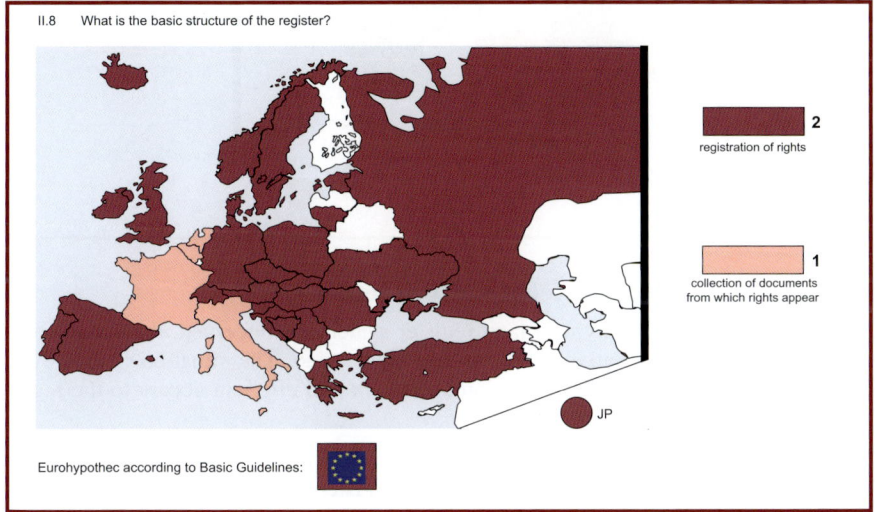

II.8   What is the basic structure of the register?

2
registration of rights

1
collection of documents from which rights appear

JP

Eurohypothec according to Basic Guidelines:

9.   Can anyone inspect the list of current rights in the land register (excluding the actual registered documents)?

Public disclosure by the land register is not possible unless the opportunity exists to inspect the published content. Therefore rights of inspection and actual access are naturally fundamental elements of a land register system.

However, there is a conflict between this right of access and protection of the privacy of those affected by the entries. The consequence of this is that in many legal systems in Europe the right to inspect the land register is restricted, in particular to those persons who can credibly claim to have a legal interest in the inspection. Legal systems that restrict access to particular persons often only grant free access to the individual plot of land and do not allow a search for all the plots of land held by a particular person. In addition, public access to the documents on which an entry is based is limited or even excluded in many countries.

An assessment of the efficiency of a land register system must take these distinctions into account if the protection of the owner, frequently a consumer, is to be given adequate consideration.[43]

---

42   With the reform of the register in 1955 the *"fichier immobilier"* was introduced in France which is intended to show the actual legal circumstances of real properties as indicated in the published documents; cf. *Stöcker*, Die Eurohypothek [*The Eurohypothek*], p. 94 et seq.

43   Here too the EBRD's study has deficiencies in so far as it does not assess this factor at all. Cf. D.I.2.

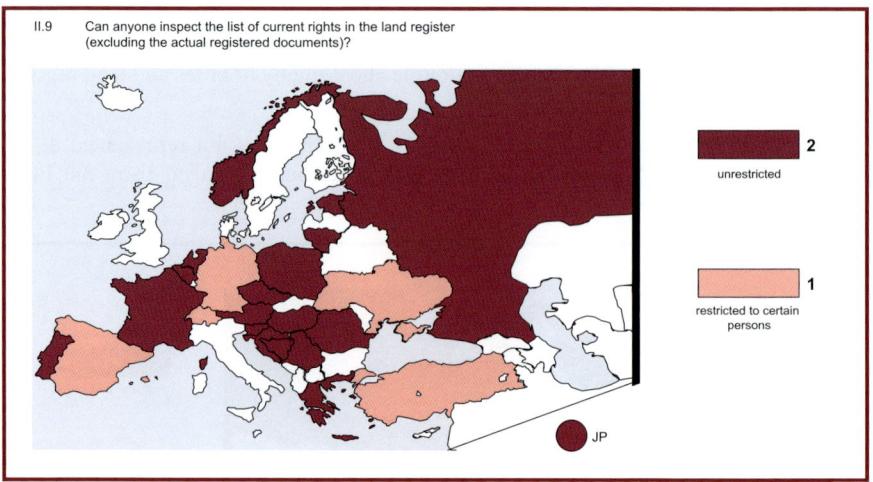

II.9   Can anyone inspect the list of current rights in the land register
        (excluding the actual registered documents)?

2 — unrestricted

1 — restricted to certain persons

10.   How is the register technically designed?

As far as the legal certainty of a land register system is concerned, the status of its computerisation is of relatively little informative value. The situation is, however, different when the speed of registration and quick and efficient access to the registered data are being assessed.

The legal systems investigated exhibit a great variety of responses in relation to the status of computerisation. Computerised land registers are today predominantly run as national electronic databases. But regionally restricted land register inspection is also still to be found in several countries.

The most advanced version of computerisation, namely fully electronic conveyancing (e-conveyancing), where the parties input their applications electronically into an electronic system that processes them automatically, checks the requirements as far as can be ascertained from the land register and triggers the changes in the land register, has up to now only been developed for England/Wales and Scotland.[44] Other countries are, however, moving towards this goal. The extent, to which this notable development will prove to be of value in practice over the long-term, remains to be seen. Longer term the question arises as to its relationship to the precautionary administration of justice in the area of land register law, which is unknown to English law in this way. By reason of the speed and efficiency gain, particularly in the mass market business of small-scale housing finance, the transfer of such a comprehensive electronic transaction system to continental European land register systems should be looked at very closely, with particular regard, however, being paid to compatibility with the security factors provided by the notarial system.

---

44   Cf. in detail *Biederer*, Die rechtlichen Voraussetzungen elektronischer Grundstückstransaktionen in rechtsvergleichender Sicht [*The legal requirements for electronic property transactions from a comparative law standpoint*], Berlin 2006 (vdp's publication series, Volume 22).

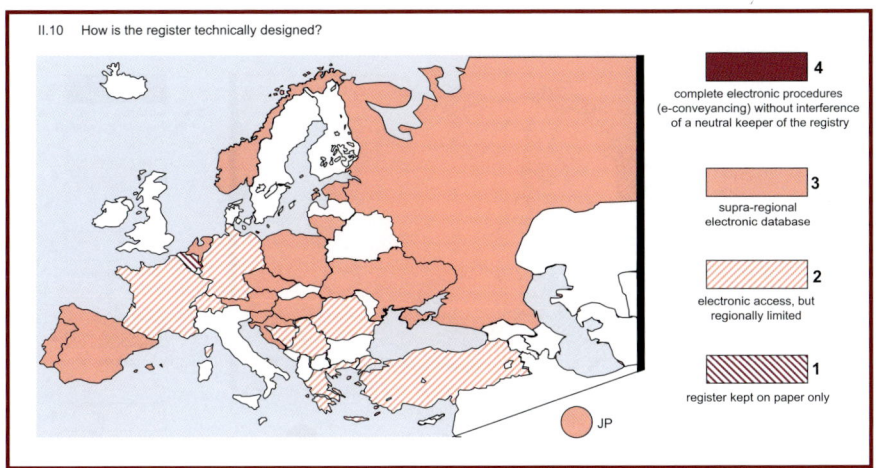

II.10   How is the register technically designed?

4 complete electronic procedures (e-conveyancing) without interference of a neutral keeper of the registry

3 supra-regional electronic database

2 electronic access, but regionally limited

1 register kept on paper only

JP

11. Is electronic access from other countries via EULIS possible?

Even specialist publications have paid little attention as yet to the trailblazing work of the "European Union Land Information System" (EULIS) project. This project was initiated by land registry bodies in Northern European countries. Meanwhile a multitude of European countries are involved.[45] The aim of the project is to create a common internet portal allowing access to European land registers and records. With this aim in mind, not only were land registration and recording systems systematically examined and compared at conferences across Europe, but an in-depth comparative law review of registered rights, including mortgages, was also carried out. EULIS has been in active operation since November 2006. Cross-border inspection of the land register on the networks of various countries in Europe has now become possible.

In 2006/2007 the EU project EULIS+ was carried out. This involved a study which investigated whether and how various Central European countries could be connected to EULIS; some have subsequently opted for a connection. Other countries are looking into involvement in EULIS. A fundamental problem are the differing conditions for inspection of the land register in the individual legal systems; but this can be resolved without standardising all systems.

---

45 *Ploeger/van Loenen,* EULIS – At the Beginning of the Road to Harmonization of Land Registry in Europe, European Rev. of Private Law 2004, 379, 382: "EULIS is a project within the eContent programme of the Directorate-General Information Society of the EU. It is a collaboration between the organizations that provide computerized access to the legal information on real estate of eight European jurisdictions: Austria, England and Wales, Finland, Lithuania, the Netherlands, Norway, Scotland and Sweden. Also, Lund University is involved in the project." On the German side, along with the vdp only representatives from the Federal Chamber of Notaries were involved in EULIS. Cf. also the EULIS website: www.eulis.org; *Zevenbergen,* Registration of property rights; a systems approach – Similar tasks, but different roles, Notarius International 2003, p. 125 (136 et seq.); *European Mortgage Federation,* Mortgage Info October 2007, Computerisation of land registers and of registration of land and mortgage collateral in Europe; *Biederer,* Die rechtlichen Voraussetzungen elektronischer Grundstückstransaktionen in rechtsvergleichender Sicht [*The legal requirements for electronic property transactions from a comparative law standpoint*], Berlin 2006 (vdp's publication series, Volume 22).

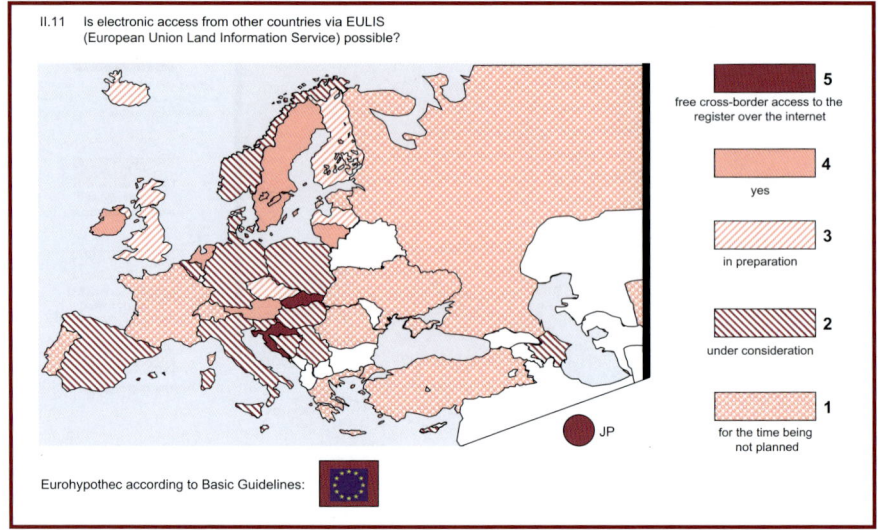

II.11   Is electronic access from other countries via EULIS
        (European Union Land Information Service) possible?

5 — free cross-border access to the register over the internet
4 — yes
3 — in preparation
2 — under consideration
1 — for the time being not planned

JP

Eurohypothec according to Basic Guidelines:

12.   Is the validity of conveyance of real property dependent on registration?

What legal effect registration has is of vital importance for legal certainty in real property law and for the significance of the reliability of a land register system. If, for instance, registration of the conveyance has constitutive effect, a contractual conveyance can only be effected by registration; it is an essential element of the legal transaction transferring the property. Until registration has taken place, the person acquiring the property cannot become the owner either within the relationship between the parties ("inter partes") and certainly not vis-à-vis third parties.

If, on the other hand, registration only has declaratory significance, contractual agreements alone, i.e. processes external to the land register, are constitutive in respect of legal changes between the parties. Nevertheless, registration may, either wholly or partially, protect third party reliance in the declared legal situation, which is of crucial significance for the degree of security of the legal transaction.

It is also in line with economic thinking that mutual trust between market participants is decisive for the proper functioning of an economy (transaction cost motive).[46] While one may accept in relation to many other types of transaction that trust may occasionally be misplaced, the financial significance of land ownership for the parties involved is usually so great that they must be certain of a proper exchange of real property rights and committed capital. At the same time, the legal relationships in real property can be particularly complex. It therefore seems sensible in relation to legal transactions involving real estate to augment the parties' trust in each other by providing a state guarantee for legally binding information. The binding character of this information is decisive for the proper functioning of the real estate industry and accordingly a considerable part of a national economy.[47]

Regulations on protection of trust are closely connected with this topic, as will be seen again later.[48]

---

46   Cf. *Knack/Keefer*, Does Social Capital Have an Economic Payoff? The Quarterly Journal of Economies, Harvard 1997, p. 1251 et seq.
47   Cf. also C.II.3.
48   Cf. C.II.17. et seq.

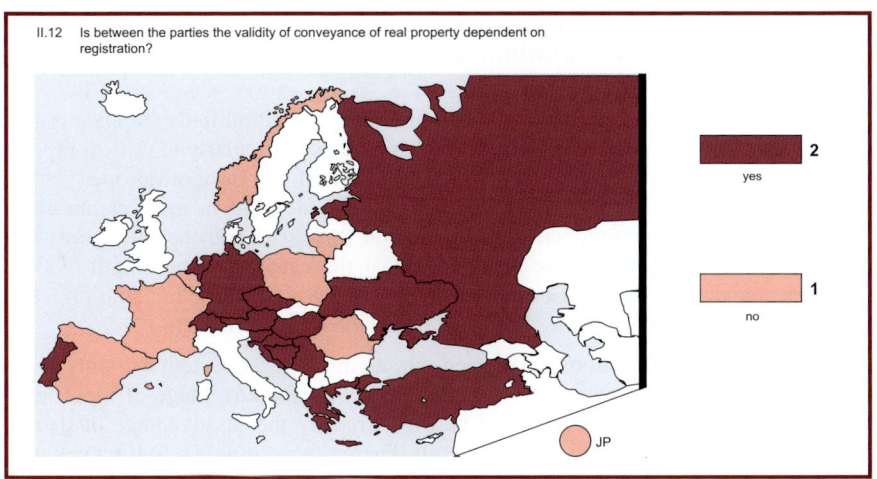

II.12   Is between the parties the validity of conveyance of real property dependent on registration?

13.   Is the validity of the establishment of a mortgage dependent on registration?

The same basically applies here as in relation to the previous slide. However, some legal systems attach greater importance to the need for adequate protection of the legal transaction creating a mortgage than the transaction implementing the sale of a property. Thus, some countries give constitutive effect to registration upon creation of a mortgage while the registration of the conveyance only has declaratory effect.

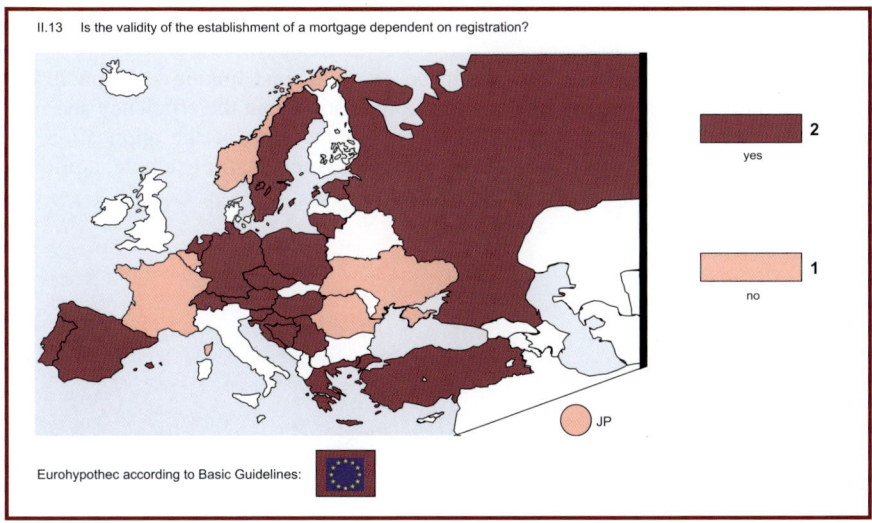

II.13   Is the validity of the establishment of a mortgage dependent on registration?

14. If registration of a mortgage is applied for with all the necessary documentation, how long does registration usually take?

When land register systems are evaluated and analysed simplified reference is frequently made to the speed of registration. This applies particularly to critical reports on the deficiencies in property conveyancing in Central and Eastern Europe.[49] However, too little regard is paid in the process to the fact that in most countries in Europe there are no comprehensive statistics on this issue and the little statistical data there does not differentiate on the basis of the causes for the length of time taken for registration or at least on the basis of the purpose of the registration (constitutive or declaratory, warning function, provisional protection etc.).

However quickly registrations are carried out, a land register system can only serve its purpose if the registrations are reliable. Otherwise the advantage of rapid legal security in the individual case would be countered by the disadvantage of dented confidence in the land register system overall. There is accordingly a conflict between speed, which is certainly a vital aim, and the security of the registration process. In the interests of the functioning of the register, most European countries accord most importance to security, whereas in many parts of the USA, for example, speed is prioritised and the disadvantage that the land register there cannot fulfil the requirements of a secure determination of the legal circumstances is accepted. This means that the services of private providers (title research and title insurance)[50] must be used, who then oppose the introduction of a sound register on business grounds.

Any assertion regarding the duration of the registration process when a mortgage is created can only reproduce an expert's estimate and this is, in any event, made on the assumption that the application for registration is complete and accurate when it is lodged.

In this connection a warning must again be given against linking any conclusion about the duration of registration alone to a conclusion about the efficiency and reliability of a land register system because the legal effects of the application for registration and of any expeditious security devices (such as, for example, a priority notice) are essential for an overall evaluation.[51]

---

49   The EBRD's study, Mortgages in transition economies, also follows this all too simple approach. Cf. D.I.2.
50   Cf. *Baur/Stürner*, Sachenrecht [*Law of Property*], 18th ed. 2009, section 64 marginal note 50 et seq.
51   Cf. also C.II.6.

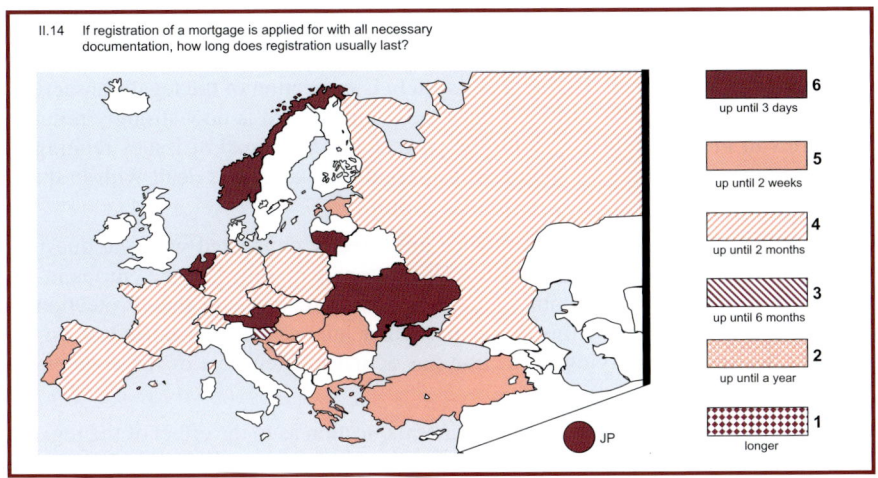

II.14 If registration of a mortgage is applied for with all necessary documentation, how long does registration usually last?

15. Is the validity of the transfer of a security right over real property, which is not connected to a mortgage certificate, dependent on registration?

With complex transactions such as, for example, the sale of mortgage debt in the course of secondary syndication or the sale of loan portfolios, the profitability and, accordingly, the feasibility of a transaction are dependent not least on the amount of expenditure necessary for its implementation. Of no little consequence in this regard is the question of whether registration is constitutive for the transfer of non-certificated mortgages, i.e. whether registration is mandatory for the validity of the transfer of a mortgage or whether other less onerous means guarantee legal effect inter partes and adequate validity towards third parties.

This question is also closely connected with the legal certainty and protection of confidence that the land register can guarantee. Looking at the speed of the transaction in isolation is therefore also not particularly useful here.

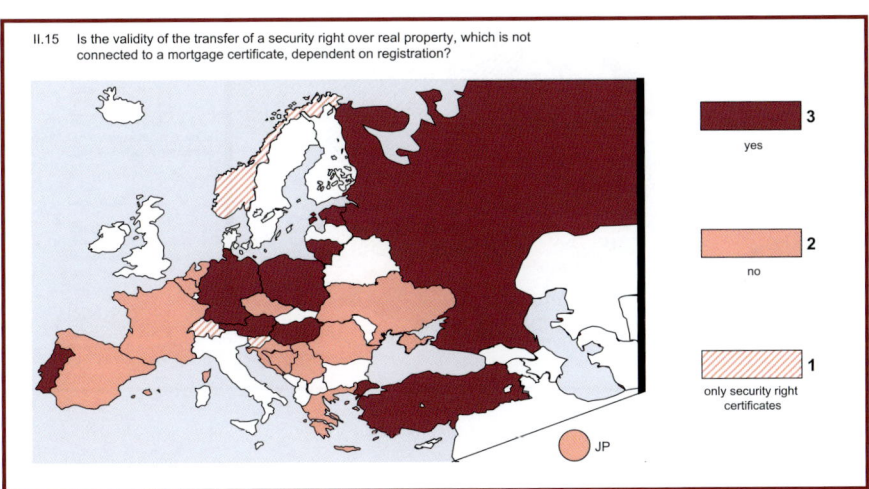

II.15 Is the validity of the transfer of a security right over real property, which is not connected to a mortgage certificate, dependent on registration?

16.   Is the reliance of the acquirer of a mortgage on the contents of the register legally protected?

The central concern of any land register system is protection of the legal transaction. The key question and most difficult question in this regard is how strongly reliance on entries in the land register should be protected. The spread of issues relating to the protection of reliance for the benefit of legal transactions is dealt with in questions 16 to 20.

Regulations on the protection of reliance are directly connected with the question as to what requirements must be fulfilled by anyone who relies on the entries in the land register and wishes to claim a legal position on the basis of this. Protection of reliance in most countries – this merits particular interest – is not dependent on the fact that the person deserving protection has actually taken note of the contents of the land register.[52]

The slide presented here deals with the general question as to the effect of the register system for protecting legal transactions. A major requirement is to avoid, as far as possible, simple disputes about property, e.g. the issue of who the owner of a property or holder of a mortgage is, by means of a public disclosure device.

Both of the following slides concern the key issue as to whether the legal transaction can rely on legal validity and ownership of a right in rem as they are published in the land register, i.e. whether the right in rem was validly created and whether the person disclosed in the land register is entitled to the right. Thus is presumed that the deed creating or transferring the right is effective.

Another question is whether the security right over real property may possibly not exist or be subject to a defence and not enforceable because the secured claim does not exist or no longer exists. This question concerns the effect of public faith in relation to the accessoriness of the security right over real property. Public faith in the land register may also be given priority here. Question C.IV.1 deals with that.

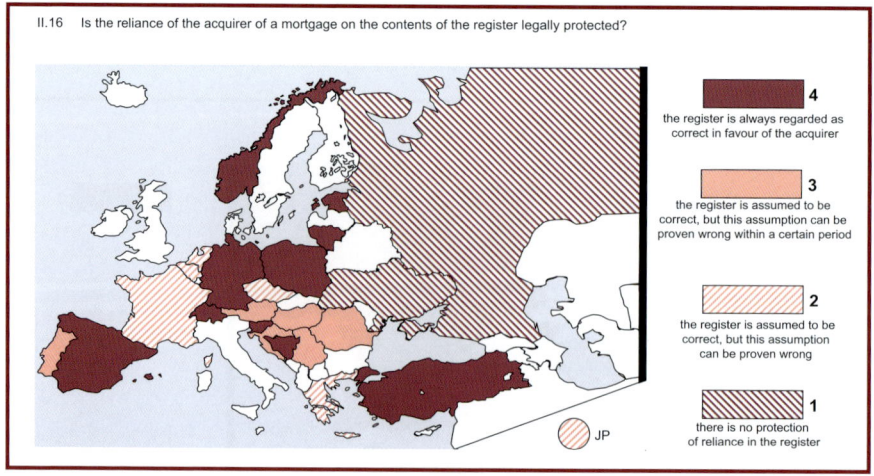

II.16   Is the reliance of the acquirer of a mortgage on the contents of the register legally protected?

4
the register is always regarded as correct in favour of the acquirer

3
the register is assumed to be correct, but this assumption can be proven wrong within a certain period

2
the register is assumed to be correct, but this assumption can be proven wrong

1
there is no protection of reliance in the register

---

52   In the Scandinavian countries, however, the view that good faith is doubtful if the acquirer has not inspected the land register has a strong following.

17. Is the creation of a mortgage effective if done by a mortgagor who is registered as owner but is not the true owner?

The question addressed here is whether the acquirer of a mortgage can rely on the registration of the creator of the mortgage as owner also in the event that this person is not the beneficially entitled party.

In view of the great importance of real estate business for a national economy[53] it is not without consequence that most countries go as far as protecting reliance on the contents of the land register even in the case where a holder of rights who is not registered loses his right or must accept its encumbering with a right in rem without any fault on his part. Where the protection of legal transaction and protection of the beneficially entitled person conflict, protection of the legal transaction is given priority in those places where the law confers positive public faith in the land register. Where this does not happen, the person with true entitlement is in principle given prior protection unless he himself failed to carry out his registration (reliance on the 'silence' of the register, negative disclosure).

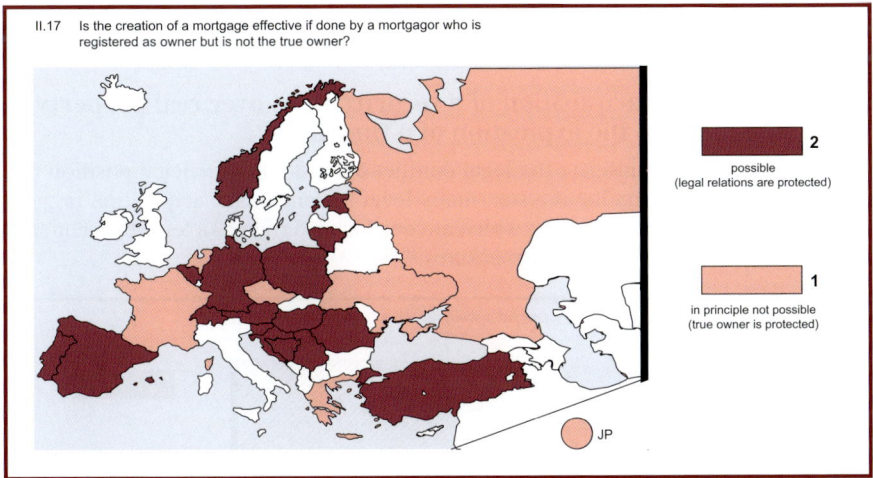

II.17 Is the creation of a mortgage effective if done by a mortgagor who is registered as owner but is not the true owner?

2 possible (legal relations are protected)

1 in principle not possible (true owner is protected)

JP

18. Is the transfer of a security right over real property effective if done by a registered mortgagee who is not the true mortgagee?

The same question arises in relation to the acquisition of a mortgage from a person who is not the beneficial holder of the mortgage but is, however, registered as such. It is interesting that not all answers to this question are the same as the answers given to the question regarding the creation of a mortgage in the previous slide.[54]

---

53 Cf. C.II.12.
54 On the question of protection of reliance where there is no secured claim cf. C.IV.1.

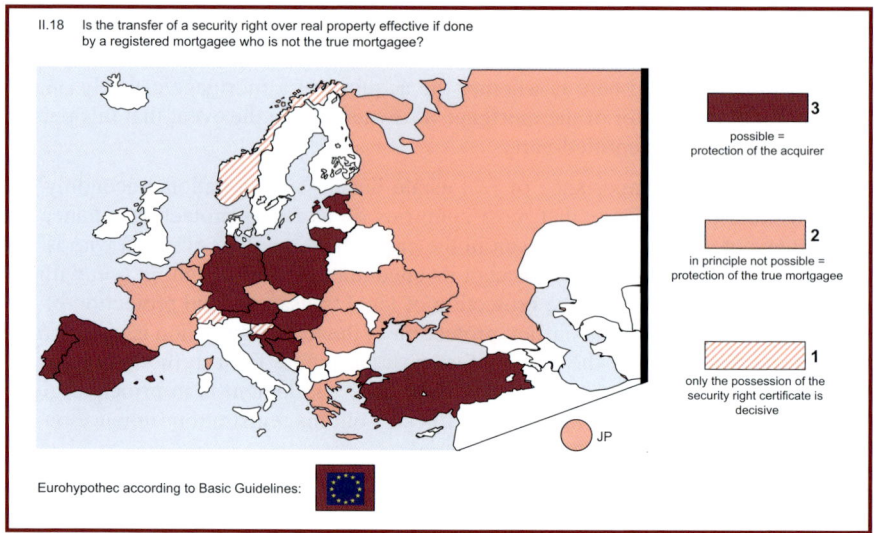

II.18   Is the transfer of a security right over real property effective if done
         by a registered mortgagee who is not the true mortgagee?

3
possible =
protection of the acquirer

2
in principle not possible =
protection of the true mortgagee

1
only the possession of the
security right certificate is
decisive

JP

Eurohypothec according to Basic Guidelines:

19. Is good faith acquisition of a security right over real property dependent on the expiration of a time limit?

In order to somewhat mitigate the legal conflict between the true legal position and the position as shown by the register, many legal systems make acquisition in good faith subject to a time limit during which anyone losing a right as a legal consequence of good faith can initiate counter measures.[55]

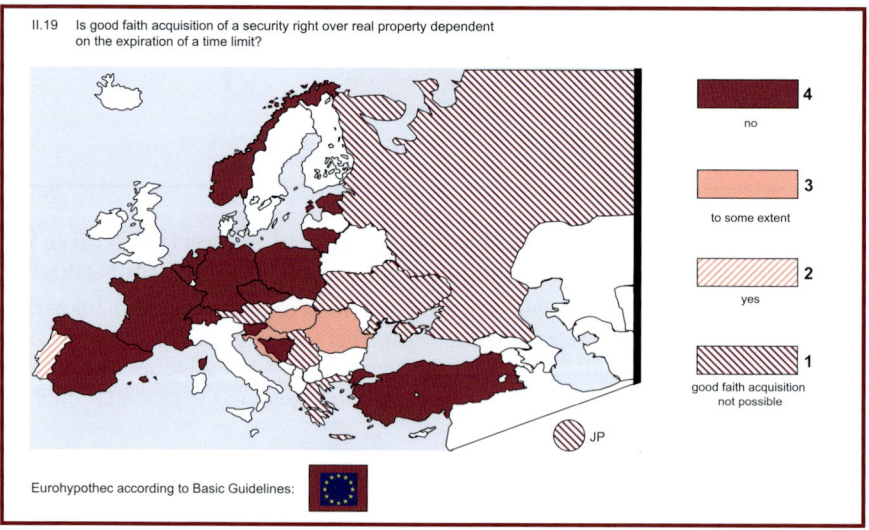

II.19   Is good faith acquisition of a security right over real property dependent
         on the expiration of a time limit?

4
no

3
to some extent

2
yes

1
good faith acquisition
not possible

JP

Eurohypothec according to Basic Guidelines:

---

55   In relation to this question, after expiry of the time limit there is no distinction between the two previous questions 17 and 18.

20. Does an acquirer of property who is in good faith regarding the fact that there is no security right over real property acquire the property unencumbered? (Extinction of a contractual security right over real property)

The question of protection of reliance arises also in the opposite case, namely where the security right over real property does materially exist but is not (or no longer) registered (e.g. because of erroneous cancellation) – and the property is now being sold. In most of the legal systems examined here the acquirer can rely on the completeness and accuracy of the entries in the land register in this respect.

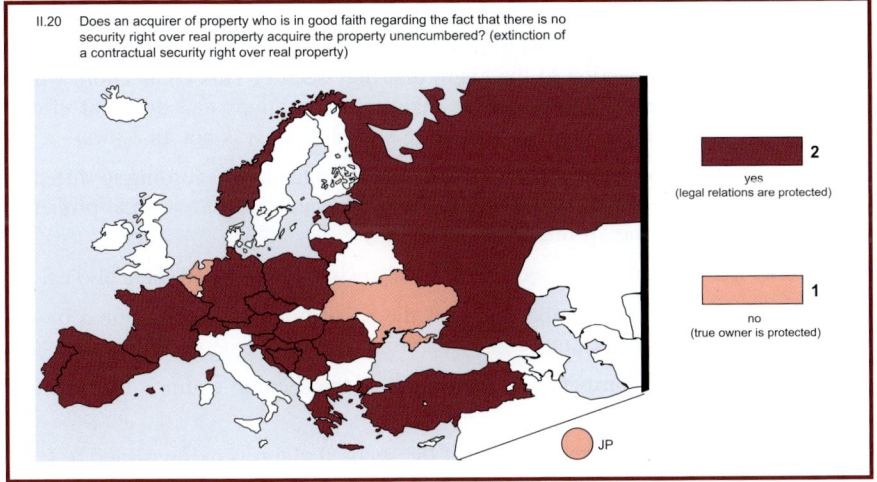

II.20 Does an acquirer of property who is in good faith regarding the fact that there is no security right over real property acquire the property unencumbered? (extinction of a contractual security right over real property)

2 yes (legal relations are protected)

1 no (true owner is protected)

JP

III. Effects of accessoriness

The crucial issue for the legal construction of a security right over real property is its relationship to the secured claim. In classifying security rights over real property both nationally and on a European level, the nature of the legal connection between the security right over real property and the secured claim is therefore also the decisive factor. Accessoriness should not be confused with the issue of whether the creation of the security right over real property must be based on a valid *causa* [legal basis] and whether its absence has an impact on the validity of the security right over real property. This, however, frequently happens in discussions on European level, in particular in connection with the Eurohypothec.[56]

Nearly all European legal systems have security rights over real property that feature a very close legal connection to the claim that they secure. This connection, which is called "accessoriness", has, however, many manifestations and different effects so an approach that does not consider all the varied aspects is not an option.

The types or effects of the accessoriness can be distinguished according to differing conflict situations in which the "secondary" right (security right over real property) has to be adjusted to the "primary" right (claim):[57]

(1) Accessoriness of **origin**: the security right only exists if the secured claim also exists.

(2) Accessoriness of **scope**: the scope of the security right is determined by the scope of the secured claim, e.g. by its amount.

(3) Accessoriness of **competency**: the holder of the secured claim is also entitled to the security right.

(4) Accessoriness of **extinguishment**: if the secured claim is extinguished (e.g. by amortisation[58]) the security right is also extinguished.

(5) Accessoriness of **enforcement**: the security right is only capable of enforcement if the secured claim is also capable of enforcement.[59]

---

56 Regarding the distinction between the accessoriness and abstract nature of the security right and the question of a valid *causa* for its creation cf. *Soergel/Stöcker*, EU-Osterweiterung und dogmatische Fragen des Immobiliarsachenrechts – Kausalität, Akzessorietät und Sicherungszweck [*Eastward expansion of the EU and doctrinal issues of real property law – Causality, Accessoriness and Purpose of Collateral*], ZBB 2002, 412-420; Köndgen/Stöcker, Die Eurohypothek – Akzessorietät als Gretchenfrage? [*The Eurohypothec – Accessoriness, the crucial question?*], ZBB 2005, p. 112 et seq. (114); *Stadler*, Gestaltungsfreiheit und Verkehrsschutz durch Abstraktion – eine rechtsvergleichende Studie zur abstrakten und kausalen Gestaltung rechtsgeschäftlicher Zuwendungen anhand des deutschen, schweizerischen, österreichischen, französischen und US-amerikanischen Rechts [*Freedom to arrange legal relationships and protection of reliance through abstraction – a comparative law study of the abstract and causal formation of contractual appropriations using German, Swiss, Austrian, French and American law*], Tübingen 1996, p. 7 et seq., 600 et seq.; *Baur/Stürner*, Sachenrecht [*Law of Property*], 18th ed. 2009, section 5 marginal note 40 et seq. and section 36 marginal note 76a et seq.

57 Cf. above *Medicus*, Die Akzessorietät im Zivilrecht [*Accessoriness in Civil Law*] JuS 1971, p. 497 et seq.

58 Repayment of the claim then leads to the extinguishment of the mortgage where the mortgage is "accessory in existence", such as, for example, is still the case today in principle (i.e. except for the hypothèque rechargeable) in France. As a result of repayment, however, a subordinate case of accessoriness of competency can also be involved, as, for example, in the case of the German *Hypothek* where extinguishment of the claim leads to the owner acquiring the *Hypothek* which is then converted into an owner's land charge (*Eigentümergrundschuld*) (section 1163 (1) sentence 2 and section 1177 (1) sentence 1 BGB); the German *Hypothek* is thus described as "accessory in competence".

59 A security right over real property that is non-accessory ("abstract") in existence and scope as a general rule lacks enforceability if a claim does not exist or does not exist for this amount, e.g. in the case of the German *Grundschuld*. Another question is whether enforcement under the security right over real property is possible when the secured claim has already become time barred through prescription.

This relationship between primary right (secured claim) and secondary right (security right over real property) cannot be understood by means of a simple question regarding accessoriness or non-accessoriness[60]; it requires an approach that looks at all the varied aspects.

The following slides show how the legal systems investigated here structure the accessoriness of security rights over real property in different ways. As there are several types of security rights over real property in most of the countries, the answers displayed are for the most flexible type, if it is of sufficient importance in practice.[61]

1. If a security right over real property has been created, is it effective even if there is not yet a secured claim? (accessoriness of origin)

The accessoriness of origin addressed here is a characteristic of security rights over real property that is frequently assumed but only actually fulfilled in a few countries. The reason for this is that generally an unspecific inquiry is made regarding the existence of the claim and the security right over real property whereas, if the matter were considered more precisely, preliminary stages of the existence of a claim could suffice and would thus be the more suitable theoretical starting point.

a) Economic interests and practical case studies suggest that the existence of a security right over real property should not be made dependent upon the existence of a claim to be secured, but instead a legal relationship should be allowed to suffice from which the claim to be secured will arise. Even in legal systems in which a concrete claim is necessary, a future claim is also usually sufficient. Drawing a dividing line between a future claim and the legal relationship forming the basis for a claim may frequently be extremely difficult. What is important for this investigation is that it could be established that practically everywhere full accrual of a concrete claim to be secured is not treated as the determining factor enabling formation of a security right over real property.

In several legal systems the security right over real property is designed as non-accessory. This means that neither a claim to be secured nor a legal relationship from which a claim may arise is required for its existence. This legal construction does not change the fact, however, that today the practical purpose of creating a non-accessory security right over real property is to secure one or more claims. The non-accessoriness is merely a legal means of achieving the greatest degree of flexibility between the collateral, i.e. the security right over real property, and the secured claim. It is, however, also clear that a legal connection must be established between security right over real property and claim; this occurs in the security contract or agreement.

---

60   This is the most important and most frequent mistake, regularly leading to a lack of understanding and confrontation in discussions on the Eurohypothec. When accessoriness or non-accessoriness is dealt with in simplified terms as one-size-fits-all doctrine, it makes it very difficult to produce a detailed consideration of the different types of accessoriness or, to put it another way, the effects of accessoriness. It would be better to examine the individual effects of accessoriness in terms of what advantages and disadvantages they have for the parties involved. It would then be possible to develop recommendations on this basis for the structuring of accessoriness or non-accessoriness of a Eurohypothec and also of a national mortgage.

61   Cf. also C.I.1. and 4.

b) This shall quickly be made clear using the example of the German *Grundschuld*.[62] The *Grundschuld*, earlier also known as the "*selbständige Hypothek*"[63], was developed as a technically isolated security right over real property predominantly for funding purposes, i.e. for use by private persons in capital transactions. The aim of it was to make an in rem claim saleable and tradeable on capital markets.[64] This required, on the one hand, its easy transferability; its certificated form served this purpose.[65] It was, on the other hand, important that a subsequent acquirer of the *Grundschuld* (the capital investor) was protected as the new creditor against pleas/objections over which he had no influence. It accordingly enjoyed the greatest marketability and security of circulation among all types of mortgage.[66] Even where it was intended to secure a claim, the choice of the *Grundschuld* meant that the contracting parties wished to favour marketability interests over security interests.[67]

Whilst the draftsman of the Civil Code gave the *Hypothek* priority over the *Grundschuld*[68], the relationship between these two types of security right over real property was soon reversed. In credit practice today the *Grundschuld* is overwhelmingly used by credit institutions, i.e. in considerably over 90% of cases, albeit in the form of the *Sicherungsgrundschuld* [*claim-securing land charge*].[69] With the *Sicherungsgrundschuld* a security agreement stipulates the purpose for which the *Grundschuld* is being created and the length of time the owner must make it available for, i.e. when he can get it back or request its cancellation. This gives rise to a type of contractual accessoriness[70] in a security right that is constructed as non-accessory.

62　For more detail see *Baur/Stürner*, Sachenrecht [*Law of Property*], 18th ed. 2009, section 45; *Stöcker*, Die Eurohypothek [*The Eurohypothec*], Internationale Juristenvereinigung Osnabrück, Annual Report 2007, p. 71 et seq.

63　*Buchholz*, Abstraktionsprinzip und Immobiliarrecht – Zur Geschichte der Auflassung und der Grundschuld [*Abstraction principle and real estate law – the history of the conveyance and the Grundschuld*], Frankfurt a.M. 1978, p. 11 and p. 395. The term *Grundschuld* was favoured as a neutral term in the work on the German Civil Code in preference to the *Realobligation*, the *Realwechsel* and the *Grundwechsel* (*Buchholz*, p. 345). The *Grundschuldbrief* [certificated land charge] was also described as a "bill of exchange [*Wechsel*] in the realm of real estate conveyancing" (*Buchholz*, p. 343, footnote 18 with further references).

64　By reason of its character as isolated security right over real property it was to be free and independent of its loan claim. The legal relationship between owner and acquirer of the isolated *Grundschuld* may appear functionally to be a credit transaction, but legally it corresponds more to a partial acquisition of the property or more accurately to the acquisition of the right of realisation. The *Sicherungsgrundschuld* only developed later, through the contractual commitment of in rem legal power (fiduciary character), from which a contractual limitation on the in rem legal position follows; cf. *Buchholz*, Abstraktionsprinzip [*Abstraction principle*], p. 12.

65　Of all types the certificated land charge made out to the bearer offers, section 1195 BGB, the greatest marketability. It has, however, no practical significance, as little as the *Wertpapierhypothek*; cf. *Staudinger/Wolfsteiner* (2002), section 1195, marginal note 1; *Baur/Stürner*, Sachenrecht [*Law of Property*], 18th ed. 2009, section 47. These types of mortgage with very high marketability were developed in many countries, but today are found very rarely in practice.

66　*Buchholz*, Abstraktionsprinzip [*Abstraction principle*], p. 11.

67　*Buchholz*, Abstraktionsprinzip [*Abstraction principle*], p. 347.

68　*Buchholz*, Wissenschaft und Kodifikation [*Scholarship and Codification*], p. 218 et seq. paints a striking picture of the developmental history of the *Grundschuld* from the 18th Century up to the reform work for the BGB. Doctrinal debates on principles and most notably changes in legal policy had the result that at some stages the *Grundschuld* was to be the dominant type of security right over real property, but at other stages it was to be abolished altogether.

69　Cf. on the unclear statistical position *Stöcker*, Die Eurohypothek [*The Eurohypothec*], p. 25 et seq., with further references.

70　On this term see *Baur/Stürner*, Sachenrecht [*Law of Property*], 18th ed. 2009, section 36, marginal note 77a et seq. and section 45, marginal note 9 et seq.

c) A somewhat different construction arises in cases in which an accessory mortgage is linked to a so-called abstract claim, such as, for example, a bill of exchange or an unconditional promise of payment. So-called parallel debt, which is very common in present day international lending operations, can likewise be grouped in this category. The security right itself must, it is true, be rated as strictly accessory but only in relation to an unconditional promise of payment that exists independently of the parallel debt claim. As in the case of non-accessory security rights over real property, this security structure makes it necessary to stipulate the security purpose and extent of the abstract claim (bill of exchange, unconditional promise of payment, parallel debt) in a security agreement.[71]

Security rights over real property in combination with unconditional promises of payments are found in Norway (gjort pantobligasjon) and Sweden (pantbrev)[72]; the special form of mortgage in Denmark in favour of the landowner (ejerpantbrev) may also belong here.[73] These structures display a clear parallel with the German "abstrakte Hypothek".[74] The linking of an English or American mortgage to a debenture or promissory note shows a similar characteristic.[75]

The combination of a security right over real property with an unconditional promise of payment is also found in Switzerland (Schuldbrief, cédule hypothécaire)[76], in Turkey (ipotekli borç senedi)[77] and in Argentina (letra hipotecaria)[78]. With these rights there exists, in addition, a statutory regulation in terms of which the original loan claim is replaced with an unconditional promise of payment; the loan claim is thus extinguished by novation[79] so that only the non-accessory claim embodied in the security paper is preserved alongside the security right over real property.

---

71 *Lassen*, Russia, in: *Stöcker*, Flexibilität [*Flexibility*], Volume II, p. 108 et seq., critical on the linking of a Russian mortgage with an unconditional promise of payment (parallel debt).

72 In Sweden the mortgage is not created to secure the loan but instead a "skuldebrev", which runs alongside the loan as a separate obligation.

73 The *ejerpantebrev* is not statutorily regulated, but instead was developed by Danish banking lawyers out of the principles of the general law of the *pantebrev* (the Danish certificated mortgage [*Briefhypothek*]). It comes into existence by the owner of a property pledging the property in respect of a claim that is directed towards himself and in respect of this claim and the pledge the land registry issues a security paper, the *ejerpantebrev*. This security paper is pledged by the owner to the creditor by way of security, with the pledge being recorded in a separate agreement. There are thus two pledges: the pledge of the plot of land and the pledge of the *ejerpantebrev*.

74 On this see *Stöcker*, Die Eurohypothek, Internationale Juristenvereinigung Osnabrück, Jahresheft 2007, p. 71 et seq.

75 In many US Federal States it is common to create a mortgage for a promissory note that also produces an obligation that exists independently alongside the loan. In German credit practice too the combination of an unconditional promise of payment along with security by means of a mortgage (Hypothek) was occasionally used, but then given up due to greater ease of use of the Sicherungsgrundschuld; cf. on this "abstrakte Hypothek" *Baur/Stürner*, Sachenrecht [*Law of Property*], 18ᵗʰ ed. 2009, section 36 marginal note 76, section 37 marginal note 18 and section 40 marginal note 45 et seq.

76 On novation with the Swiss *Schuldbrief* cf. *Stürner/Stadler*, Hypothekenpfandbriefe und Deckungs-werte in der Schweiz [*Mortgage bonds and cover assets in Switzerland*], Berlin 2007 (vdp's publication series, Volume 31), p. 13; *Stöcker*, Die Eurohypothek [*The Eurohypothec*], p. 243.

77 This mortgage, whose orientation towards the Swiss *Schuldbrief* follows the receptive influence of the Swiss civil code on the Turkish civil code, is apparently not used in Turkish credit practice. Under the Turkish consumer credit law it may not be created by consumers. Academic research is currently being undertaken into the issue of the extent to which this prohibition is justified. Cf. also C.I.4.

78 Cf. *Cristiá/Stöcker*, Structured "covered bonds" in Argentina, Immobilien & Finanzierung 2007, p. 318.

79 It is undisputed, at least in Switzerland, that this novation effect applies flexibly and so can be excluded contractually (also tacitly), which is the common practice of credit institutions. On the comparable legal position in Russia prior to 1917 cf. *Lassen*, Die Hypothek nach russischem Recht als Kreditsicherungsmittel [*The mortgage under Russian law as loan collateral*], p. 77 et seq.

This short overview with examples shows that, on closer examination, accessoriness and non-accessoriness appear in a variety of forms. This very differing basic structuring of the accessoriness of origin has decisive influence on practical cases, as will be explained under C.VII.

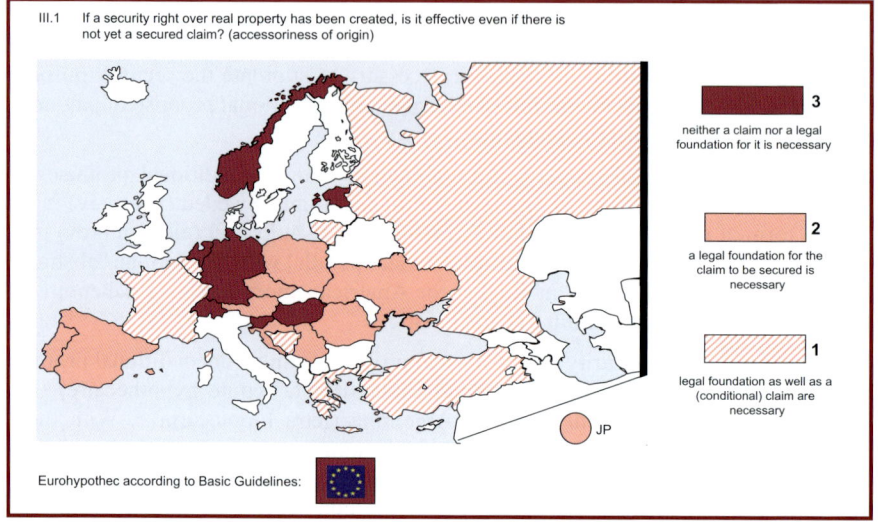

2. Is it possible to register a higher amount for the security right over real property than the size of the secured claim? (accessoriness of scope)

Accessoriness of scope is also generally accepted as an implied characteristic of mortgages and is sometimes even postulated as vital in order to protect the consumer. A study of the legal situation shows, however, that practically everywhere in Europe exceptions are found which predominate in practice without as yet being noticeably problematic or even risky for the consumer.

The most widespread type of mortgage in Europe that is an exception as regards accessoriness of scope is the so-called maximum amount hypothec. Here the accessoriness of scope is relaxed because the secured claim can fluctuate in terms of amount. In Belgium, where for many years the French example of the strictly accessory mortgage was followed, the "hypothèque pour toutes sommes" was created by statute as recently as 1996. By means of the Belgian mortgage "pour toutes sommes" future claims can also be secured, provided they are ascertained or can be ascertained when the mortgage is created. This type of mortgage has quickly become popular in Belgian credit practice.[80]

The problem with many maximum amount hypothecs (e.g. under German and Austrian law) is that a standard maximum amount of liability must be agreed for capital and interest. These maximum amount hypothecs are not subject to interest so the interest that needs to be secured along with the capital and, should the case arise, be enforced compulsorily, must also be included in the capital sum. This has consequences for the setting up of costs and fees.

---

80   The Belgian "hypothèque pour toutes sommes" was modelled on the Dutch bank mortgage but goes beyond its scope of application: it can also secure claims other than bank claims and may also convey its flexibility to an assignee pro rata.

Another important disadvantage in practice may concern the efficiency of any enforcement proceedings. As the capital is only a maximum amount, prevailing opinion in, e.g. Germany is that a maximum amount hypothec cannot be declared to be for immediate execution. This means that the possibility provided in principle in many legal systems for the owner to submit to immediate execution with effect in rem for each future owner (e.g. by means of a notarially recorded declaration) does not exist. Thus, the bank must in principle first of all obtain title by litigation before it can institute compulsory enforcement proceedings. However, many legal systems are not affected by such restrictions, e.g. where each notarially authenticated mortgage deed is executable by operation of law without any further action. The matter of the actual amount of the claim is then determined in accordance with the general rules on the allocation of the burden of proof in relation to the accrual and expiry of claims.

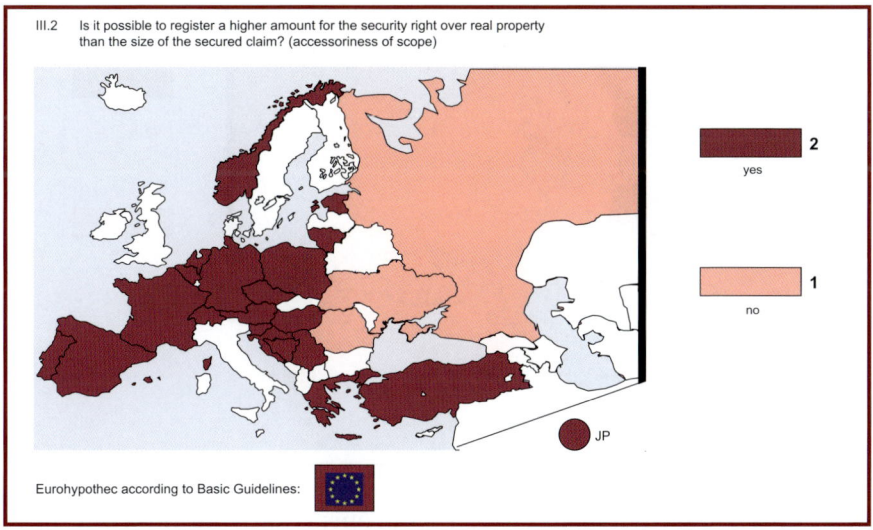

III.2 Is it possible to register a higher amount for the security right over real property than the size of the secured claim? (accessoriness of scope)

2 yes

1 no

JP

Eurohypothec according to Basic Guidelines:

3. Is the creditor of the secured claim by operation of law always the mortgagee? (accessoriness of competence)

This accessoriness of competence can more easily be regarded as an essential core element of the classic accessory mortgage than the other two effects of accessoriness analysed above. It is at least generally accepted that a divergence in the position of mortgagee and holder of the secured claim is not compatible with the principle of accessoriness.[81]

---

81 For the German *Hypothek Staudinger/Wolfsteiner* (2002), Preliminary note 7 on section 1113 et seq. with further references; *Baur/Stürner*, Sachenrecht [*Law of Property*], 18th ed. 2009, section 37 marginal note 11. The reference in *Becker-Eberhard* is, however, interesting: Die Forderungsgebundenheit der Sicherungsrechte [*The binding nature of the claim towards security rights*], Bielefeld 1993, p. 329 et seq.; it is stated here that no justification for the identification rule is to be found in the materials on the BGB; he is of the view that the binding nature of the claim and divergence between proprietorship of the security right and creditorship of the secured claim go very well with each other (p. 331). Similarly, along ago as 1891 *Dernburg*, p. 61: "An advantage that its independence gives the *Grundschuld* is that a different creditor to the personal creditor may be registered as the *Grundschuld* creditor, who can then enforce the *Grundschuld* as fiduciary. ... Certainly a "*Hypothek*" can be established in the same way; for it is not to be expected that the proposition of "gemeines Recht" (19th century German law) whereby a *Hypothek* can only be granted to the personal creditor also applies to the modern *Hypothek*."

This applies both in relation to the creation and the transfer of an accessory mortgage. The maximum amount hypothec thus displays its limited flexibility particularly in the case of a transfer to a new creditor because here the accessoriness applies in the form of accessoriness of competence and does not allow the separation of the security right over real property from the claim. Consequently the claim and the security right over real property must, in principle, be transferred together and claims that are not transferred along with the security right over real property are no longer secured in rem. The broad flexibility within the accessoriness of origin and, particularly, the accessoriness of scope are thereby again restricted. This hampers syndication and accomplishment of the case situations mentioned in C.VII.10. and 11.

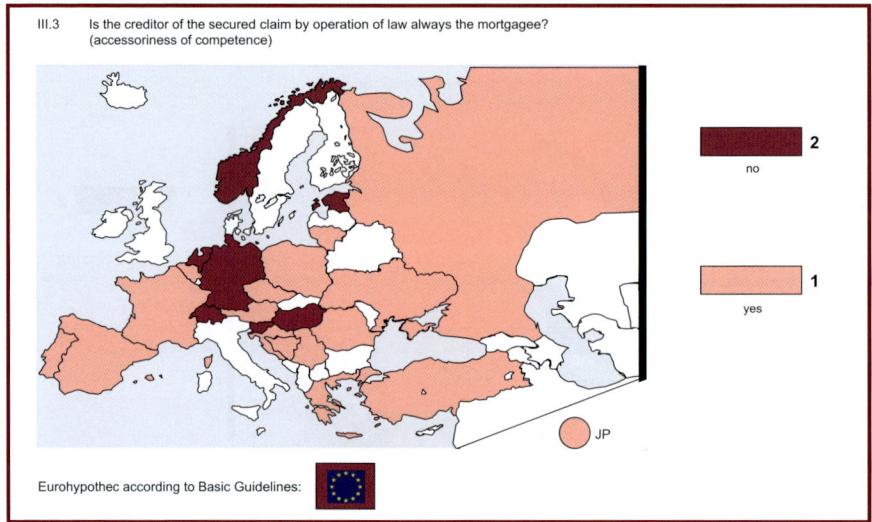

III.3   Is the creditor of the secured claim by operation of law always the mortgagee? (accessoriness of competence)

2 no

1 yes

JP

Eurohypothec according to Basic Guidelines:

4.   Can the security right over real property only be enforced if the secured claim can be enforced?[82] (accessoriness of enforcement)

The accessoriness of enforcement ought to play a greater role in the overall view of the legal doctrine than is usually the case, unfortunately. It may, admittedly, not be of material importance in the view of credit institutions. But it is perhaps the most important element of in rem liability from the owner's point of view if he has to defend himself against unjustified enforcement proceedings. The possibility on the part of the owner to prevent the enforcement of the registered security right over real property where a secured claim is lacking is, from the point of view of legal policy, an important factor on which assessment of the whole system of the statutory regulation of mortgages as balanced and fair depends.

It can be stated in respect of all the legal systems examined, both in relation to accessory and non-accessory mortgages alike, that an owner can defend himself against execution under the mortgage if a secured claim is lacking. However, it must be taken into account in relation to this that the conflict of interest between protection of the transaction and protection of the owner is resolved quite differently. This becomes apparent when the mortgage is transferred, i.e. when there is a change of

---

82   In this regard the question as to whether the enforcement of the mortgage continues to be possible when the claim has become time barred or is inhibited by the time barring of the claim is not considered here.

creditor, and this is wholly irrespective of whether the mortgage is constructed as accessory or non-accessory. In the case of the accessory mortgage, (good faith) acquisition without a claim can be permitted and in the case of the non-accessory mortgage, (good faith) acquisition free of the defence under the security agreement can be excluded, as has recently been introduced in Germany.[83]

In the course of modernising the finance industry and the lending system it was realised some hundred years ago in Europe that too close a link between loan and security right over real property is a constraint on the flexibility of the credit relationship and also hampers funding. Many lawmakers in Europe have therefore considered how they can make mortgages more flexible and, in particular, more easily transferable in order to improve their national lending system. The same interests have always been in conflict here:

- Low cost loans should be facilitated, which necessitated a workable mortgage in order to minimize risk – the law on mortgages and the land register addressed this.

- Third party acquisition of loan claims and mortgages should be made easier for funding purposes – in the law on mortgages and the land register the priority topics of pleas/defences, transferability and the issuing of a deed were involved.

- Protection of the owner/debtor against unjustified compulsory measures should be ensured – this addressed the question as to how the owner can enforce his justified pleas or objections in execution proceedings and how he can safeguard himself against surprise execution.

The national objectives of the individual legislative measures naturally had consequences for the setting of priorities among often completely conflicting interests. When faced with the impact of wretched experiences of a huge demand for capital that could scarcely be satisfied, e.g. for the (re-)development of their country after a war or during an intensely competitive phase of industrialisation, lawmakers focussed on strengthening the legal position of capital investors who were prepared to make a loan or acquire a mortgage from a mortgagee. If one bears in mind the obstacles that had to be overcome in earlier centuries in relation to money and capital movements without an elaborate and comprehensive banking system, without a bank supervisory authority and without a cashless payment system, it is understandable that paramount importance was attached to the mortgage deed when the large-scale monetary economy was in its infancy; and with regard to the matter of pleas and defences following sale and transfer of mortgages, it is understandable that the example of the earlier developed bill of exchange could be seen as very attractive.

In addition, the problem of protection of reliance in the land register and records must be considered in relation to the subject of accessoriness of enforcement and must be included in the assessment.[84]

---

83 Cf. section 6 RisikobegrenzungsG [*Law on Risk Mitigation*] of 12.8.2008, BGBl. (Federal Law Gazette I) 2008, 1666 et seq., inserted into the BGB by section 1192 subsection 1a. On this see also C.IV.1.

84 Cf. section 6 RisikobegrenzungsG [*Law on Risk Mitigation*] of 12.8.2008, BGBl. (Federal Law Gazette I) 2008, 1666 et seq., inserted into the BGB by section 1192 subsection 1a.

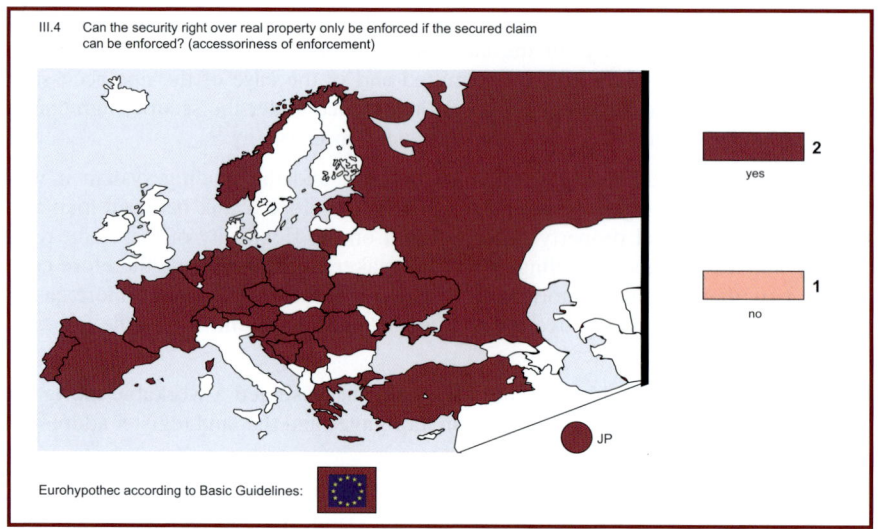

III.4   Can the security right over real property only be enforced if the secured claim
         can be enforced? (accessoriness of enforcement)

2 yes

1 no

JP

Eurohypothec according to Basic Guidelines:

5.   Does the extinguishment of the secured claim lead to the extinguishment of the security right over real property by operation of law? (accessoriness of extinguishment)

Full accessoriness of extinguishment is only preserved with security rights over real property that are strictly accessory in existence, which are found less and less often in practice and in many countries have disappeared completely.

Many legal systems go as far as maintaining the in principle "accessory" maximum amount hypothec when the secured claim or all secured claims are fully extinguished. The maximum amount hypothec thereby becomes non-accessory as regards the accessoriness of extinguishment. This applies, for example, in the case of the Dutch bank hypothec and the Austrian maximum amount hypothec which, moreover, can secure a multiplicity of variable claims.

A distinction must be drawn between the question as to whether the security right over real property is extinguished with the claim and the additional question as to whether the creditor nonetheless still has the possibility of taking compulsory measures against the debtor. The accessoriness of extinguishment of the security right over real property is frequently inferred in order to make it impossible for the creditor to institute – certainly then unjustified – compulsory enforcement. However, the possibility of levying execution against a property is, in fact, often solely dependent on whether the security right over real property is still registered.[85] Irrespective of how the accessoriness of extinguishment is regulated, lack of authority to institute compulsory enforcement because a claim does not exist or no longer exists must then be asserted by the owner by judicial means, as the onus of initiating proceedings lies with him.

---

85   This is the outcome of the provisions on public reliance in the land register, cf. C.II.16. et seq.

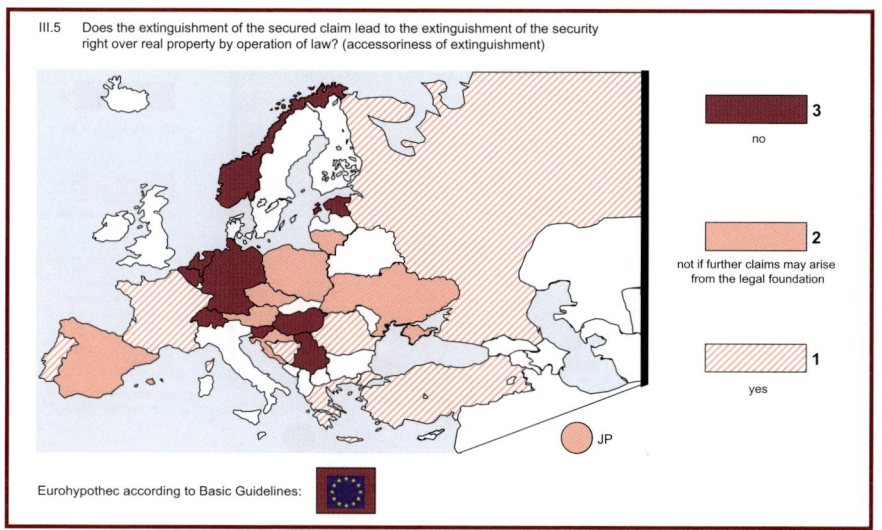

III.5 Does the extinguishment of the secured claim lead to the extinguishment of the security right over real property by operation of law? (accessoriness of extinguishment)

3 no

2 not if further claims may arise from the legal foundation

1 yes

JP

Eurohypothec according to Basic Guidelines:

6. Is the security right over real property linked to the secured claim by a security agreement on the scope of the secured claims?

A security agreement that contains an obligation to create a security right over real property as security is the basis of every security right over real property, whether accessory or non-accessory, because otherwise the security right over real property would be obtained without legal cause.[86] Another question is whether *causa* and the formation agreement are united or are separate. Legal systems answer this question differently according to their fundamental starting point (single contract for obligation and disposition or separation principle). With a non-accessory security right over real property or, as often is the case, where there is relaxed accessoriness, the security agreement also has the additional function, however, of establishing the legal relationship between the secured claim and the security right over real property: ascertainment of claims involved, termination of the security relationship, the owner's rights of defence in the event of enforcement of the security right over real property contrary to contract etc.

86　On this and the following point *Soergel/Stöcker*, EU-Osterweiterung und dogmatische Fragen des Immobiliarsachenrechts – Kausalität, Akzessorietät und Sicherungszweck [*Eastward expansion of the EU and doctrinal issues of real property law – Causality, Accessoriness and Purpose of Collateral*], ZBB 2002, 412 et seq.; further, *Baur/Stürner*, Sachenrecht [*Law of Property*], 18th ed. 2009, section 5 marginal note 40 et seq., section 36 marginal note 76a et seq., section 45 marginal note 9 et seq.

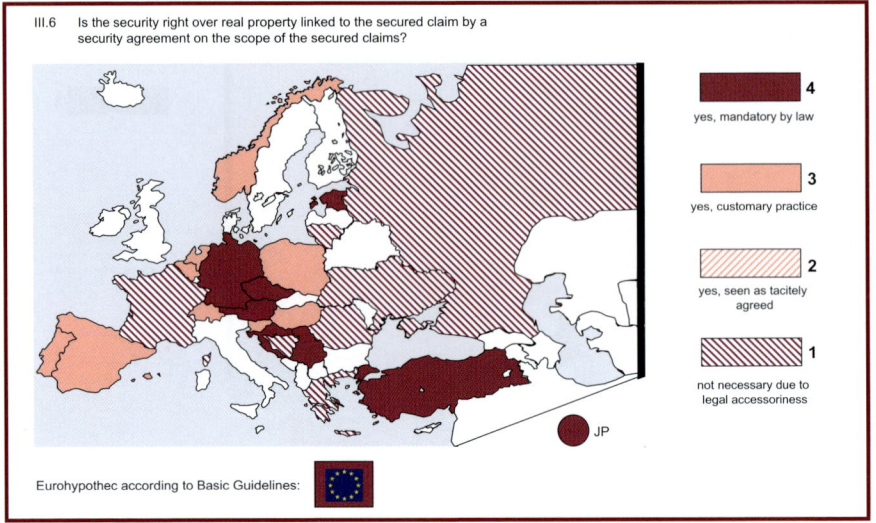

III.6   Is the security right over real property linked to the secured claim by a
         security agreement on the scope of the secured claims?

4 yes, mandatory by law

3 yes, customary practice

2 yes, seen as tacitely agreed

1 not necessary due to legal accessoriness

Eurohypothec according to Basic Guidelines:

7.   How can subordinate (junior) mortgagees or unsecured creditors acquire the position of the free parts of the first ranking mortgage?

Real estate financing frequently requires the cooperation of several credit institutions who in each case receive their own mortgages with differing ranking. For subordinate mortgagees the question arises as to whether and how they can take over the position of a prior ranking creditor. In most legal systems this is possible contractually (e.g. by assignment of the rank) or through statutory succession by way of promotion to a higher position upon repayment of the prior ranking secured claims.

In most legal systems it is also possible for unsecured creditors to obtain a security right on a plot of land by means of enforcement. This provides a compulsorily registered mortgage but it is, of course, subordinate in rank in relation to mortgages that have already been registered. In many countries where only the accessory mortgage is known, this position may improve over time: if, for example, a prior ranking secured claim is repaid, the prior ranking mortgage is thereby reduced in extent and the compulsorily registered subordinate mortgage in this way achieves an upgrading effect through promotion to a higher position.

Other legal systems do not, however, provide for such promotion to a higher ranking position but instead grant the owner himself a right in the parts of a prior ranking mortgage that become free following repayment of the claim. This is also described as the "fixed rank system". In these countries the position of the subordinate creditor thus does not automatically improve with the repayment of the prior ranking mortgage. Instead, however, there is, potentially, the possibility of acquiring the legal position of the owner in the prior ranking secured mortgage. The owner achieves an increasing position in the prior ranking secured mortgage with amortisation (in Germany in the form of the right to restitution [Rückgewähranspruch] – comparable to the equity of the redemption in English law) and this position may be acquired either contractually in advance or also by later pledging. The subordinate creditor then has an effective possibility of enforcement as he acquires an existing, better ranking mortgage without having to create and register a new mortgage.

It is noticeable, however, that countries with non-accessory mortgages do sometimes make reference to ranking promotion but in the case of non-accessory mortgages such ranking promotion can be frustrated by the ever possible renewal of an existing loan facility. A similar position of conflict can arise in relation to maximum amount hypothecs.

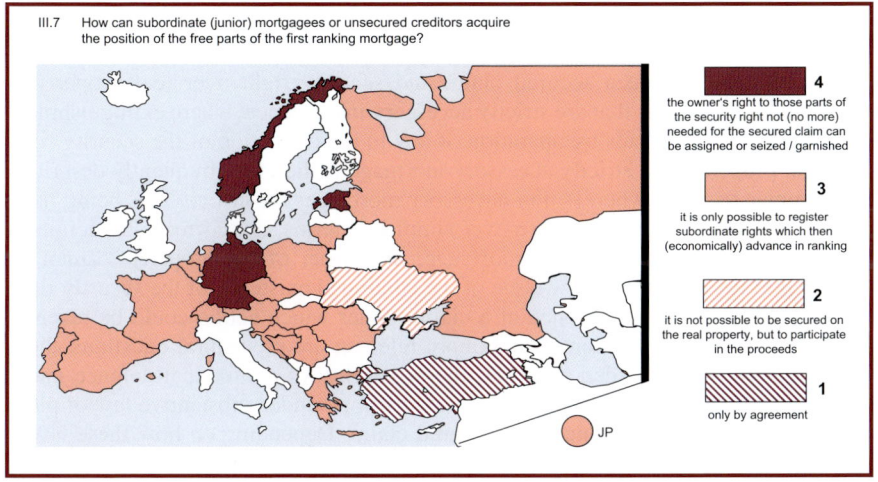

III.7   How can subordinate (junior) mortgagees or unsecured creditors acquire the position of the free parts of the first ranking mortgage?

4 the owner's right to those parts of the security right not (no more) needed for the secured claim can be assigned or seized / garnished

3 it is only possible to register subordinate rights which then (economically) advance in ranking

2 it is not possible to be secured on the real property, but to participate in the proceeds

1 only by agreement

JP

IV. Protection of the owner

For many years aspects of consumer protection have been increasingly central to the interests both of many national legislatures but particularly also of the European Commission with the development of new regulations applicable across the European Union providing minimum standards of protection. In the area of real property law and mortgages the owner of the property is regarded as being in need of protection. It must be taken into account at the same time, however, that as a rule real property law in Europe does not differentiate according to the person of the owner. Whether he is a consumer or not an owner's rights against unjustified enforcement action by a mortgagee are always the same.

The closest link between secured claim and security right over real property is exhibited by mortgages that are strictly accessory in existence, where extinguishment of the secured claim leads by operation of law to the extinction of the security right over real property. The strictly accessory mortgage is therefore frequently described as consumer-friendly, whereas non-accessory mortgages are criticised as being risky for the consumer. This is, in these over-simplified terms, not correct. Protection of the consumer (in relation to the mortgage: the owner of the property) cannot be restricted to the substantive law issue of the continued existence of the security right over real property in the absence of a claim, under which action could be taken in the context of an enforcement. Much more relevant are procedural questions about the allocation of the burden of proof, the possibility of contractual defence under the security agreement or good faith "disacquisition" under substantive law of pleas or defences due to the absence of a secured claim. Depending on how these issues are regulated in a legal system, a non-accessory mortgage can be by all means less "risky" for the owner than an accessory mortgage.

As could be stated in C.III.4., the principle of accessoriness of enforcement applies everywhere, though in many countries there are regulations that serve transactional interests by making the transfer of mortgages easier. These facilitate the good faith acquisition, free of pleas and defences, of a security right over real property or at least pass on the burden of proof in many cases to the owner. The following slides and also slide C.V.4. deal with this.

1.   Can the owner object that there is no secured claim due if the acquirer of the security right over real property is in good faith?

Whereas in C.II.18. above the question of reliance on the accuracy of the land register was addressed in relation to the case where someone other than the registered holder is entitled to an existing mortgage, the question being looked into here is whether the protective effect of the land register also extends to the case where the claim secured by the security right over real property is lacking.

In credit practice the good faith acquisition of security rights over real property without claims may well happen only rarely. But for an acquiring credit institution it is important to know during the process of the transfer of a mortgage what legal facts have to be investigated in order to minimise the risk of acquiring a security right over real property that cannot be enforced – and this in turn determines both the relevant operational time and costs expended in connection with credit checking and also the likelihood of the risk of not even having acquired a right at all, which in turn represents a factor in risk management and in the calculation of margin. The credit institution must address these issues with particular care when, in implementation of Basel II, it chooses the Internal Ratings Based Approach (IRBA) for risk weighting and capital requirements.[87]

From a legal policy point of view the issue of the risk of a double demand under the loan claim and the security right over real property attracts the greatest attention. In fact, cases of this type happen very seldom in practice. The discussions about the Eurohypothec have shown, however, that the basic doctrinal issue of the degree of accessoriness of a mortgage is often largely discussed against the backdrop of this risk. But the risk of a double demand was properly based not on the non-accessoriness of, for instance, the earlier German *Grundschuld*, but on the previous possibility of the good faith acquisition, free of pleas and defences, of a mortgage generally, so that this risk applied in equal measure in respect of the conventional mortgage [Verkehrshypothek] and the *Grundschuld*.[88] In the meantime, in 2008, the German legislature has largely excluded the good faith acquisition of a *Grundschuld* without the existence of a claim, though not, however, the good faith acquisition of a conventional mortgage without the existence of a claim.[89] Nothing could demonstrate more convincingly how little the risk of a double demand depends on fundamental accessoriness or non-accessoriness.

However, this does not mean that the risk of a double demand does not exist where the law does not give the option of acquisition in good faith. This is because issues concerning the allocation of the burden of proof are also relevant in this regard. In many countries with accessory security rights over real property it is customary for the bank to have the disbursement of the loan (notarially) attested in a mortgage deed; only then does disbursement take place.[90] This, to some extent, achieves a similar effect as is achieved with the creation of a non-accessory Grundschuld prior to disbursement of the loan which, in the view of the financing bank, may be completely legitimate and necessary. Advocates of the consumer protection effect of the strict accessoriness of a mortgage, however, as a general rule do not respond to this widespread practice.

In conclusion, it can be seen in relation to the legal systems examined, that in this situation of conflicting interests most of them more readily protect the owner, others, however, the mortgagee.

---

87   Cf. D.I.2.
88   On this see *Baur/Stürner*, Sachenrecht [*Law of Property*], 18th ed. 2009, section 36 marginal note 76a et seq., and section 45 marginal notes 61 et seq. and 67a et seq.; further, *Kircher*, Grundpfandrechte in Europa [*Mortgages in Europe*], p. 295 et seq. and p. 391.
89   In detail on the new law *Baur/Stürner*, section 45 marginal note 67a et seq. *Stürner*, Festschrift für Dieter Medicus zum 80. Geburtstag, 2009, p. 513 et seq.; *Nietsch* NJW 2009, 3606; *Langenbucher* NJW 2008, 3169, 3172; *Habersack* NJW 2008, 3173, 3176.
90   Cf. C.V.4.

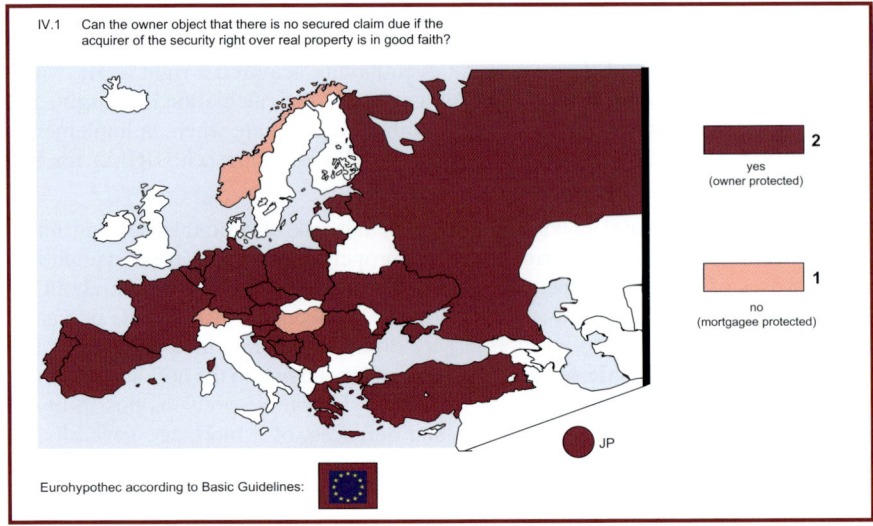

IV.1   Can the owner object that there is no secured claim due if the
        acquirer of the security right over real property is in good faith?

2
yes
(owner protected)

1
no
(mortgagee protected)

JP

Eurohypothec according to Basic Guidelines:

2.   Is it possible for the owner to have the registered amount of the security right over real property reduced when it is clear that only a part of the set maximum amount of the security right over real property will be used?

Many legal systems provide the possibility for the capital sum of the security right over real property to be reduced, in accordance with repayment, in the land register or on the deed, and the creditor is obliged to cooperate. In this way the owner is protected against unjustified action on the part of a mortgagee, which can be of particular importance with security rights where good faith acquisition of a security right over real property without the existence of a claim is possible. In practice, however, in making his decision as to whether he should make use of this right, the owner should weigh the rather theoretical risk of good faith acquisition against the loss of the flexibility of his security right. Higher costs could arise later if the creditor, for example, wishes to augment his loan.

What is surprising is that several legal systems only permit a reduction when the secured claim has been completely repaid, for in this case the security right over real property could also be completely cancelled. In these countries a reduction is also not possible in face of the creditor's opposition as long as any residual debt exists.

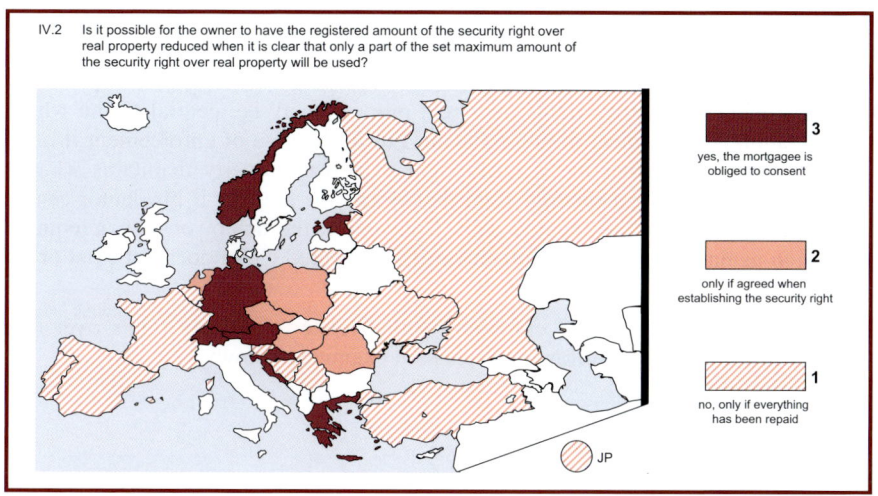

IV.2   Is it possible for the owner to have the registered amount of the security right over
       real property reduced when it is clear that only a part of the set maximum amount of
       the security right over real property will be used?

3
yes, the mortgagee is
obliged to consent

2
only if agreed when
establishing the security right

1
no, only if everything
has been repaid

JP

3.   Is there statutory regulation or court practice (case law) protecting the owner of a real property who has established a security right over real property to secure another person's debt? (protection of a third party mortgagor)

Another just as important problem area, which is frequently discussed in connection with consumer protection issues, is the establishment of a security right over real property by a different (third party) real property owner from the mortgagor.[91] In these cases of third party security right creation there may be protection provisions, particularly if the third party, in addition to liability under the security right over real property, is also to assume personal liability under extended form or if the security right over real property is intended to secure a plurality of claims against the debtor.

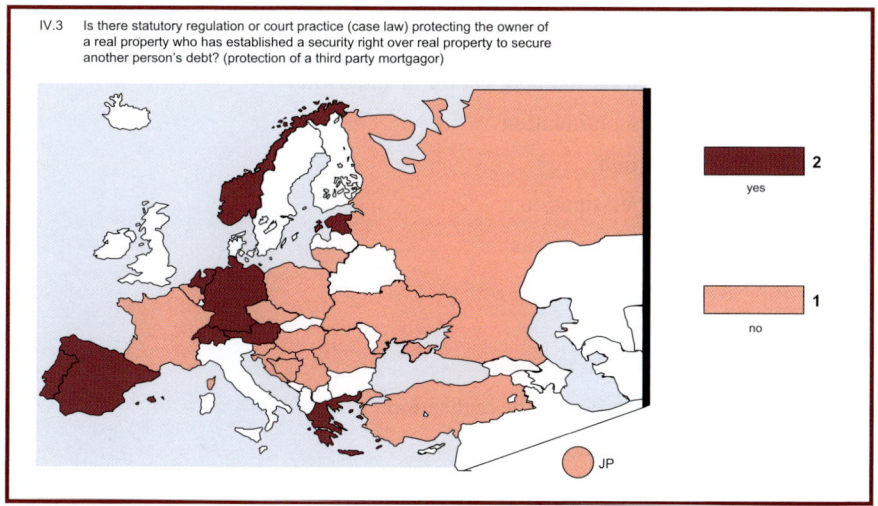

IV.3   Is there statutory regulation or court practice (case law) protecting the owner of
       a real property who has established a security right over real property to secure
       another person's debt? (protection of a third party mortgagor)

2
yes

1
no

JP

---

91   In connection with his deliberations about a Eurohypothec, this is dealt with in particular detail
     by Kiesgen who, for the legal systems investigated by him regarding mortgages and more,
     reappraises the fundamentals of the case law, which result everywhere in restrictions in respect
     of such third party cases. Cf. in particular his comparative law analysis, (footnote 1) p. 157 et seq.

V.   Enforcement

However important all the doctrinal questions regarding the formation, transfer and extinguishment of security rights over real property may be, central to the whole consideration is the subject of enforcement. For in the case of enforcement it must become apparent whether the security right over real property maintains what it promises, namely to be a security right that assists the creditor if his debtor can or will no longer service the secured debt. Conversely, the debtor or owner requires protection against unjustified enforcement if the secured claim does not exist or no longer exists.

Issues surrounding the law of enforcement that relate to security rights over real property and concern the following topics are examined below:

- Executory title
- Executory clause
- Owner's rights – onus of initiating proceedings against enforcement
- Owner's rights – burden of proof
- Rights of subordinate creditors
- Realisation of mortgages
- Attachment of the income from real property
- Expulsion of the owner from the property
- Effect of the award in forced sale proceedings
    - Cancellation of rights
    - Realisation on the application of subordinate creditors
    - Unsatisfied claims
    - Agreement on survival of the mortgage
- Discontinuation of the compulsory enforcement
    - Discontinuation on the application of the owner
    - Duration of discontinuation
- Procedure – valuation
- Protection against dissipation
- Alternative realisation options
    - *lex commissoria*
    - Value equalization
    - Acquisition by the creditor
- Distribution of the proceeds of realisation
- Building contractors' mortgages
- Interest and costs
- Duration of the proceedings

1. How is an executory title for enforcement of the mortgage obtained?

Nearly all the legal systems covered here require the existence of an executory title in order for enforcement proceedings to be commenced. In principle what is required is in fact a judgment following contentious proceedings which orders the payment of a sum of money from the real property or acquiescence to the compulsory enforcement. In the case of mortgages it is, however, often useful on efficiency grounds to avoid proceedings regarding the payment obligation where this obligation is clear on the merits and ascertainable as regards amount. This, on the one hand, avoids a delay in the enforcement proceedings which would reduce the financial value of the security right over real property; and on the other hand the courts are not burdened with proceedings with a foreseeable outcome. In relation to security rights over real property with clearly ascertainable amounts, many countries therefore completely avoid the judicially pronounced executory title and leave the notarial deed creating the security right over real property to suffice as title, or else provide specially simplified and quick court proceedings.

Indeed there is a huge variety of different methods[92] whereby a creditor may procure "rapid" title without having to bring preliminary proceedings. In conclusion it is evident that all countries offer the possibility for title to be procured at the stage when the security right over real property is created or later in simple proceedings.[93]

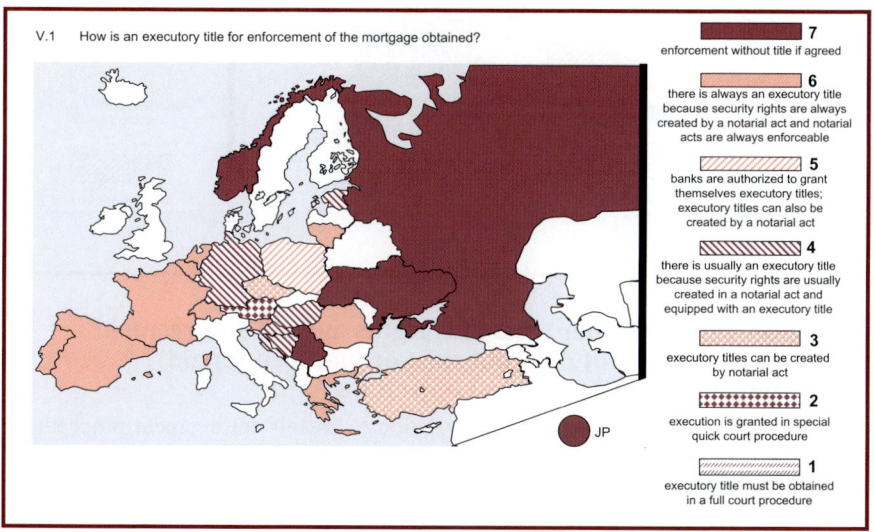

V.1   How is an executory title for enforcement of the mortgage obtained?

7 enforcement without title if agreed

6 there is always an executory title because security rights are always created by a notarial act and notarial acts are always enforceable

5 banks are authorized to grant themselves executory titles; executory titles can also be created by a notarial act

4 there is usually an executory title because security rights are usually created in a notarial act and equipped with an executory title

3 executory titles can be created by notarial act

2 execution is granted in special quick court procedure

1 executory title must be obtained in a full court procedure

---

92   Many countries offer several types of proceedings for realisation, e.g. Czech law.
93   In the first edition of this book answer 1 was given for Russia. For information on legal changes since then see *Lassen*, Reformen im russischen Recht: Stärkung der Pfandgläubiger, WiRO 2009, p. 321 et seq.

2. Is a statement that the copy of the executory title can be used for enforcement necessary (executory clause), and if so, how can it be obtained?

The formal requirements for enforcement, often in the form of a so-called executory clause, which is found in many legal systems, based on the French model, are easily and quickly fulfilled. This applies also in countries where special court proceedings are necessary for this.

In principle the enforceable official copy of an executory title is only issued once, whereas multiple copies of the mortgage deeds may be issued. The reason for this is that the whole point of one enforceable official copy is precisely to ensure that only one lot of enforcement proceedings are carried out using that executory title. This serves to protect the owner from multiple, parallel proceedings and also promotes legal certainty.

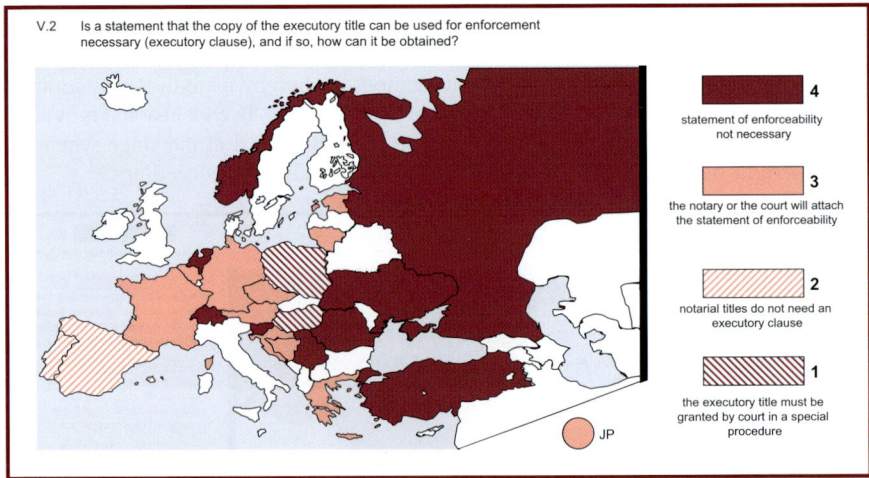

V.2 Is a statement that the copy of the executory title can be used for enforcement necessary (executory clause), and if so, how can it be obtained?

4 — statement of enforceability not necessary

3 — the notary or the court will attach the statement of enforceability

2 — notarial titles do not need an executory clause

1 — the executory title must be granted by court in a special procedure

3. How can the owner assert his rights against enforcement (e.g. that the debt does not exist or has been repaid)? (substantive or procedural objections)

The elementary principle applicable in relation to all fair enforcement proceedings is that the debtor or the owner has the possibility of defending himself against enforcement if he is of the view that the enforcement is either completely unjustified or at least not justified in the amount claimed. This right is accorded to him in all the legal systems examined here. However, they also impose on him the burden of conducting litigation. This means that he must actively defend himself if he considers his rights are being infringed. He thus bears the burden of initiating legal proceedings: as is generally the rule in civil proceedings, anyone who wishes to assert a right or a right of defence must take active steps to do so.

Whether the owner can defend himself in the ongoing enforcement proceedings or whether he must initiate separate legal proceedings is regulated in different ways, but in most cases this is of formal significance if anything.

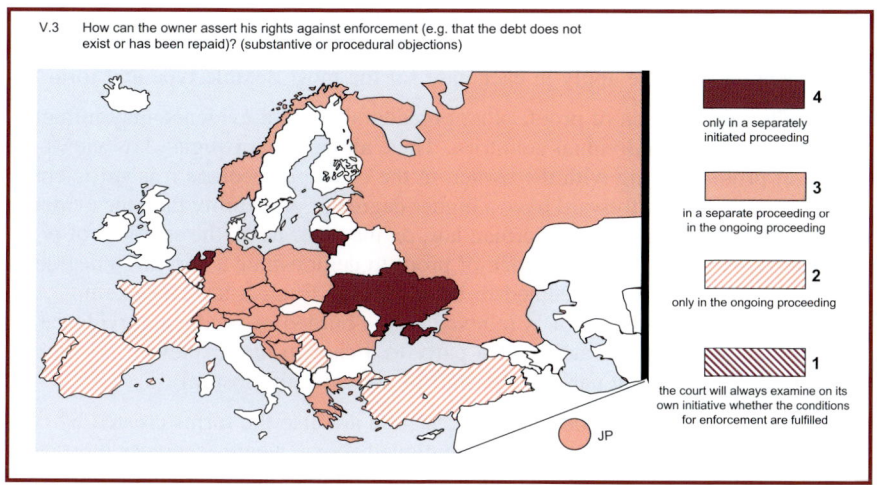

4. When disputed, who has to prove that the secured debt has come into existence and/or is due? (no change of mortgagee)

Very different sets of priorities are evident in the individual legal systems in relation to the issue of the allocation of the burden of proof.

Countries that prioritise the creditor's interests assign the burden of proof to the owner. Where protection of the owner is more highly rated than protection of the mortgagee, the law provides that the creditor must furnish proof if the owner disputes that the secured claim has come into existence and/or is due.

It is particularly striking that the issue of the burden of proof is only influenced to a limited extent by accessoriness or non-accessoriness. At the starting point of the discussion it is indeed true that in the case of the accessory mortgage the creditor bears the burden of proving that the debt has come into existence and is due, whereas in the case of the non-accessory mortgage the owner must prove the use of the security right contrary to contract, i.e. that the claim does not exist and is not due. This basic approach is, however, often so bound up by covenants and representations that often not much is left of it.

In many countries with accessory mortgages, as already mentioned above (in C.IV.1.) the creditor acquires a standard form notarial confirmation of disbursement prior to disbursement which largely passes the burden of proof to the owner in the event of dispute. On the other hand, even in countries with non-accessory mortgages, the creditor is not always given such unilateral protection. An example of this can be found in German law. In the case of the claim-securing land charge [Sicherungs-grundschuld], a narrow or broad security purpose may be agreed. If a narrow security purpose is agreed, the land charge may only be used to secure a particular claim. A broad security purpose, which is widespread in practice, can be used to secure a number of future claims, as is also possible with many maximum amount hypothecs in Europe. In accordance with German case law, the burden of proof for the exist-ence of more claims than the originally secured claim is, however, borne by the creditor where a broad security purpose has been agreed.[94]

---

94   See *Baur/Stürner*, Sachenrecht [*Law of Property*], section 45 marginal note 12.

It must be borne in mind that in many countries the answer may be different depending on what type of mortgage has been chosen or the precise contractual wording. The answers given here apply in each case for the most flexible type and form.[95]

Despite the same burden of proof, other procedural rules of evidence may influence the actual results of individual countries. Thus, although Norwegian law views the burden of proof as being with the owner, in the court proceedings it is sufficient to show that the facts put forward have a higher degree of probability than the evidence submitted by the other side. In German law, on the other hand, the standard of proof requires the party that has the burden of proof to demonstrate a very high degree of probability for proof to be deemed to be shown. In English law, for example, the party with the burden of proof is relieved of the burden of producing evidence by the very wide-ranging obligation of a party to a case to make relevant documents available to the opposing party at the start of the case (disclosure).

Worthy of close consideration in this connection are also the forms created by contractual covenants and representations mentioned above, where accessory mortgages are established for abstract claims, such as, for example, unconditional promises of payment, certificates of indebtedness or bills of exchange.[96]

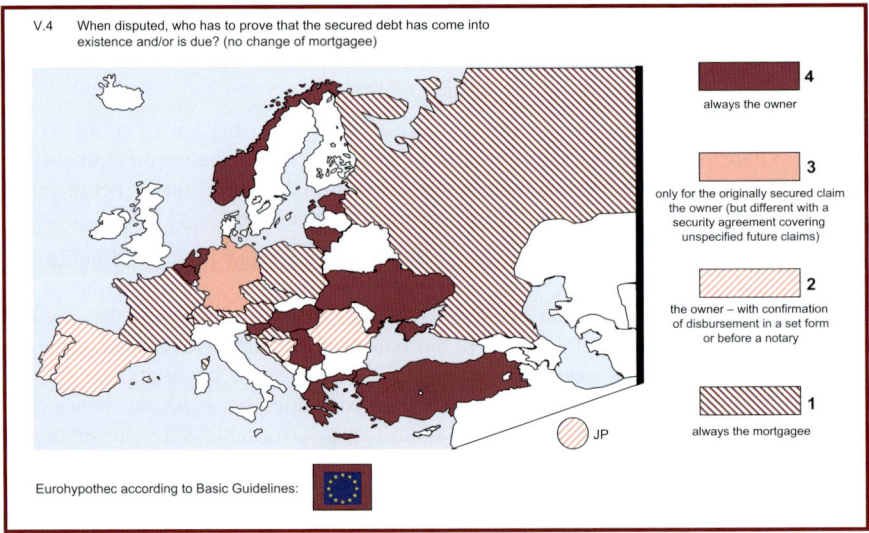

V.4 When disputed, who has to prove that the secured debt has come into existence and/or is due? (no change of mortgagee)

4 always the owner

3 only for the originally secured claim the owner (but different with a security agreement covering unspecified future claims)

2 the owner – with confirmation of disbursement in a set form or before a notary

1 always the mortgagee

JP

Eurohypothec according to Basic Guidelines:

5.   When the burden of proof is with the owner, must the mortgagee cooperate by submitting documents?

Even though many countries impose the burden of proof on the owner, the weight of this burden is often mitigated. A degree of protection of the owner is also achieved in countries where the owner does bear the burden of proof because the creditor must practically always cooperate by producing documents that establish the factual and legal situation. In this way, the bank's documents, which are subject to extensive statutory retention obligations, are as a rule also available to the owner for his production of evidence. This is of particular significance when there is a dispute about whether the debt has been discharged.

---

95   Cf. C.I.4.
96   Cf. C.III.1.

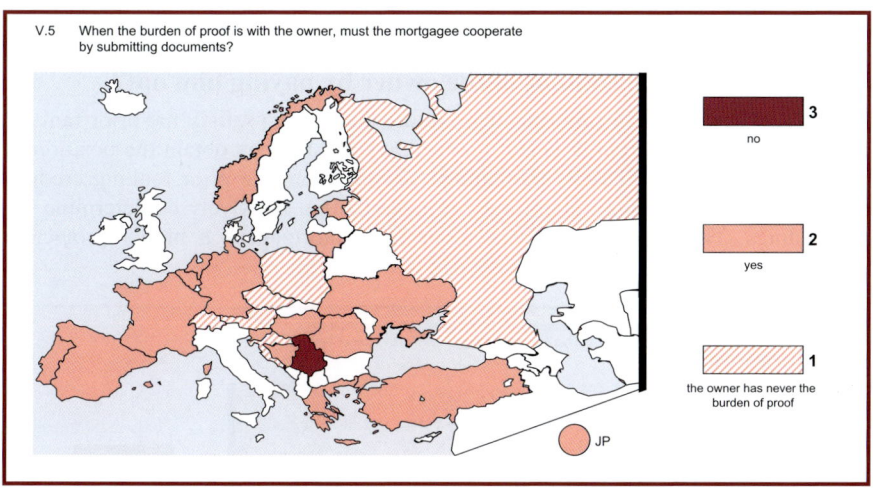

V.5 When the burden of proof is with the owner, must the mortgagee cooperate by submitting documents?

3 no

2 yes

1 the owner has never the burden of proof

JP

6. Can subordinate mortgagees separately initiate enforcement of the mortgage?

A very important question for evaluating a mortgage is whether a subordinate creditor can separately initiate enforcement, meaning without the involvement or consent of the prior ranking mortgagee. All the legal systems presented here permit this and consequently also grant subordinate mortgagees the full and independent right to initiate enforcement proceedings.

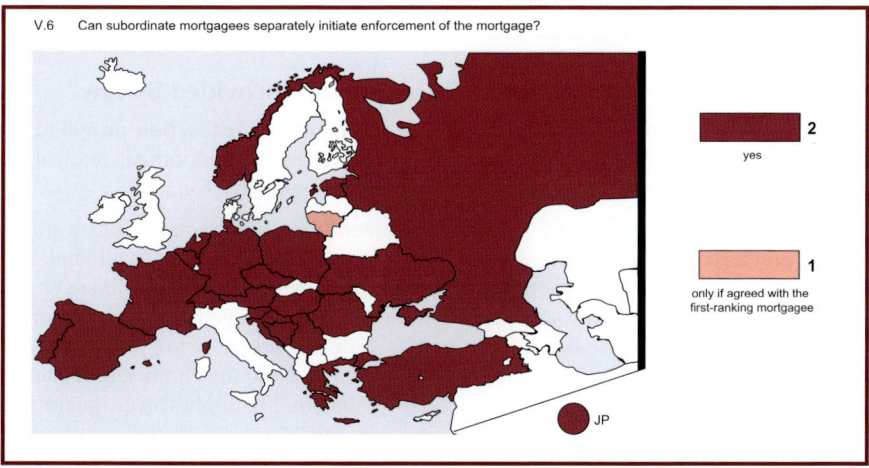

V.6 Can subordinate mortgagees separately initiate enforcement of the mortgage?

2 yes

1 only if agreed with the first-ranking mortgagee

JP

7. During enforcement proceedings, can subordinate mortgagees obtain the position of the first-ranking mortgagee without his consent or the consent of the owner by paying him out?

Many legal systems give subordinate creditors the right to satisfy the prior ranking creditor or creditors in enforcement proceedings and thereby obtain the position of prior ranking creditor. This is particularly useful where the prior ranking creditor only has a relatively small claim but can nevertheless decisively co-determine the proceedings. This possibility gives subordinate mortgagees a higher protective effect.

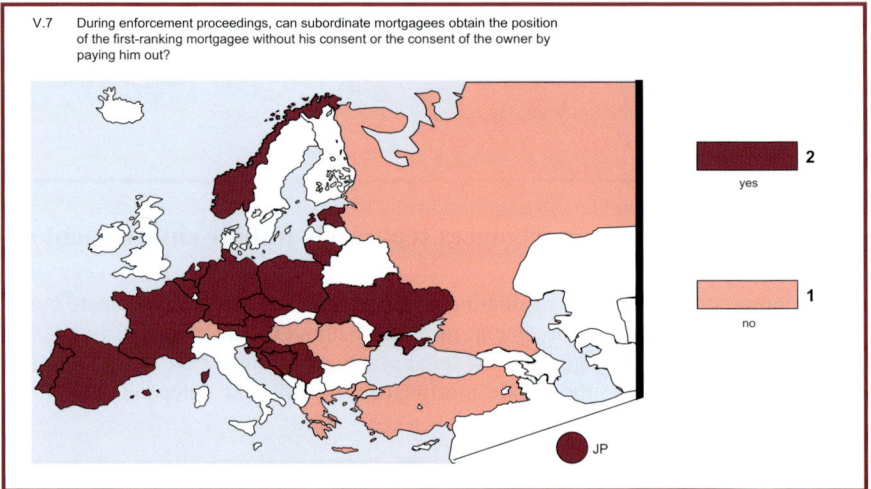

V.7 During enforcement proceedings, can subordinate mortgagees obtain the position of the first-ranking mortgagee without his consent or the consent of the owner by paying him out?

2 yes

1 no

JP

8. Which other options for enforcement are provided by law?

Public auction by a public appointed body is the means of realisation provided by statute in Western Continental Europe. In Eastern Europe, by contrast, realisation by means of private sale, also at a public auction, is generally found.[97]

The advantage of an auction by a public appointed body is that it provides a transparent, precisely regulated process where the system can take account of and balance the interests of the enforcing mortgagee, the debtor/owner and the subordinate creditor. On the other hand, a free sale can be more flexibly managed and a higher price can be achieved, which also benefits the parties. Sale at a privately run public auction is an attempt to find a compromise and on the one hand avoid the cumbersome nature of a process carried out by a public body and on the other hand, however, guarantee a certain means of control.

---

97   See also C.V.19. on *lex commissoria*.

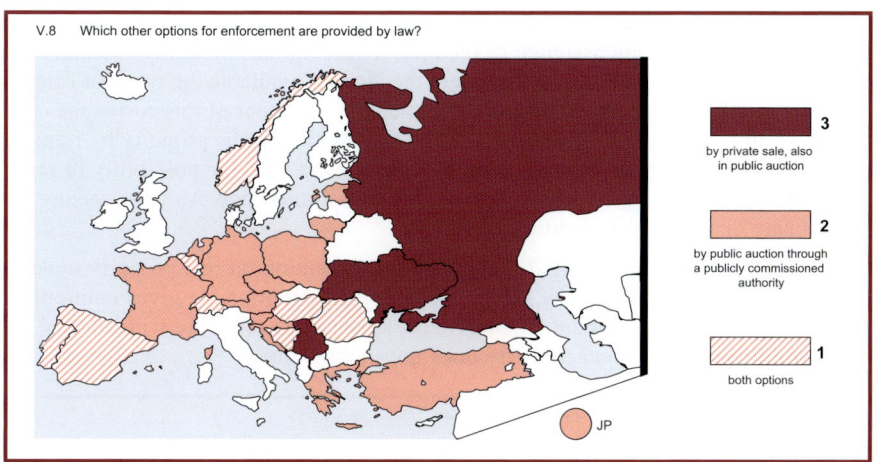

V.8   Which other options for enforcement are provided by law?

3
by private sale, also
in public auction

2
by public auction through
a publicly commissioned
authority

1
both options

JP

9.   During enforcement, can the yields of the property be seized before the sale of the property?

It is of considerable importance, particularly during extended enforcement proceedings, whether a mortgagee can seize the (rental) yields of a property. Most of the countries shown here do provide this possibility, whether in the form of a special form of enforcement, or by permitting a claim to the yields to be assigned or pledged. The creditor must, nonetheless, be aware that the means of seizure differ fundamentally.

Many countries provide a separate type of procedure within the law of enforcement which, unlike the compulsory auction or forced sale, does not have the aim of the final realisation of the property by transfer to a purchaser but instead allows the mortgagee to seize the yields of the property. In most cases, management of the property is, for this purpose, transferred to an administrator who pays the surpluses to the creditors. This type of procedure is available to every holder of a mortgage; an additional agreement alongside the mortgage is not necessary.

Normally this enforcement form of forced administration does not exclude the compulsory auction or forced sale forms of enforcement. The mortgagee may thus, on the one hand, exclude the owner from access to the property and gather in the yields himself and, on the other hand, at the same time pursue the final realisation of the property. This will mostly be the case where the claim is fairly large and the creditor does not want to get involved in long-drawn-out realisation proceedings.

In many countries direct seizure of the yields of the property can be secured by the conclusion of agreements to this effect. So in English law, for example, a charge over all the assets of the company holding the property can be agreed (floating charge). This then permits special, separate proceedings in the insolvency concerning the property, with the yields able to benefit the creditor. In this way the yields of the property can indeed be seized but this happens on the basis of a security which is not necessarily registered in the land register but may instead, like the English floating charge, be entered in the commercial register (Companies Register).

Also external to the land register are contractual agreements in terms of which the yields of the property are assigned or pledged. These options probably exist and are frequently used in all countries even where the law has available the types of seizure already described. In many countries a contractual agreement of this sort is the only way to secure seizure of the yields. Until final realisation of the property by transfer to a third party, the yields firstly benefit the person who used the possibility of separate, secured seizure; many legal systems set time limits, however, for seizure by subordinate or unsecured creditors.

Finally, it must be borne in mind that outside of execution on real property under a security right over real property, every executory title in principle gives entitlement to carry out direct attachment of individual assets (e.g. rents etc.) insofar as the execution levied on the real property does not include these.

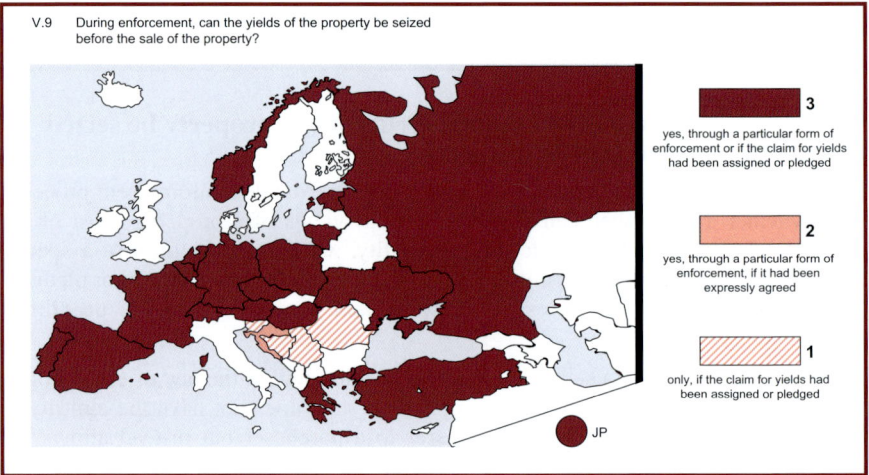

V.9   During enforcement, can the yields of the property be seized before the sale of the property?

3 — yes, through a particular form of enforcement or if the claim for yields had been assigned or pledged

2 — yes, through a particular form of enforcement, if it had been expressly agreed

1 — only, if the claim for yields had been assigned or pledged

JP

10.   Can the owner be entirely deprived of control of the property before a forced sale?

It is sometimes useful to remove actual control of the property from the owner, e.g. where it is feared that he is managing the property badly or even damaging it. The mortgagee's possibilities for intervention are certainly regulated very differently.

In many countries the form of enforcement of forced administration just described in 9. above can also be used in order to deprive the owner of access to the property if this could be important for maintaining or enhancing its financial value or the yields. Although seizure of the yields is primarily important in relation to let property and commercial property, the additional effect of the exclusion of the owner from the management may lead to the special form of execution of forced administration sometimes being used also in relation to owner-occupied properties; however, forcing the owner to move out of his own house is not usually permitted.

In Great Britain, as already mentioned in 9. above, there is the option of a special administrative procedure relating to the property in the interests of the creditor in whose favour a multiple lien (floating charge) over all assets of the company holding the property is created. It must, however, be separately agreed and the financing transaction must be correspondingly structured.

In other countries, if the property is threatened by the conduct of the owner, the only possibility is to obtain court orders in the individual case.

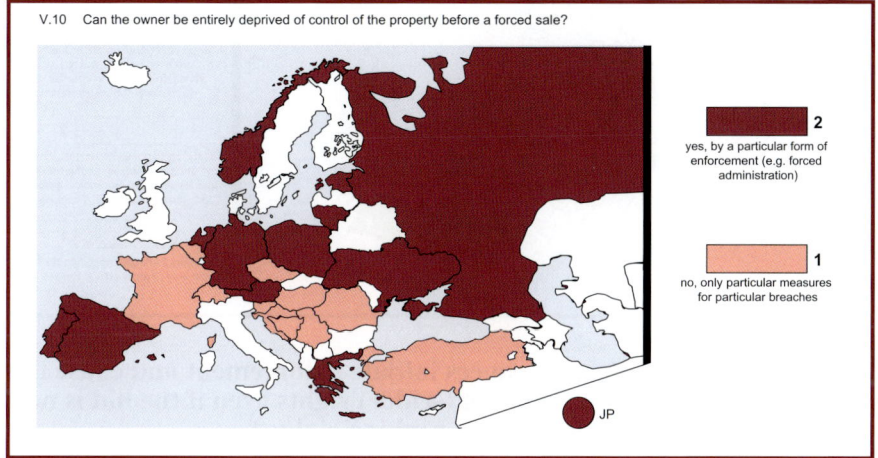

V.10   Can the owner be entirely deprived of control of the property before a forced sale?

2 yes, by a particular form of enforcement (e.g. forced administration)

1 no, only particular measures for particular breaches

JP

11. What are the effects of the decision to transfer the real property in forced sale proceedings on the rights over the property?

The effect of the court order in the compulsory auction transferring ownership (award) is of fundamental importance. Particularly in the situation where the property is encumbered with several mortgages, the question arises as to whether equal or sub-ordinate ranking mortgages continue or whether they are extinguished within the framework of an auction. Many countries permit only prior ranking mortgages to persist; others release the property completely from all charges.

One statutory approach is to safeguard the relative rights of the entitled parties in the forced auction so that prior ranking creditors who do not attach themselves to the proceedings should not be affected. However, many countries follow the model originating from France where the property is completely purged of all encumbrances. This is intended to create an opportunity to end what was viewed in the 19th Century as the detrimental, permanent encumbering of properties and to make wholly unen-cumbered properties fully marketable and financially realisable again. The auctioning of an unencumbered property may indeed be frequently more efficient and, even taking account of the encumbrance, generate higher proceeds overall than the realisa-tion of a property encumbered with a prior ranking right that may be difficult to evaluate. However, the holder of a right who possibly sees no reason at present for realisation and who, at the time his right was created, could not know of the subor-dinate rights that are now forcing a realisation, is then drawn into the realisation.

For a number of reasons most of the legal systems that provide for the extinguish-ment of prior ranking encumbrances must make exceptions in particular cases. Thus, easements for power cables and water pipes must remain secure in the interests of public infrastructure. Many countries go further and in principle exclude real servi-tudes from abolition.

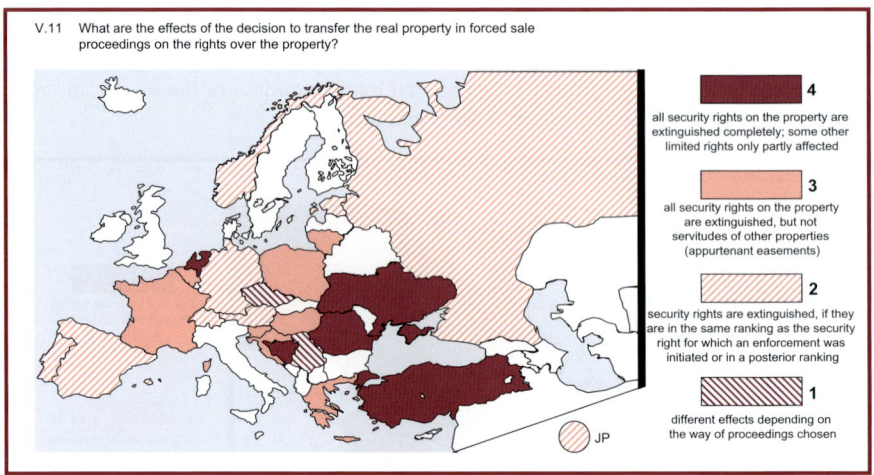

V.11   What are the effects of the decision to transfer the real property in forced sale
       proceedings on the rights over the property?

12.   Can subordinate mortgagees initiate enforcement and cause the extinction of better ranking (senior) rights even if the bid is not sufficient to cover the better ranking rights?

This question, which is of great significance for first-ranking mortgagees, arises in connection with the right of subordinate mortgagees to initiate proceedings described above in C.V.6. Most countries do not permit prior ranking rights to be endangered in this way.

Where subordinate mortgagees are permitted to carry on proceedings without regard to the adequacy of a bid for prior ranking creditors, subordinate creditors can commence enforcement proceedings and bring down prior ranking mortgagees without compensating the latter in full. However, the proceeds of enforcement will then be even less adequate for the subordinate creditors, so there is little incentive for such a course of action.

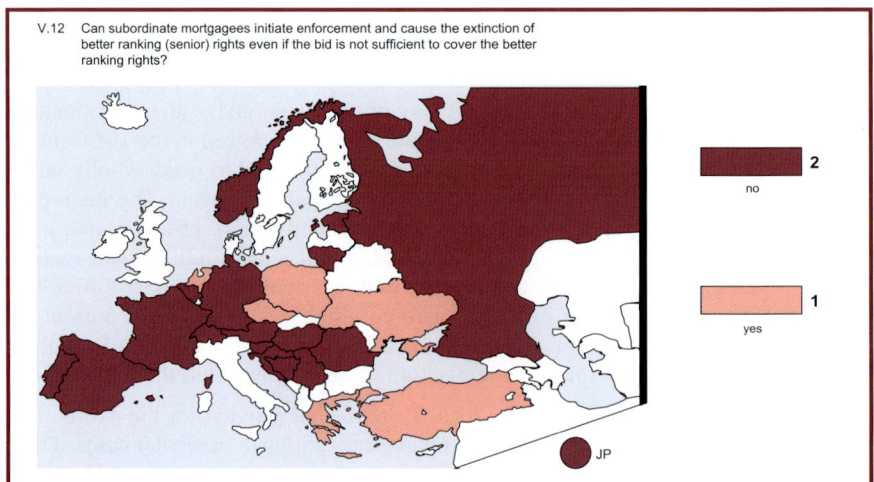

V.12   Can subordinate mortgagees initiate enforcement and cause the extinction of
       better ranking (senior) rights even if the bid is not sufficient to cover the better
       ranking rights?

13.   How does the decision to transfer the real property in a forced sale affect those claims not covered by the proceeds of the forced sale?

In nearly all countries claims that cannot be satisfied from the proceeds of the forced sale persist and can be asserted again as unsecured claims. Only in the Ukraine are these claims also extinguished.

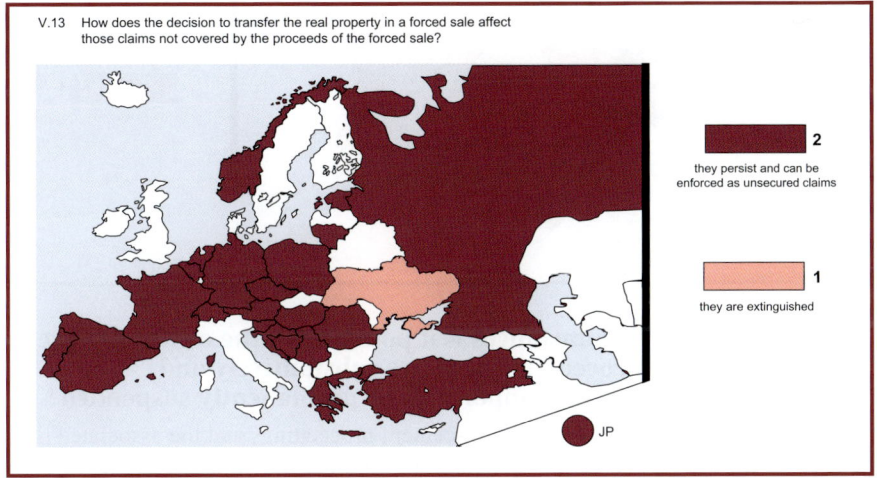

V.13   How does the decision to transfer the real property in a forced sale affect those claims not covered by the proceeds of the forced sale?

2 — they persist and can be enforced as unsecured claims

1 — they are extinguished

JP

14.   Is it possible to use the security right over real property of a mortgagee initiating enforcement to finance the acquisition of the property in forced sale proceedings by the new owner?

It can be advantageous if the mortgage of the enforcing creditor is not extinguished but can be used instead for financing the successful bidder. In this way, acquisition in the course of compulsory enforcement proceedings can be financed by a bank without a new mortgage having to be created. This may not only save costs and time. A security right over real property that could enable the financing of the acquisition is often not immediately available at the time of acquisition. This is because the property has been seized in the enforcement proceedings, so the acquirer cannot yet have a mortgage registered, although he possibly needs a mortgage immediately to finance his acquisition. This survival of the security right over real property (Liegenbelassung) is provided for or possible in many countries, but in others is not.

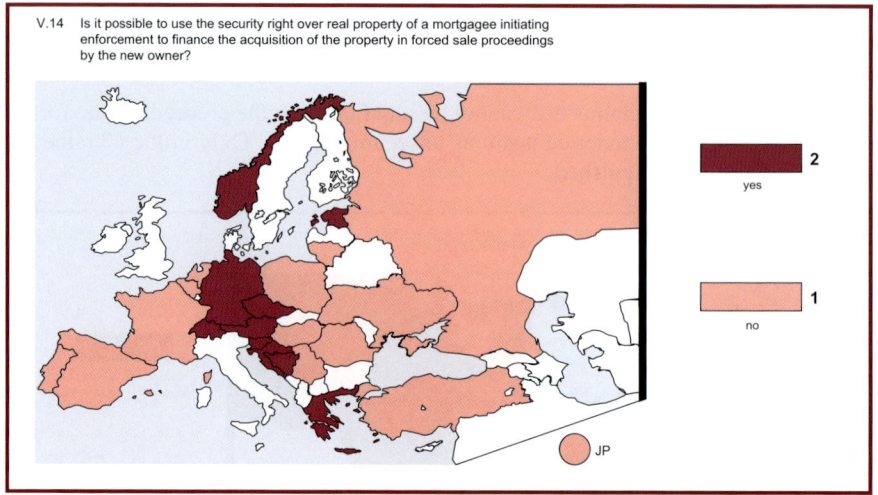

V.14   Is it possible to use the security right over real property of a mortgagee initiating
       enforcement to finance the acquisition of the property in forced sale proceedings
       by the new owner?

15. Under what circumstances is it possible for the owner to have enforcement proceedings that are substantively and procedurally lawful temporarily or permanently suspended?

In order to estimate the duration of enforcement proceedings and the associated time commitment the question as to whether and, if applicable, for how long the owner can have the proceedings suspended is important. Most countries do not permit this at all, or they permit it only with the creditor's consent or only in very exceptional cases. An exceptional case may exist where the owner can furnish prima facie evidence that life and health would be threatened if enforcement is continued.

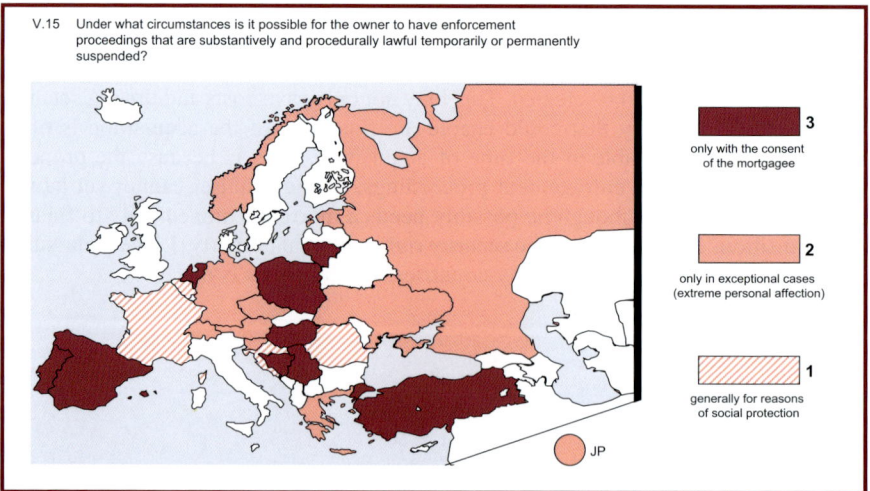

V.15   Under what circumstances is it possible for the owner to have enforcement
       proceedings that are substantively and procedurally lawful temporarily or permanently
       suspended?

16.   If the enforcement proceedings are suspended at the request of the owner, without the consent of the mortgagee, is the suspension permanent or temporary?

If it is possible to suspend the proceedings, this will only be temporary. It should be borne in mind, however, that special rules may apply where there is a danger of dissipation, as emerges from the following slides.

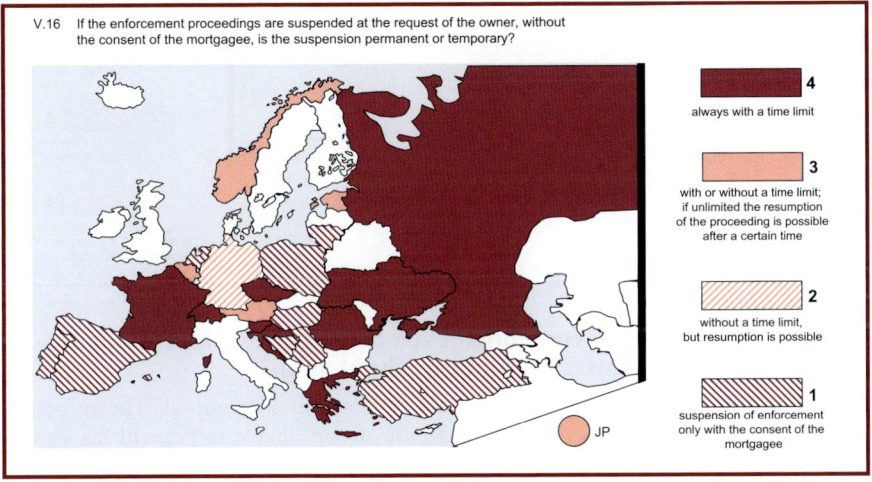

17.   Does a valuation of the property take place within the enforcement proceedings?

Many countries provide that the value of the property involved in the enforcement proceedings must be determined by an expert valuer. This serves largely to protect the owner, because the value determined can then be used as a benchmark for assessing whether the price achieved reaches the minimum prescribed by law. On a secondary basis, however, this also provides protection for the purchaser, as the valuation gives him a benchmark for his offer. It must be taken into account here that in compulsory enforcement proceedings purchasers generally do not have the same opportunities to inspect and closely examine the property as they do in an independent sale. This shortcoming can be compensated for to some extent with the help of a valuation determined beforehand by an expert valuer. An evaluation within the proceedings thus affords better provision for all the parties involved. But at the same time it has to be accepted that the proceedings will be delayed. Obtaining the valuation may cost time, particularly if the parties put forward objections or even seek legal redress against the outcome of the valuation.

Some countries therefore dispense with a valuation in the interests of a quick process. Some legal systems dispense completely with the protection of a minimum price. In other countries there is at least the possibility for the owner to have a valuation undertaken subsequently. This happens primarily if a sale on the open market is permitted.

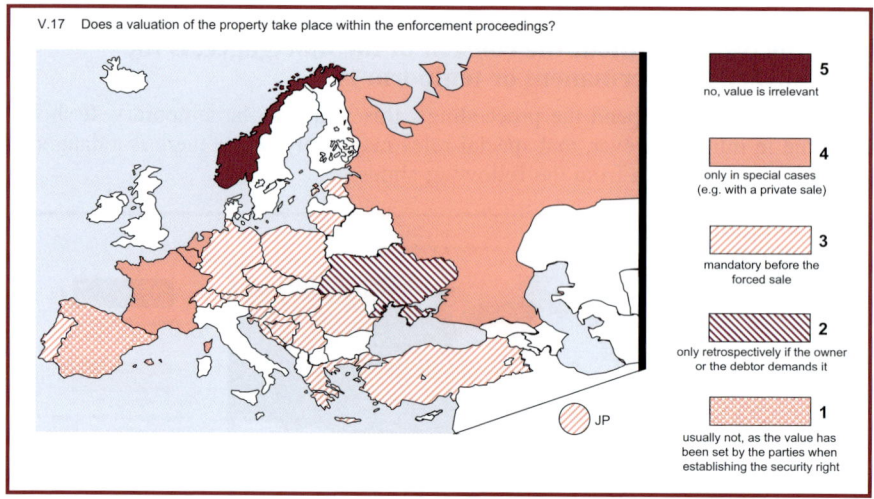

V.17   Does a valuation of the property take place within the enforcement proceedings?

18.   Is the forced sale concluded even if the price achieved for the property is below a certain threshold value?

Many conflicting interests become evident in realisation proceedings. The enforcing creditor wants to satisfy his claim. The debtor/owner, unable to prevent his loss of ownership, wants to obtain proceeds that at least cover all his liabilities or if possible exceed them. Subordinate creditors are interested in the proceeds exceeding the claims of the prior ranking creditors in order that they themselves also receive payment when the proceeds come to be divided up.

The owner and the subordinate creditors may thus be interested in preventing realisation if a certain value is not achieved in the auction. For this reason many legal systems stipulate statutory threshold values; if these are not achieved the forced sale cannot go through, or the proceedings have to be postponed and will thus be prolonged. Differing prioritisation in different countries is evident from the individual regulations dealing with this.

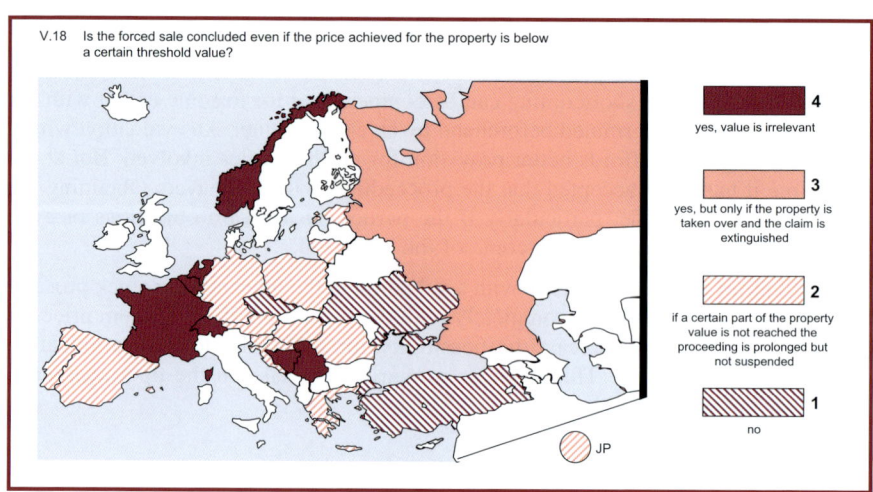

V.18   Is the forced sale concluded even if the price achieved for the property is below a certain threshold value?

19.   Can a mortgage be enforced by the mortgagee using a right to take over the property? (lex commissoria)

The takeover of the property by the mortgagee is the quickest form of realisation. But it comes up against deep-rooted legal policy concerns if the right of takeover is not restricted, in particular by a value equalisation claim on the part of the owner.

Most Continental European legal systems prohibit a takeover completely. Only in the Ukraine and Scotland, apparently, does it represent the customary form of realisation. However, France[98] and Romania also allow a takeover by prior contractual agreement.

The right of takeover is a highly explosive issue in consumer policy and thus merits closer consideration on a European level, but it has not as yet been included in the EU Commission's White Paper on consumer protection. The EU considerably extended the possibilities for realisation without recourse to proceedings in the case of chattel mortgages in the commercial sector in the Financial Collateral Arrangements Directive (implemented in Germany in section 1259 BGB), but no conclusions regarding a corresponding trend as regards real property can be drawn from this.

A comparison with US law opens up interesting prospects. If a bank carries out the foreclosure of a property including a building, in most states it can then only claim the residual debt if it opts for judicial proceedings for the realisation and then allows the residual debt to be determined by the court (so-called deficiency judgment). However, the law of many states and contractual covenants and representations generally grant options to the banks promising quicker and higher proceeds for extra-judicial enforcement. The banks usually opt for these because, in view of the high mobility in the USA and the difficulty of locating a debtor in a country without a system of registration of residents, claiming the residual debt is generally regarded as not very promising.[99]

There is no need to determine whether this more or less clear emphasis of loan structuring on liability in rem particularly when financing private purchase of land set a substantial cause for the recent financial crisis.[100] In the end, the analysis only affirms the common knowledge that real estate values decay rapidly when too many loans are too high compared with the value of the encumbered real property and are given to debtors of minor quality causing a foreseeable wave of sales and forced sales.

---

98   The *pacte commissoire* was newly introduced into the French Code Civil (sections 2459 and 2460 Civil Code) by Order No. 2006-346 of 23rd March 2006 (Journal Officiel No. 71 of 24th March 2006) in the course of the reform of the French security law. For consumers this possibility was already excluded, however, by section L 311-32 Code de Consommation, if the real property concerned is the main place of the owner's residence.

99   On the realisation of a mortgage in the USA cf. *Stürner/Kern*, Grundsatzfragen des US-Hypothekenrechts [*Key issues of US mortgage law*], p. 936 et seq.

100 See *Lutter* ZIP 2009, 197, 198; *Heun* JZ 2010, 53, 55; *Shiller*, The Subprime Solution, 2008, p. 30 et seq., *Großfeld/Heppe*, DAJV-Newsletter 2009, 175 et seq.; *Zywicki/Adamson* 80 University of Colorado Law Review 1 et seq.

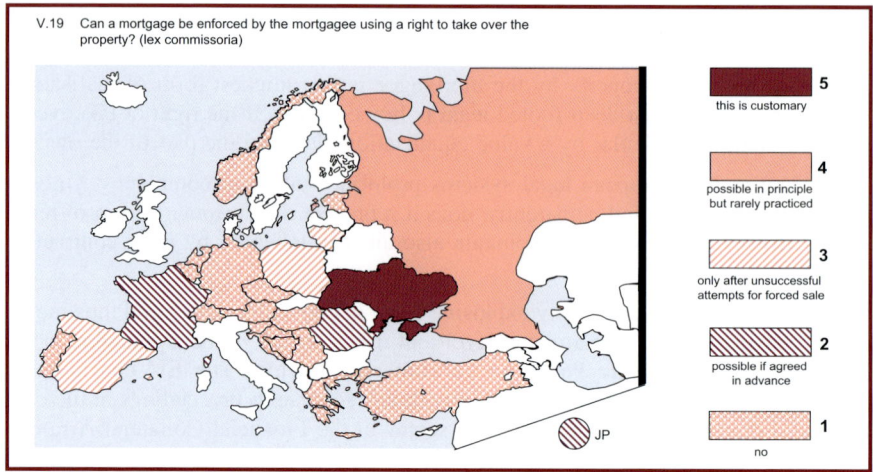

V.19   Can a mortgage be enforced by the mortgagee using a right to take over the property? (lex commissoria)

5 this is customary

4 possible in principle but rarely practiced

3 only after unsuccessful attempts for forced sale

2 possible if agreed in advance

1 no

20.   When the mortgagee takes over the property, must compensation be paid if the value of the property exceeds the debt?

This question only makes sense, of course, if there is a right of takeover. The complete absence of a right to compensation certainly has explosive effect in legal policy terms, although it is surprisingly seldom found.

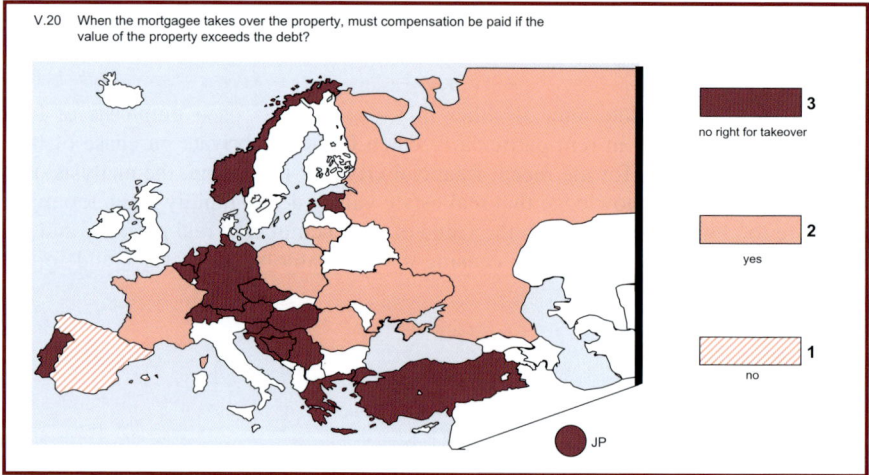

V.20   When the mortgagee takes over the property, must compensation be paid if the value of the property exceeds the debt?

3 no right for takeover

2 yes

1 no

21. Can the mortgagee himself take part in a forced sale auction and acquire the property?

The "private" right of takeover (*lex commissoria*) must be distinguished from purchase at auction by the enforcing creditor. The owner or debtor is not in need of protection to the same degree here as with a takeover without judicial action because the formalisation of the process will largely put a stop to any manipulation. However, the danger also exists that the mortgagee will seize this opportunity to his advantage and buy at auction cheaply. Some countries protect against this by cancelling the residual debt either in whole or in part, e.g. in Germany up to 7/10 of the assessed value of the property (section 114a Law on Compulsory Auctions and Forced Administration [Gesetz über die Zwangsversteigerung und Zwangsverwaltung: ZVG]). In other legal systems, by contrast, there is no such protection, i.e. repayment to the extent of the proceeds of the auction has to suffice. A strong but inflexible solution is a complete prohibition on self-bidding; however, this does not appear to apply anywhere among the countries examined.

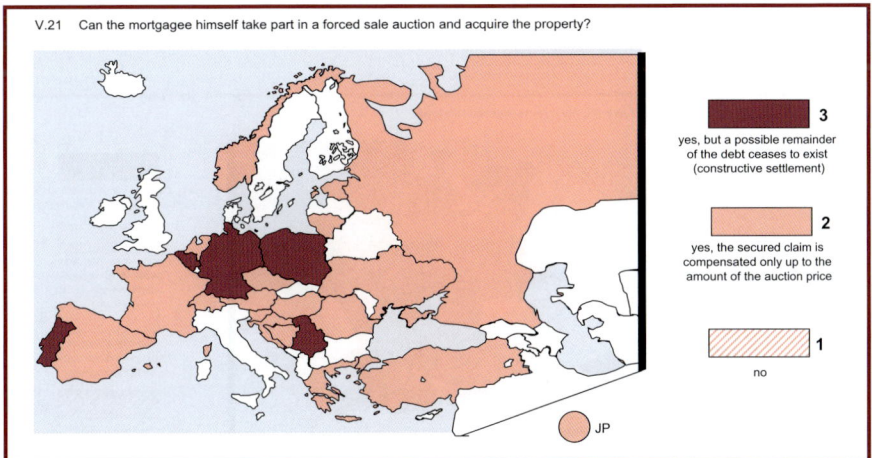

V.21 Can the mortgagee himself take part in a forced sale auction and acquire the property?

3 — yes, but a possible remainder of the debt ceases to exist (constructive settlement)

2 — yes, the secured claim is compensated only up to the amount of the auction price

1 — no

22. Which unregistered claims have priority over registered mortgages?

Distribution of the proceeds of realisation is one of the most important issues for the enforceability of a mortgage. A factor of paramount significance here is which claims take priority over the mortgages, even if they are unregistered.[101]

The transaction costs take precedence everywhere. Property taxes, public charges and maintenance costs are also usually given priority. By contrast, salary claims by employees and claims to maintenance are generally only taken into consideration in relation to mortgages within narrow limits, so are restricted, for example, to a statutory minimum wage, a short time period or to employees working on the property itself.

---

101 On preferential rights in insolvency proceedings cf. C.VI.9.

The preferential handling of all tax claims and salary claims against the current owner and all his predecessors was still the general rule in Central and Eastern Europe until the 1990s.[102] While such privileged treatment has largely been abolished by reforms, it is still to be found in one form or another in Latin law systems or systems influenced by Code Civil law. The advantage that this can bring in a few individual cases for some employees and the tax authorities is countered by the considerable restriction on the value of the security right over real property as a means of security. Lenders who cannot know the extent of preferential future claims are not going to rely in the usual way on the value of the security right over real property and thus in many cases will be more cautious in relation to financing, which may indirectly in turn reduce national income and the number of jobs.

Protection in practice against these preferential rights is sometimes achieved by commercial property being held by special purpose vehicles (SPVs) which are restricted contractually to exercise no other sort of commercial activity except to hold the property. In this way, to a very substantial extent, salary claims do not even arise and the taxes can be calculated. But the cost of these structures and their ongoing supervision by the mortgagee increases the costs of property finance and makes credit more expensive.

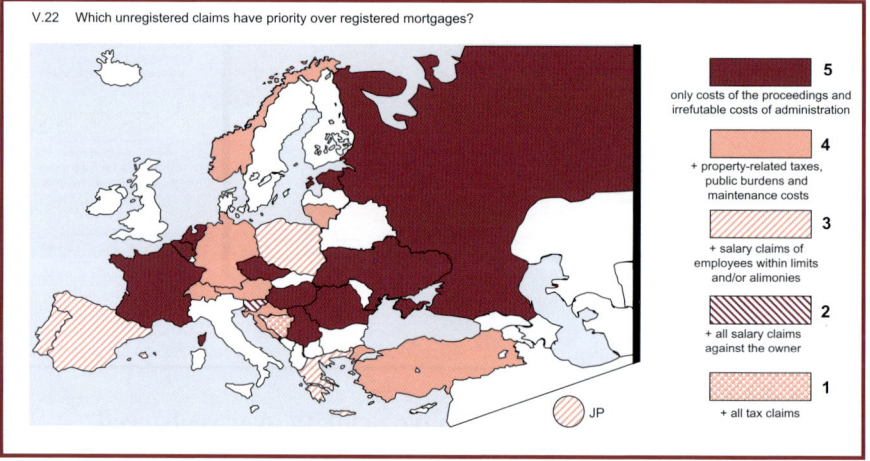

V.22   Which unregistered claims have priority over registered mortgages?

5
only costs of the proceedings and irrefutable costs of administration

4
+ property-related taxes, public burdens and maintenance costs

3
+ salary claims of employees within limits and/or alimonies

2
+ all salary claims against the owner

1
+ all tax claims

JP

23.   Can contractors and tradesmen who have contributed to the construction or renovation of the property secure priority over the property for their claims?

It is frequently requested on the political level that a legal framework is provided to give building contractors and tradesmen a preferential right ahead of mortgagees when the proceeds of realisation are distributed, in order that the creditors who produced the building and generated its value through their work input do not go away empty handed. However, it must be taken into account that, on the one hand, it is often difficult to calculate the added value and to prove which of the individual tradesmen contributed to the overall value. On the other hand there are certainly

---

102 On the innovative reforms on this matter in Polish law which in particular led to the abolition of the "secret" statutory mortgage in favour of the tax authorities, cf. e.g. *Drewicz-Tułodziecka/ Soergel/Stöcker*, Mehr Rechtssicherheit für die Hypothek in Polen [*More legal security for mortgages in Poland*], WM 2002, p. 891 et seq. (893). The taxes specified in the slide under No. 4 thus no longer take obligatory precedence over a mortgage.

other approaches, preserving public disclosure, to ensure that the companies involved can have claims that arose during the period of construction satisfied.

Individual legislatures have thus developed very different regulations in order to resolve this conflict of interests. The recent laws on this in Central and Eastern Europe refer the building contractor to having a contractually drawn up security right over real property created in order to secure his claims.

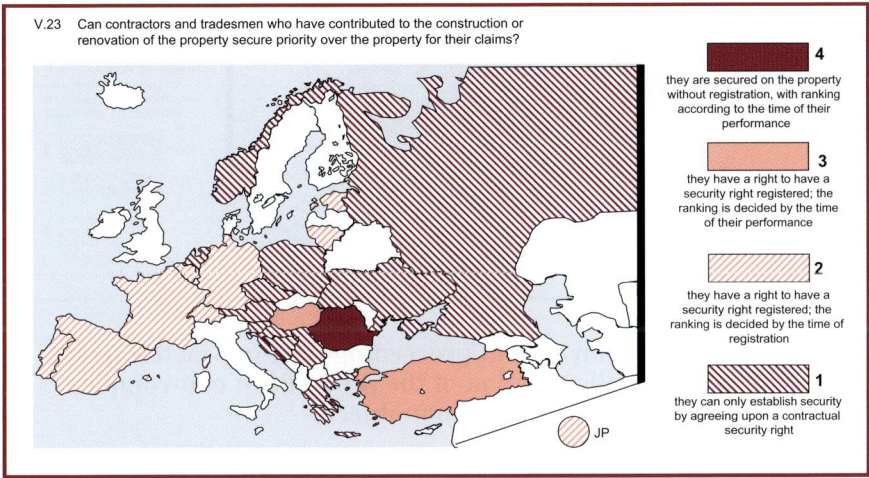

V.23 Can contractors and tradesmen who have contributed to the construction or renovation of the property secure priority over the property for their claims?

4 they are secured on the property without registration, with ranking according to the time of their performance

3 they have a right to have a security right registered; the ranking is decided by the time of their performance

2 they have a right to have a security right registered; the ranking is decided by the time of registration

1 they can only establish security by agreeing upon a contractual security right

24. To what extent can the creditor claim interest and costs from the proceeds of enforcement (excluding the cost of the proceeding)?

The regulations on the scope of liability of the property are very diverse. While some countries grant an additional amount of liability for the mortgagee which can be used for various ancillary claims, other legal systems only offer the possibility of demanding interest in accordance with the loan agreement. In between there are a number of variations along this spectrum.

With strictly accessory mortgages the amount of interest that can be claimed results in principle from the contractual loan agreement. This is, however, also to some extent the case with mortgages with strictly restricted accessoriness. Many legal systems offer the possibility within the contractually agreed framework of claiming not only the interest but also other claims and thereby provide the mortgagee with more flexibility. The drawback with such solutions is that they allow the amount that can be claimed overall in the realisation to be considerably higher than the registered capital sum. Some legal systems therefore try to protect subordinate creditors from unpleasant surprises and give them more information about the overall prior ranking amount. The most clear-cut solution is for the security rights over real property to be registered only for an amount that also has to cover interest and costs, meaning that the borrower has to opt for this correspondingly higher capital sum. Another option is for the interest secured by mortgage to be limited in amount or to provide a statutory framework for interest, costs and other possible claims instead of a contractually agreed framework.

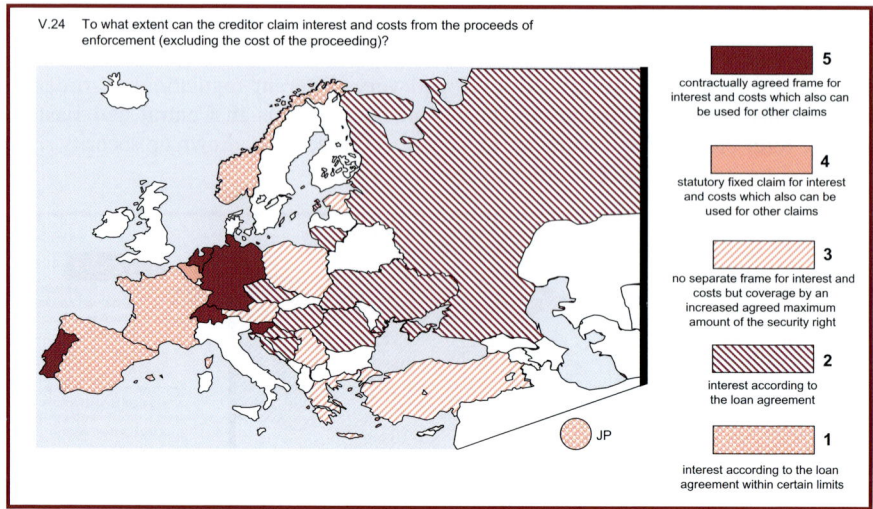

V.24   To what extent can the creditor claim interest and costs from the proceeds of
       enforcement (excluding the cost of the proceeding)?

5 contractually agreed frame for interest and costs which also can be used for other claims

4 statutory fixed claim for interest and costs which also can be used for other claims

3 no separate frame for interest and costs but coverage by an increased agreed maximum amount of the security right

2 interest according to the loan agreement

1 interest according to the loan agreement within certain limits

25. How long do enforcement proceedings last in practice from initiation until distribution of the proceeds in non-complex cases where the owner does not object?

In comparative studies with qualitative conclusions the duration of enforcement proceedings is frequently regarded as the central benchmark for the efficiency and legal effectiveness of a mortgage. Such an assessment is, however, based ultimately on a weighted factor that is not wholly convincing. The problem is that duration alone permits very little to be said about whether the mortgagees' claims are also actually capable of being completely satisfied in the enforcement proceedings. Much more relevant for the satisfactory outcome of the proceedings are rights to initiate and defend proceedings, the allocation of the burden of proof in the case of disputes and also possible priorities of other claims and issues of how far the mortgagee is in command of the proceedings.

In most countries there are no reliable statistics on the duration of proceedings. Where statistics are kept, no differentiation is made on the basis of the types of property and reasons for differing procedural duration. A distinction would certainly be useful, however, to show whether proceedings run smoothly and consequently determine the statutory standard periods, or whether the owner legitimately and for understandable reasons resists execution against his property using judicial remedies, even if ultimately he is defeated.

By and large it can be said that in most countries, in simple cases, enforcement proceedings last for less than a year, if the owner does not assert any opposing rights. In light of this, the evaluation method in the EBRD Study appears to fail to take all the factors into account.[103]

---

103 Cf. on this in D.I.2.

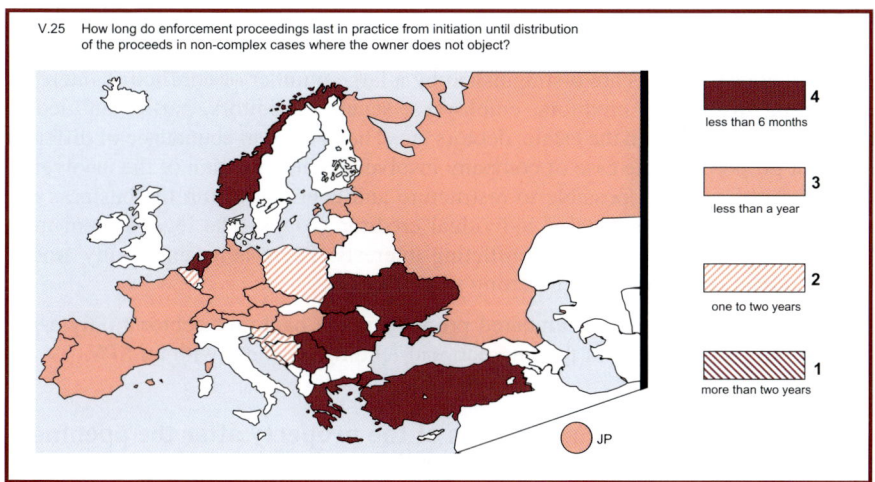

V.25 How long do enforcement proceedings last in practice from initiation until distribution of the proceeds in non-complex cases where the owner does not object?

26. How long do enforcement proceedings last in practice from initiation until distribution of the proceeds in non-complex cases if the owner uses judicial remedies?

If the owner defends himself against execution on his property, the proceedings are delayed everywhere, as a rule by one echelon of time. If the owner disputes the secured claim and therefore brings proceedings against the execution by resort to all court instances, an upper limit for the duration of the proceedings is very difficult to estimate. The duration of the proceedings then depends on the normal duration of proceedings in civil law disputes because the enforcement proceedings can only follow the subsequently initiated contentious proceedings.

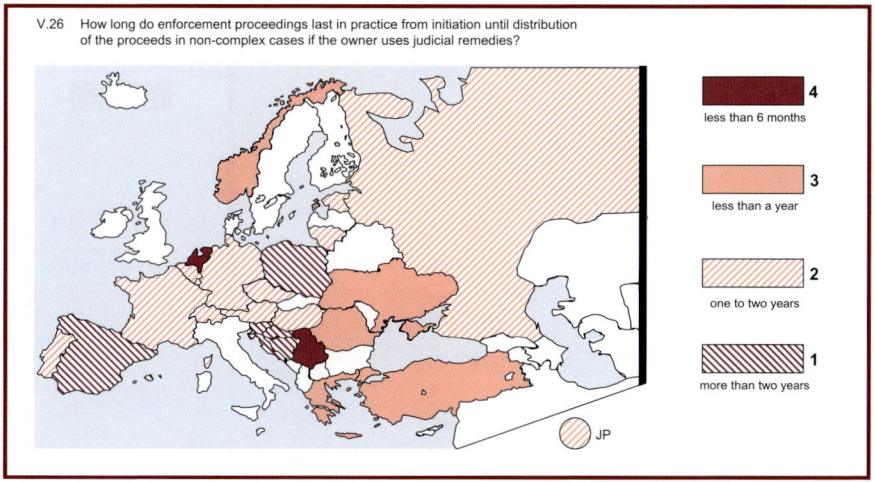

V.26 How long do enforcement proceedings last in practice from initiation until distribution of the proceeds in non-complex cases if the owner uses judicial remedies?

VI. Insolvency

Insolvency proceedings are distinguished by a large number of conflicting interests: competing insolvency creditors, employees, secured creditors, parties entitled to release of property from the estate, debtors etc. They cover an abundance of different items of property. In the case of company insolvency, the intention of the insolvency administrator as far as possible to restructure and continue to run the business can run contrary to the interests of individual creditor groups. The legal system must strike a balance between these conflicting interests. There is no uniformity among the examined countries in their setting of priorities.

The issue is easier if the encumbered property is the bankrupt debtor's only asset, as may often be the case in the international lending business with an SPV.

1. Who may initiate realisation of the property after the opening of insolvency proceedings over the owner's estate?

When insolvency proceedings are opened over the property owner's estate, power of administration and disposal over the property in principle passes to the insolvency administrator everywhere. The possibilities for mortgagees to influence further procedures do, however, differ and this will be examined in the following slides.

There are three basic possibilities for regulating the right to initiate the realisation of an encumbered property and each of these is put into practice in several legal systems. One possibility is for the right to initiate realisation to lie only with the mortgagee – most notably the Spanish solution. Alternatively, the right can lie with the mortgagee or the insolvency administrator. This, for instance, is the German solution. Or only the insolvency administrator may initiate realisation, which is the position in the majority of the legal systems examined.

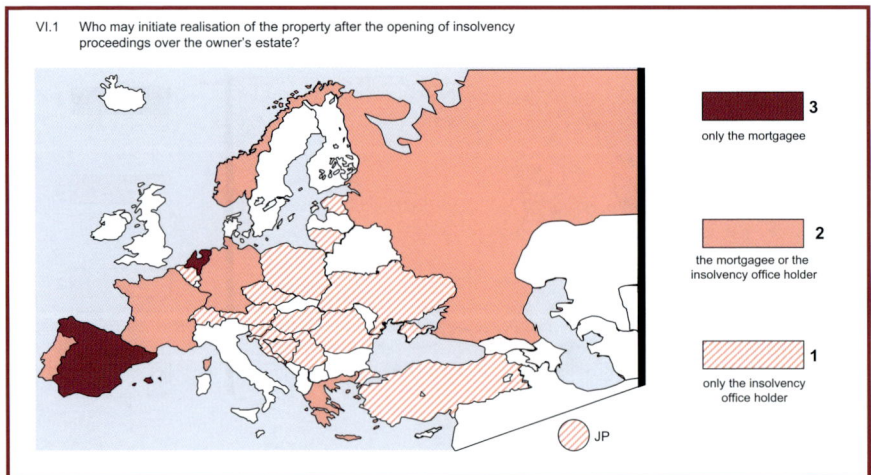

VI.1   Who may initiate realisation of the property after the opening of insolvency proceedings over the owner's estate?

3 only the mortgagee

2 the mortgagee or the insolvency office holder

1 only the insolvency office holder

2. To what extent can the mortgagee influence the realisation of the encumbered property when the owner is subject to insolvency liquidation proceedings?

Many legal systems, Germany and Spain, for example, allow the implementation of separate enforcement proceedings outside the insolvency proceedings or grant the creditor considerable influence over the realisation procedure. Some legal systems, primarily in Central and Eastern Europe, form a separate asset class for the encumbered property with consent requirements from the mortgagee.

By contrast, in other countries in Central and South Eastern Europe, procedural jurisdiction lies solely with the insolvency administrator so that the mortgagees can only exert indirect influence over the general supervision by the court that is competent in respect of the insolvency proceedings. The insolvency administrator is therefore largely able to act independently.

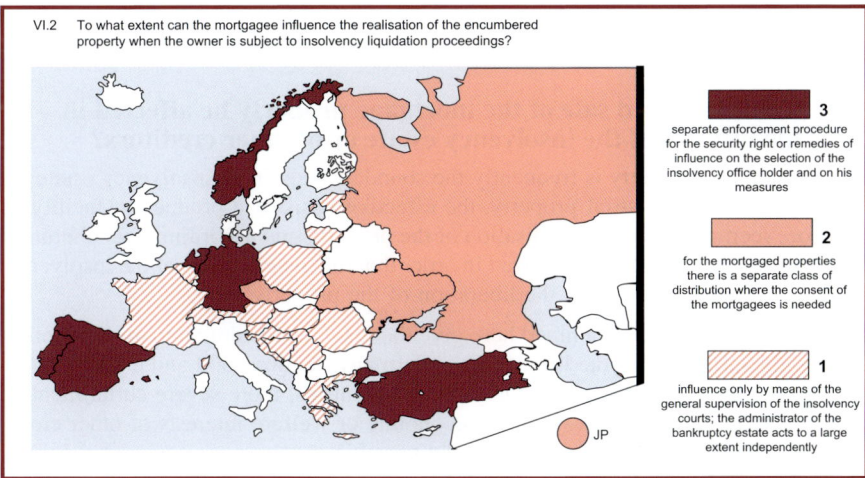

VI.2   To what extent can the mortgagee influence the realisation of the encumbered property when the owner is subject to insolvency liquidation proceedings?

3 separate enforcement procedure for the security right or remedies of influence on the selection of the insolvency office holder and on his measures

2 for the mortgaged properties there is a separate class of distribution where the consent of the mortgagees is needed

1 influence only by means of the general supervision of the insolvency courts; the administrator of the bankruptcy estate acts to a large extent independently

JP

3. To what extent can the mortgagee influence the realisation of the encumbered property when the owner is under reorganisation or composition proceedings?

In reorganisation proceedings there is a risk that a contribution may be demanded from the mortgagees in order to maintain a company, e.g. in the form of a moratorium or partial waiver. Legal systems fall into two groups in this regard. Some legal systems make such restrictions dependent on the consent of the mortgagees or a majority of them. But there are also other countries in which payment of a restructuring contribution can be forced.

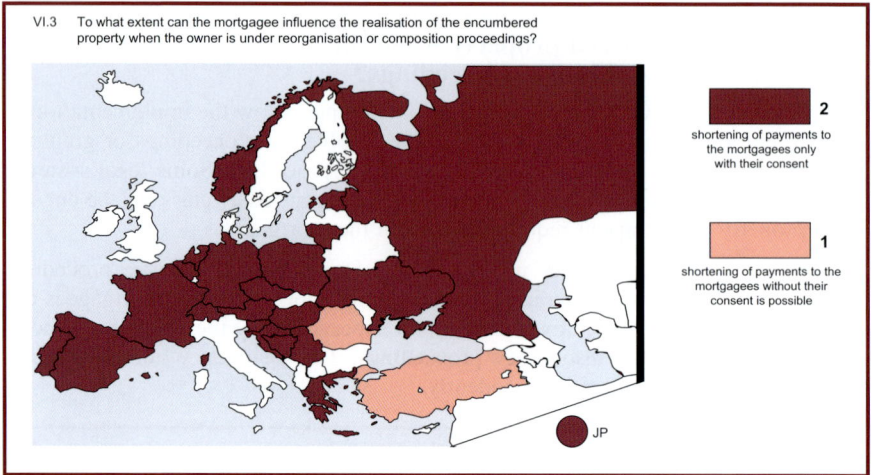

VI.3   To what extent can the mortgagee influence the realisation of the encumbered
        property when the owner is under reorganisation or composition proceedings?

4.   Can the forced sale of the mortgage property be affected in the interest of the insolvency estate or of other creditors?

The item of real property is frequently the soundest asset in an insolvency estate or, in the case of an industrial property, the effective basis of a production facility. It therefore seems obvious that realisation of the property and accordingly its liberation from the insolvency estate is deferred in order that the overall value of the insolvency estate is not compromised by the liberation of the property.

Nearly all the countries examined here give the insolvency administrator this option either only subject to a time limit (e.g. in Germany, sections 30d and e ZVG) or do not provide the possibility at all. Only in few countries, more severe curtailment of the realisation option by reason of the economic or welfare interests of other creditors does, however, generally appear to be possible.

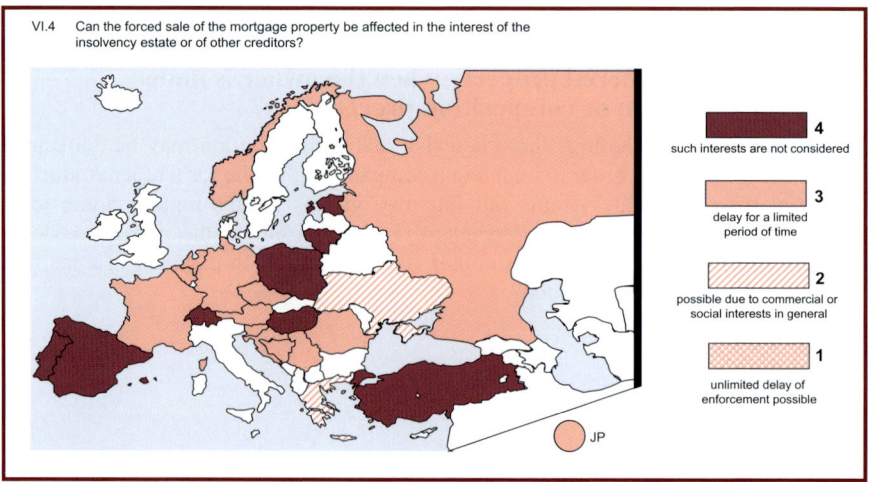

VI.4   Can the forced sale of the mortgage property be affected in the interest of the
        insolvency estate or of other creditors?

5.   If the enforcement procedure is delayed in the interest of the insolvency estate, must the insolvency estate compensate the mortgagee's loss?

Western European countries sometimes give mortgagees a right to compensation in the event that realisation of the estate by the insolvency administrator is delayed. But it appears that most legal systems do not provide for this. The notion of compensation in relation to any intervention affecting security rights has primarily been developed in American insolvency proceedings.[104]

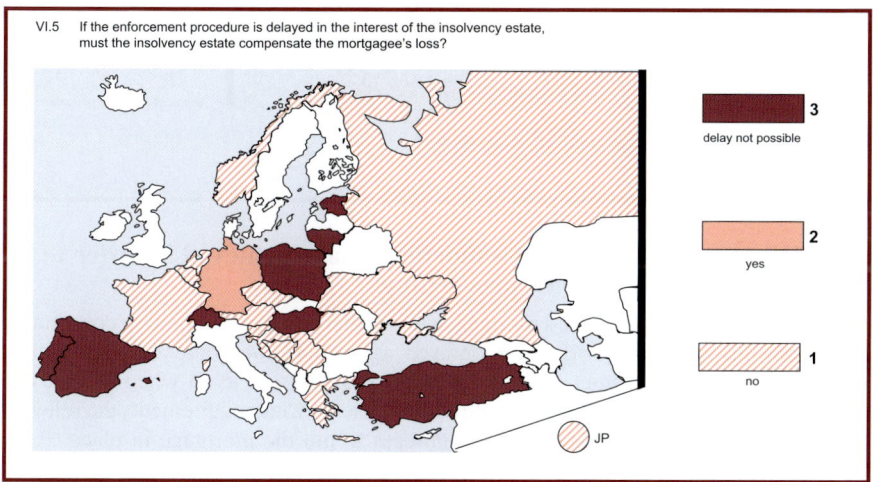

VI.5   If the enforcement procedure is delayed in the interest of the insolvency estate, must the insolvency estate compensate the mortgagee's loss?

3 — delay not possible

2 — yes

1 — no

6.   When does the insolvency take effect? (disregarding possible rescissions)

Of great significance to all creditors of an insolvency estate is the precise time at which the insolvency takes effect. Only in a few countries is the opening of the insolvency proceedings of sole importance in this regard.

Most legal systems assume the time of the opening of the insolvency, but provide in addition the possibility of interim restrictions or reversal periods in order to include previous disposals in the run-up of the insolvency proceedings too. A mortgagee must be informed of these periods if he wants to be sure that his mortgage will actually continue to apply in the insolvency. But important in this regard is also the status of the mortgage creation process at the time in question (see VI.7.)

---

104 See *Baur/Stürner*, Zwangsvollstreckungs-, Konkurs- und Vergleichsrecht [*Compulsory enforcement, bankruptcy and composition law*], Vol. II Insolvency Law, 12th ed. 1990, marginal note 39.89; *Stürner/Kern*, Deutsche Hypothekenpfandbriefe und U.S.-amerikanische Deckungswerte [*German mortgage bonds and US cover assets*], 2007, p. 93 et seq. (for securities on moveable property).

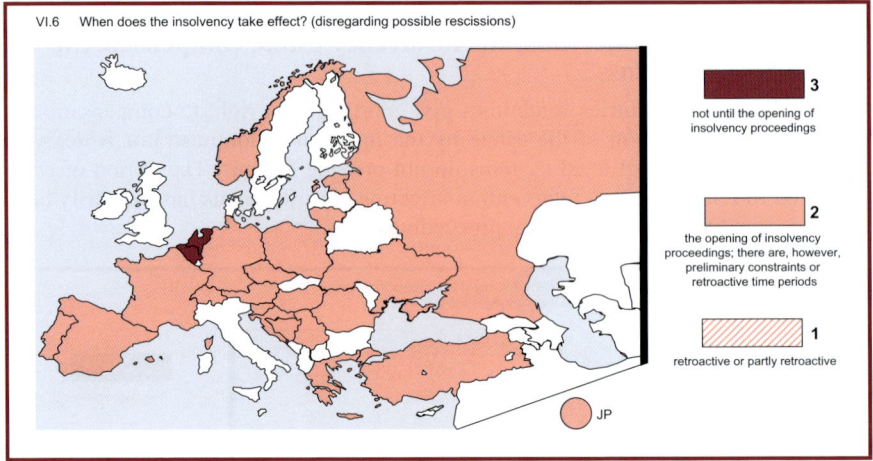

VI.6   When does the insolvency take effect? (disregarding possible rescissions)

3
not until the opening of
insolvency proceedings

2
the opening of insolvency
proceedings; there are, however,
preliminary constraints or
retroactive time periods

1
retroactive or partly retroactive

JP

7.   What legal status must a mortgage have achieved in order to be effective in insolvency proceedings?

Of fundamental importance for a mortgagee is whether and on what precise constitutive conditions his mortgage will be recognised as such in the context of insolvency proceedings. This has direct consequences for the decision as to when a bank can disburse the loan. This depends in the individual case on what requirements the relevant legal system places on the status of the process to put the mortgage in place.[105]

In many countries a security right over real property is only taken into account in insolvency proceedings if its registration in the land or property register has already taken place. Other legal systems move this point in time forward and allow the lodging of the application for registration or the application for a priority notice, an annotation or a pre-registration to suffice. Only very occasionally is it sufficient for the creation of the mortgage inter partes to have taken place.

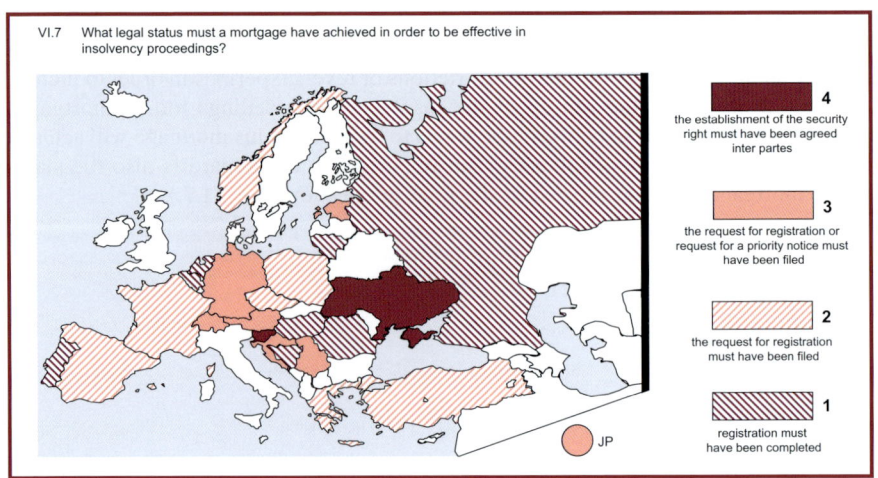

VI.7   What legal status must a mortgage have achieved in order to be effective in
        insolvency proceedings?

4
the establishment of the security
right must have been agreed
inter partes

3
the request for registration or
request for a priority notice must
have been filed

2
the request for registration
must have been filed

1
registration must
have been completed

JP

---

8. How is the revenue from the forced sale distributed?

In a range of countries the creditor receives the realisation proceeds due to him directly out of the realisation proceedings that are carried out specifically in relation to the real property. In many countries the realisation proceeds are seized by the insolvency administrator, but are then paid out to the mortgagees without first becoming part of the insolvency estate. Another solution encountered is where the proceeds accrue to the insolvency estate and the mortgagee is then provided for preferentially from the estate for distribution.

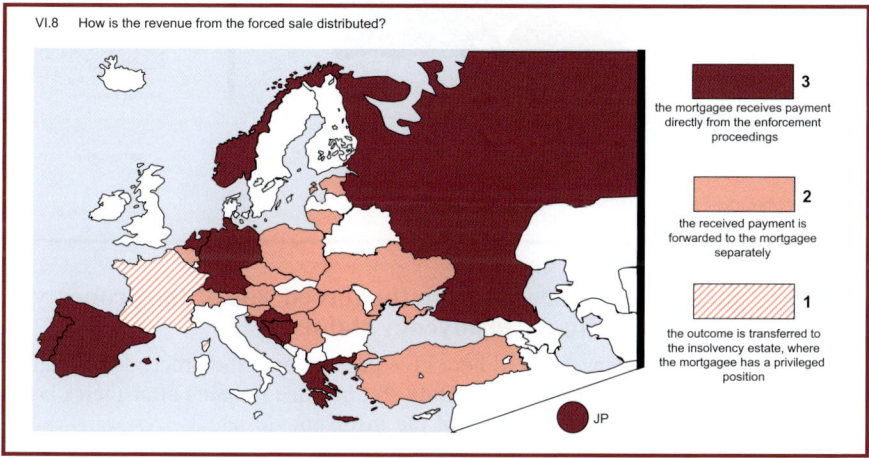

VI.8   How is the revenue from the forced sale distributed?

3 the mortgagee receives payment directly from the enforcement proceedings

2 the received payment is forwarded to the mortgagee separately

1 the outcome is transferred to the insolvency estate, where the mortgagee has a privileged position

9. Which unregistered claims have priority over mortgages?

As with the right of enforcement[106], the question as to whether claims that have not been registered can take precedence over a mortgage is of paramount importance in insolvency proceedings. These preferential rights, frequently described as privileges or secret mortgages, can seriously compromise the security value of a security right over real property or even erode it altogether if they are not foreseeable, verifiable or otherwise calculable.

Some years ago security rights over real property in Central and Eastern Europe were still jeopardised by numerous preferential rights of this sort. It is very gratifying that security rights over real property are now assigned a good ranking position in insolvency proceedings in all the legal systems examined here. Indeed in Central and Eastern Europe their codified position is often better than in many Western European countries.

---

106 Cf. C.V.22.

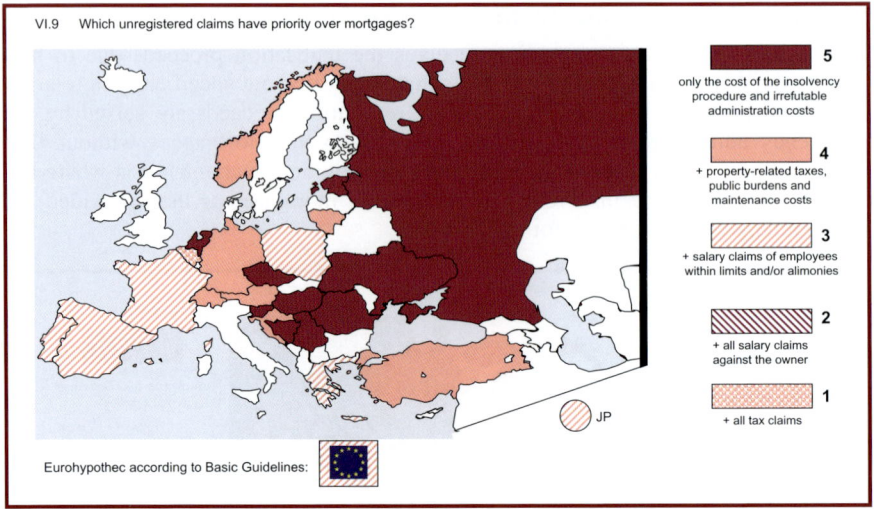

10. Are parts of the proceeds from the forced sale of the property used to cover ordinary insolvency claims?

Nearly all the legal systems covered here give priority over the proceeds of realisation of the property to the mortgagees. Only if a balance remains after their claims have been satisfied does this form part of the insolvency estate.

Only a very few countries make an exception to this and give a flat rate share of the realisation proceeds directly to the insolvency estate, thereby reducing the realisation proceeds for the mortgagees.

Using the example of German law it can be seen that these regulations can be extremely complicated: under section 171 of the German Insolvency Regulations [Insolvenzordnung: InsO] in conjunction with section 10 I 1a Act on forced sales proceedings [Gesetz über die Zwangsversteigerung und Zwangsverwaltung: ZVG], 4% of the proceeds from the realisation of moveable items that have joint liability under the mortgage (i.e. the fixtures and fittings) is deducted from the proceeds of realisation as a lump sum contribution to costs and brought into the insolvency estate. This deduction reduces the mortgagees' proceeds to this extent. In practice, however, this sum is generally not of any great relevance and can thus be disregarded.

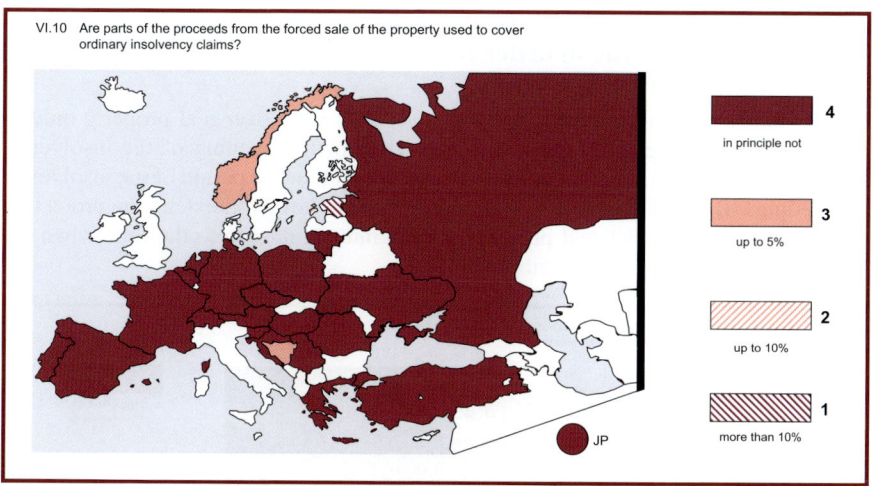

VI.10   Are parts of the proceeds from the forced sale of the property used to cover
        ordinary insolvency claims?

4 — in principle not
3 — up to 5%
2 — up to 10%
1 — more than 10%

11.   Does the mortgagee receive payment for interest and costs from the proceeds of the forced sale of the property?

By far the majority of the legal systems shown here provide for the mortgagee to receive the full amount of his interest and costs from the proceeds of realisation, i.e. in so far as the security right over real property also covers such costs outside of an insolvency. The insolvency then has no diminishing effect on the scope of the security.[107] Only very few countries curtail this basic principle.

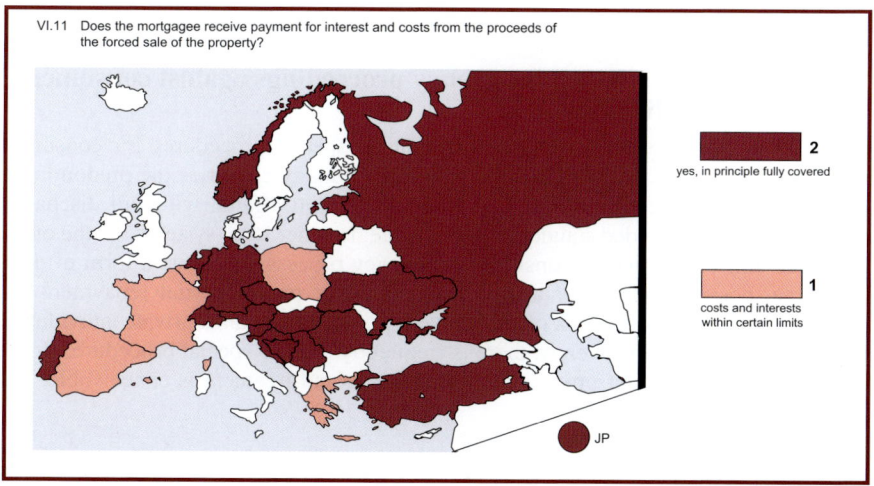

VI.11   Does the mortgagee receive payment for interest and costs from the proceeds of
        the forced sale of the property?

2 — yes, in principle fully covered
1 — costs and interests within certain limits

---

107 Cf. also C.V.24. on individual enforcement action.

12. Until which point in time must interest covered under the mortgage be due in order to be paid from the proceeds of the forced sale?

Some countries grant the protection of the security right over real property only in respect of loan interest that falls due up to time of the opening of the insolvency proceedings. The mortgagee thus has no interest yield for the period of the insolvency proceedings. By far the majority of legal systems do, however, extend the protection of the security right over real property also to interest due up to the time when the proceeds of realisation are distributed.

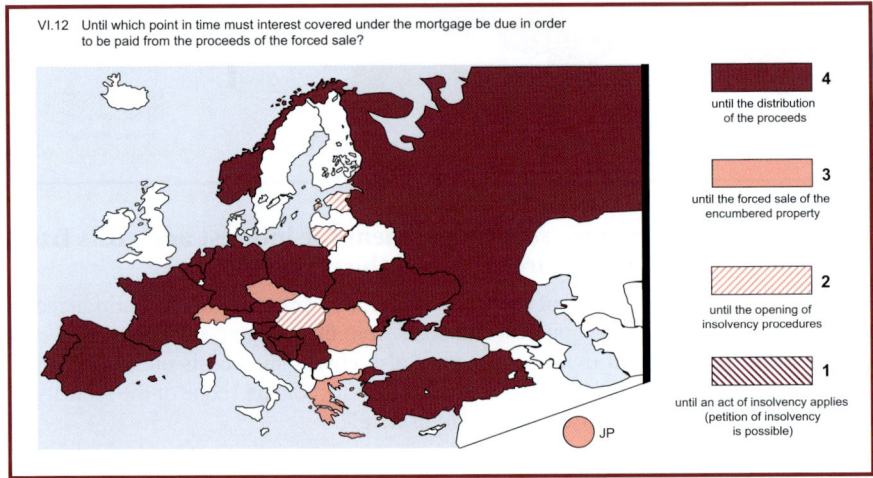

VI.12   Until which point in time must interest covered under the mortgage be due in order to be paid from the proceeds of the forced sale?

4 — until the distribution of the proceeds

3 — until the forced sale of the encumbered property

2 — until the opening of insolvency procedures

1 — until an act of insolvency applies (petition of insolvency is possible)

JP

13. What is the effect of insolvency proceedings against consumers (private individuals)?

In recent times many countries have introduced special procedures for consumer insolvency. The aims of such procedures differ. In many countries the predominant objective is simplification of the individual's financial affairs, with full discharge from debt not the intended standard consequence. In other legal systems, on the other hand, the aim of the special consumer insolvency process is at least a form of debt discharge, possibly only after a probation period of proper partial repayment. In countries where, due to the lack of an insolvency procedure against private individuals, there is no consumer insolvency, there is frequently also no special procedure. However, a similar debt relief process under the law of enforcement is conceivable.

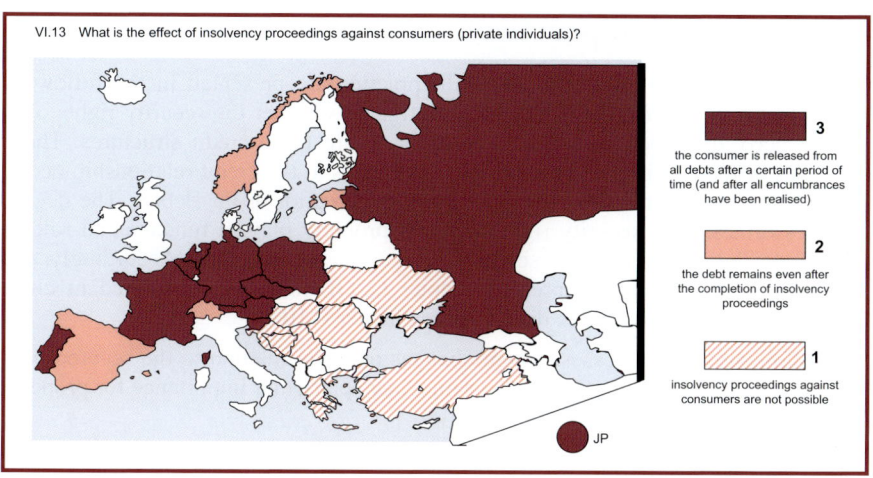

VI.13   What is the effect of insolvency proceedings against consumers (private individuals)?

3

the consumer is released from all debts after a certain period of time (and after all encumbrances have been realised)

2

the debt remains even after the completion of insolvency proceedings

1

insolvency proceedings against consumers are not possible

JP

14.   Do consumers in insolvency proceedings enjoy stronger protection in relation to mortgages compared to debtors/owners in insolvency proceedings generally?

In legal systems where there is a special consumer insolvency process a decision must be made as to whether the owner of encumbered property is to be given greater protection in such proceedings than he would receive in ordinary insolvency proceedings. It appears, however, that this does not happen or very rarely happens. It would also impact negatively on the banks' readiness to lend.

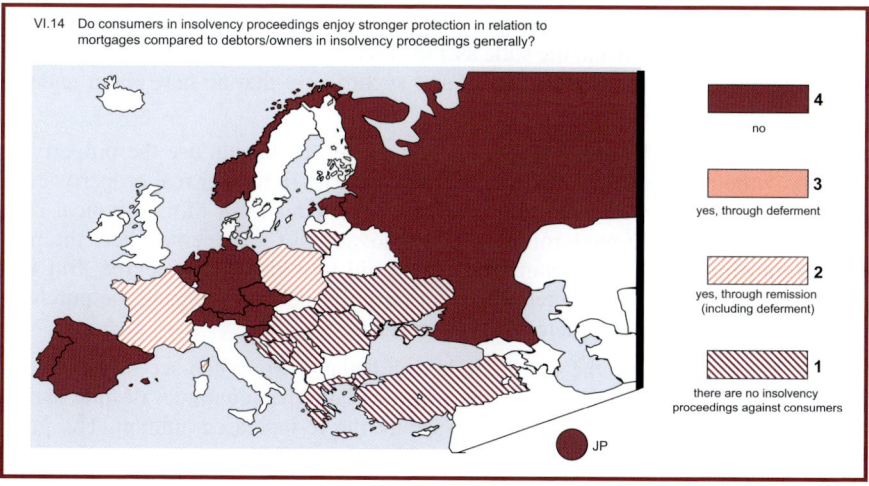

VI.14   Do consumers in insolvency proceedings enjoy stronger protection in relation to mortgages compared to debtors/owners in insolvency proceedings generally?

4

no

3

yes, through deferment

2

yes, through remission (including deferment)

1

there are no insolvency proceedings against consumers

JP

VII. Utilisation in practice

Some important case studies from credit practice are presented in the following slides. In the course of this it will be investigated whether the security rights over real property described here can be used to secure these credit structures. These examples primarily concern cases in which changes in the credit relationship occur. These changes can affect the secured claim, the creditor or the debtor. The degree of accessoriness of a security right over real property plays a fundamental role in relation to the flexibility of a security right over real property. Accordingly, the questions dealt with in the present chapter C.VII. must be considered in close association with the questions discussed in chapter C.III.

The following first five cases, where changes occur in relation to the secured debt but the creditor and debtor remain the same, have particular importance for property financing, both commercial and residential.

1.   Is it possible to structure a security right over real property in such a way that the amount of an existing secured claim can be increased without changing the security right over real property itself?

Credit facility enhancements and consequently loan increases take place frequently in credit practice. From a mortgage law point of view these pose no problem if an already partially repaid loan is to be "replenished" and brought up, either wholly or partially, to the level of the initial capital amount again. Frequently, however, the amount of the ultimate loan capital is left open and only limited to a maximum amount, e.g. in the form of a credit facility arrangement. It is essential in this regard that the security right over real property is created for a sufficient amount from the outset. Both the question and the slide assume that such an arrangement was included in the credit agreement from the outset and accordingly that no new claim under a new loan agreement arises.

For the owner such flexibility offers the advantage that he can use the property as security without the expense of creating a new security right over real property, even for liabilities that are only later of economic significance for him. A typical case might be a loan for the modernisation and renovation of a property where the purchase financing has in the meantime been repaid to a significant degree. But this could also be used for completely different purposes such as securing the purchase of another property or completely different assets.

All that is necessary is that the security right over real property is non-accessory in terms of its scope and extinguishment, for the secured claim then continues despite partial extinguishment and can also be used to secure the re-increased amount. The great majority of the legal systems presented here offer this possibility – in any event with the most flexible form of a security right over real property examined here in each case.

In many countries this possibility only exists, however, if the original contractual basis for the loan relationship still exists and can be accommodated by restructuring to the financial requirements. Once the contractual relationship is extinguished, however, in these countries the security right over real property can no longer be used either.

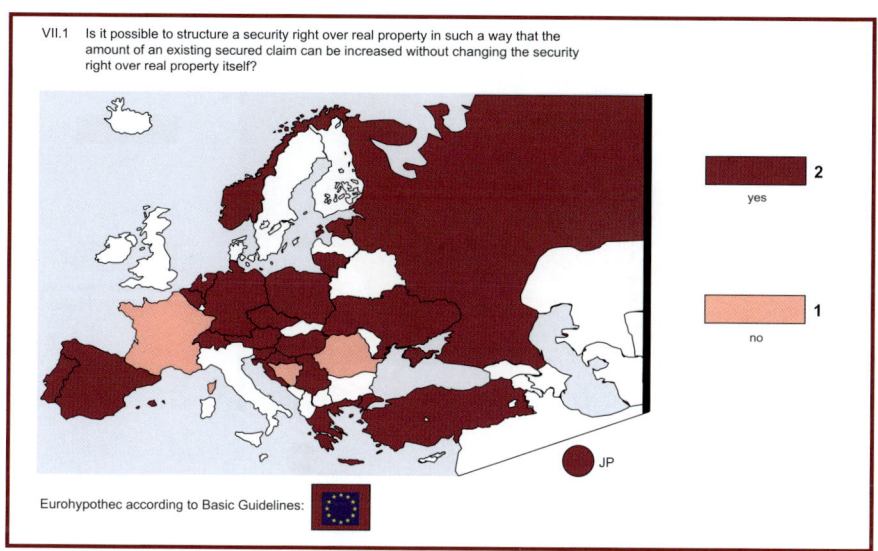

VII.1 Is it possible to structure a security right over real property in such a way that the amount of an existing secured claim can be increased without changing the security right over real property itself?

2. Is it possible to replace the existing secured claim with another claim against the current debtor – without affecting or changing the security right over real property? (the new claim immediately replacing the old one – novation, subrogation)

There is often a need in practice to replace one or more claims under a loan relationship with a new claim, often under another, new loan relationship. The textbook case is rescheduling. This is where the debtor takes out a new loan with the same creditor in order to be able to pay off another loan or several other loans. The economic background may be, for example, a change from a short-term variable interest rate loan to a long-term fixed one.

From a legal point of view a new claim is constituted and the earlier claims are extinguished. A security right over real property with strict accessoriness of extinguishment would consequently also expire and a new security right over real property would have to be created to secure the new claim, which in turn would trigger the usual costs. Nearly all countries have, however, developed possibilities for avoiding this.

Many legal systems generally permit debt replacement and thereby breach the principle of strict accessoriness as regards the accessoriness of extinguishment. Others only allow debt replacement if the underlying legal relationship at least continues, e.g. the framework loan agreement continues in force – the accessoriness of extinguishment is strongly relaxed here. Legal systems that wish in principle to adhere as far as possible to the principle of accessoriness must have complicated legal constructions available in order to achieve the same aim, such as, for example, the technique of back-to-back novation and subrogation.

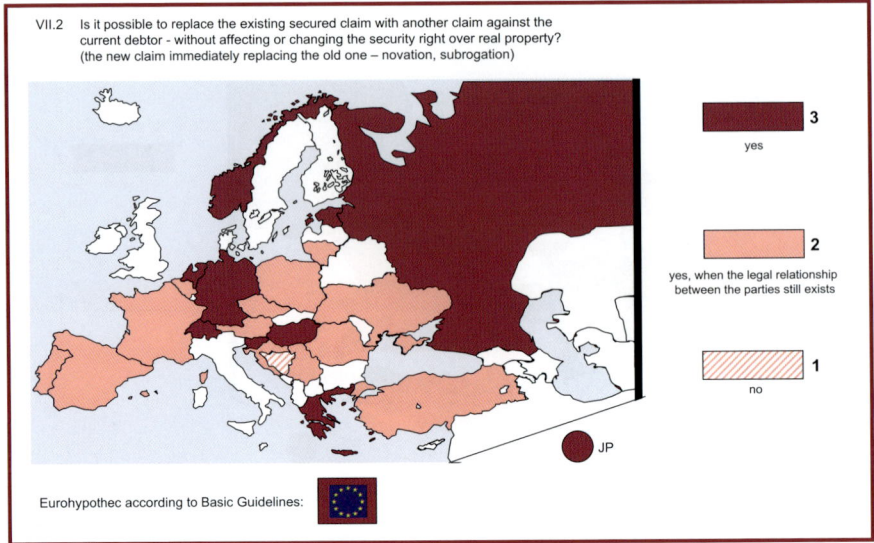

VII.2 Is it possible to replace the existing secured claim with another claim against the
current debtor - without affecting or changing the security right over real property?
(the new claim immediately replacing the old one – novation, subrogation)

3 — yes

2 — yes, when the legal relationship between the parties still exists

1 — no

JP

Eurohypothec according to Basic Guidelines:

3. Is it possible to secure new claims under the security right over real property once the original claims have been extinguished completely?

The technical "trick" of avoiding the pitfalls of the accessoriness of extinguishment by the use of novation and subrogation cannot therefore succeed if there is a time gap between extinguishment of the previous claim and establishment of the new claim. In any legal system where the principle of accessoriness is strictly maintained and no exceptions are permitted in this situation, the security right over real property cannot be used to secure a new claim as it is likewise irrecoverably extinguished with the old claim.

The strength and flexibility of security rights over real property that are structured as non-accessory as regards extinguishment, as is the case in around half of the countries examined, is apparent here.

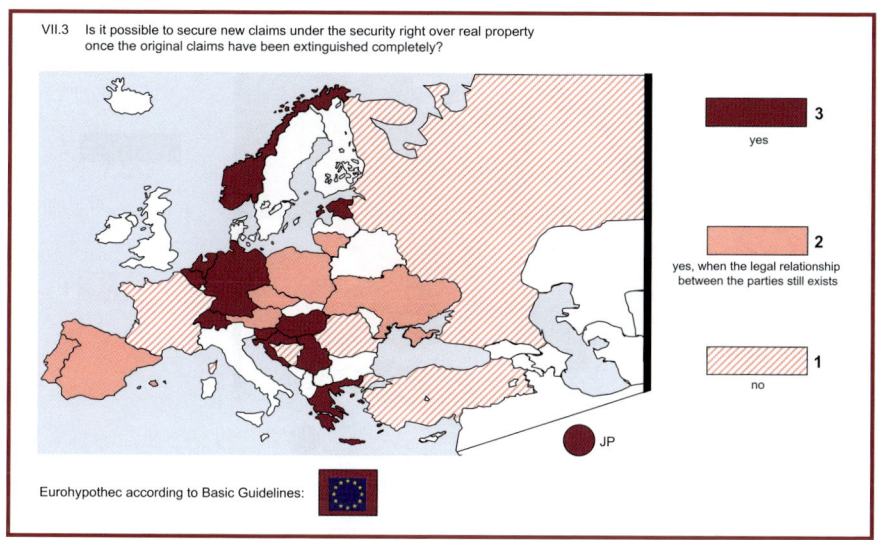

VII.3 Is it possible to secure new claims under the security right over real property once the original claims have been extinguished completely?

4. Is it possible to secure a revolving credit line without further action and without necessitating alterations to the security right over real property itself?

A credit line, as a general rule, is a credit agreement under which the level of the credit can fluctuate and only a maximum figure is specified. A credit line of this kind can be secured without any difficulty by security rights over real property whose accessoriness of scope and extinguishment is either relaxed or abandoned completely.

Business people and the self-employed with irregular earnings but regular outgoings have a particular economic need to provide cover for a constantly fluctuating credit requirement. Very early on, even legal systems that have a strong emphasis on the accessoriness of the security right over real property therefore developed this possibility of a more flexible mortgage arrangement. As the advantages of this more flexible form of security right over real property soon became generally apparent, it has come to be used in many countries today far beyond this customer group.

A strictly accessory mortgage may also be used to secure a credit line if it can secure a future claim which, in addition, does not have to be specified, only ascertainable. The security right over real property can then secure the future claim that exists when the credit line is terminated, e.g. in the event of termination of the credit line by the bank when the customer does not make the agreed payments.

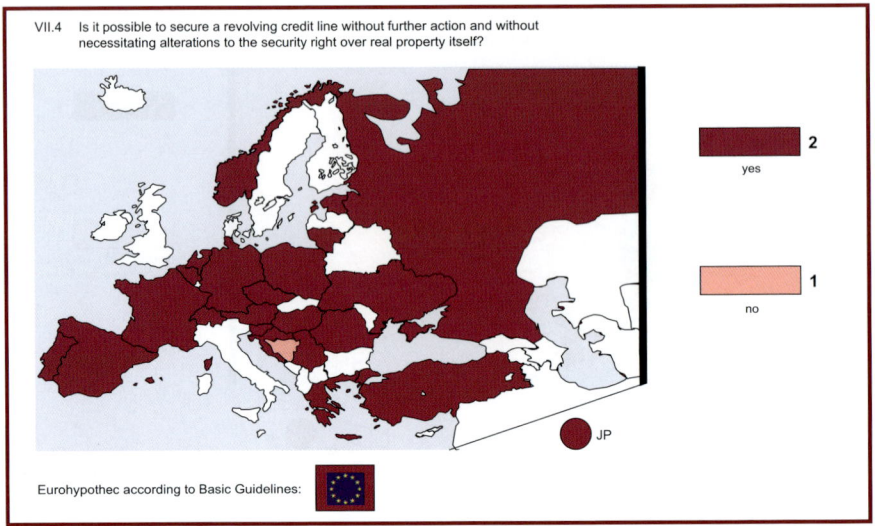

VII.4   Is it possible to secure a revolving credit line without further action and without necessitating alterations to the security right over real property itself?

5.   Is it possible (without alterations to the security right over real property) to secure a long-term loan where the interest rate is only set for a part of the term and must subsequently be agreed again for shorter or longer periods? (sectioned loans)

The "sectioned loans" type of financing is very significant in many countries today because the scheduled duration of property loans, particularly in private housing finance, is very long, frequently around 30 years. But customers do not want to be bound to one interest rate for such a long period of time because they hope that it might go down in future. The banks also have problems offering such long-term fixed rates because over such a long period of time it is only in exceptional cases that they themselves can obtain funding at fixed interest rates.

For this reason the interest rate is often only fixed for part of the term and after expiry of this period a new interest rate is agreed. The emergence of a new claim does not, as a rule, amount to novation because only the level of the interest rate is being changed. As regards the security right over real property, all that is necessary is that it can be established with a maximum interest rate or with a maximum amount that can be calculated at a high enough figure also to cover future interest rate increases. Non-accessory security rights over real property naturally offer a very simple solution, as both the capital amount and the interest rate of the security right over real property can be specified independently of the capital amount and the interest rate of the secured claim.

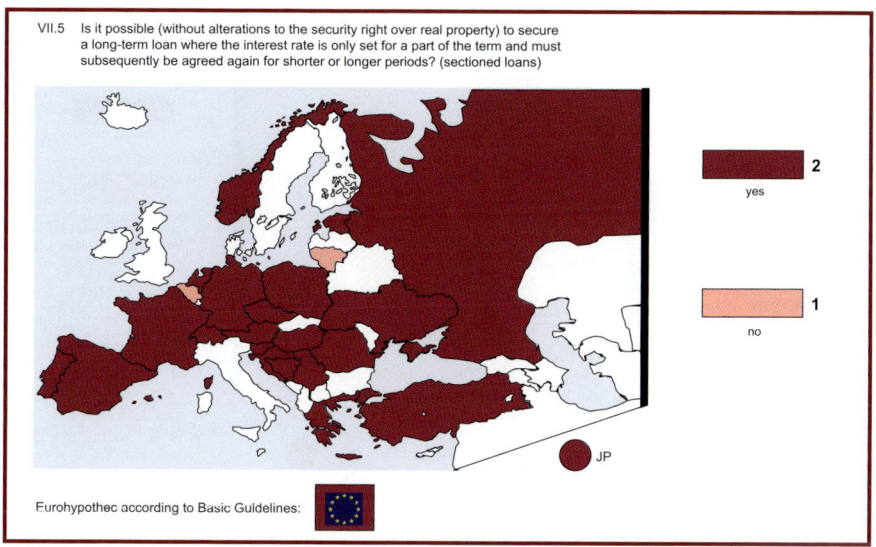

VII.5   Is it possible (without alterations to the security right over real property) to secure
         a long-term loan where the interest rate is only set for a part of the term and must
         subsequently be agreed again for shorter or longer periods? (sectioned loans)

2 yes

1 no

JP

Eurohypothec according to Basic Guidelines:

6.   Can the security right over real property be transferred from Bank A to Bank B and then secure new claims? (Change of secured claim and creditor through transfer of the security right over real property)

Cases of practical relevance where there is a change of creditor are investigated in questions 6 – 11. What these cases involve is achieving a change of creditor and secured claim while retaining the same security right over real property.

The simplest case is classic refinancing. Here the customer changes from one bank to another, thereby redeeming his loan with a new loan from the new bank. From a legal standpoint a new claim arises between new contracting parties that can only be secured by means of the same security right over real property if either the security right over real property generally permits a change of creditor and secured claim or if a special regulation allows such a substitution.

This shows the clear advantage of the non-accessory security right over real property where the secured claim can be replaced without any difficulty.

The only way some legal systems can achieve the same aim is for the old claim to be taken over by Bank B too and only then for it to be replaced with a new claim. This is the technique of novation and subrogation.

A range of countries does not offer this arrangement option. This includes the Netherlands, although without change of creditor its bank mortgage represents a very flexible type of security right over real property. Its limitations become apparent with a change of creditor, because if it is transferred to another creditor the "bank mortgage" has to be converted into a fixed mortgage [vest hypothek] and then the accessoriness of extinguishment applies so the security right over real property also expires with the extinguishment of the original secured loan. Despite the new flexibility introduced in 2007 the same is furthermore the case with the "hipoteca de máximo" in Spain.

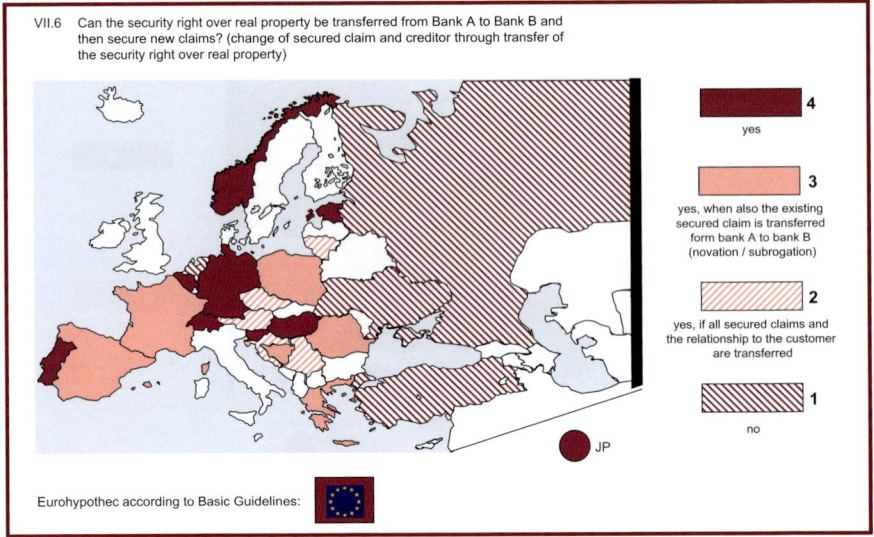

VII.6   Can the security right over real property be transferred from Bank A to Bank B and
then secure new claims? (change of secured claim and creditor through transfer of
the security right over real property)

4 — yes

3 — yes, when also the existing secured claim is transferred form bank A to bank B (novation / subrogation)

2 — yes, if all secured claims and the relationship to the customer are transferred

1 — no

JP

Eurohypothec according to Basic Guidelines:

7.   Can the security right over real property and secured claim be held by different persons?

The economic background to this question is cases in which banks cooperate with each other as happens with credit consortiums or bridging finance. While a building is in the course of construction it is a great advantage if a security right over real property that is to continue later on a long-term basis can, depending on the stage the construction project has reached, be used proportionally for the banks respectively providing the bridging and the end financing. If this is not possible, providing cover for the bridging finance with a security right over real property and coordinating this with a security right over real property for the end financing is so complicated that in most cases a coordinated approach is avoided and the consequence of more expensive bridging finance is accepted.

Where a property is jointly financed by several banks, although in most countries all the banks can have their own security rights over real property registered with the same ranking, in view of the not uncommon later addition of other banks or the later transfer of shares in the financing between banks, this is pretty inflexible. These joint forms of financing often appear to be cost effective only if one bank can also hold the security right over real property for the other banks in a fiduciary capacity.

What is required in such cases is a mortgage where the mortgage creditor does not, at the same time, also have to be the creditor of the secured claim and consequently does not have to hold all secured claims. Sameness of the creditor of the security right over real property and the secured claim is, however, an important structural feature of all security rights over real property that follow the precept of accessoriness of competence.

Even the most flexible version of accessory mortgage has the disadvantage compared to a non-accessory mortgage that the requirement of accessoriness of competence does not permit the position of creditor of the security right over real property to be separated from the position of creditor of the secured claim[108] so that it is not possible, for example, for security rights over real property to be held in a fiduciary capacity for the benefit of other holders of claims. This is ultimately the clearest and most important difference between accessory and non-accessory mortgages. However, one particular arrangement which permits a trustee to hold what is, in principle, an accessory mortgage for the creditor or creditors of a claim is the security trust which, despite fundamental accessoriness, can lead in some legal systems to a breaching of the accessoriness of competence.[109]

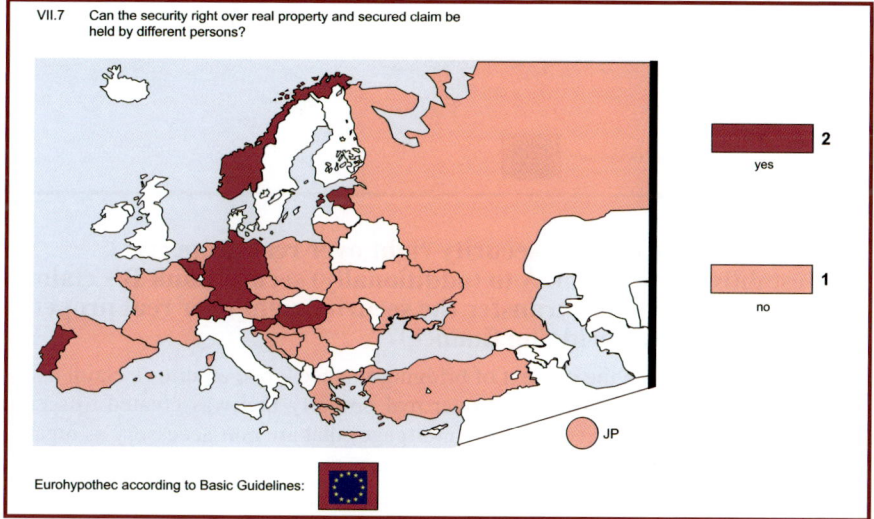

VII.7 Can the security right over real property and secured claim be held by different persons?

8. Is it possible for a Bank B as security for its outstanding loans to take over a security right over real property from Bank A, without causing the extinguishment of Bank A's secured claim or the secured claim having to be transferred to Bank B?

One type of inter-bank cooperation found is where Bank B takes over a security right over real property from Bank A in order to secure a claim of Bank B but Bank A retains its claim so that subrogation of the claim is not involved. This frequently occurs where term financing or bridging financing is planned which is to be covered with a security right over real property but where long-term financing is already in place and is to continue.

This can only be achieved without any problems by using non-accessory mortgages.

---

108 Cf. C.III.3.
109 Cf. also C.VII.10. below.

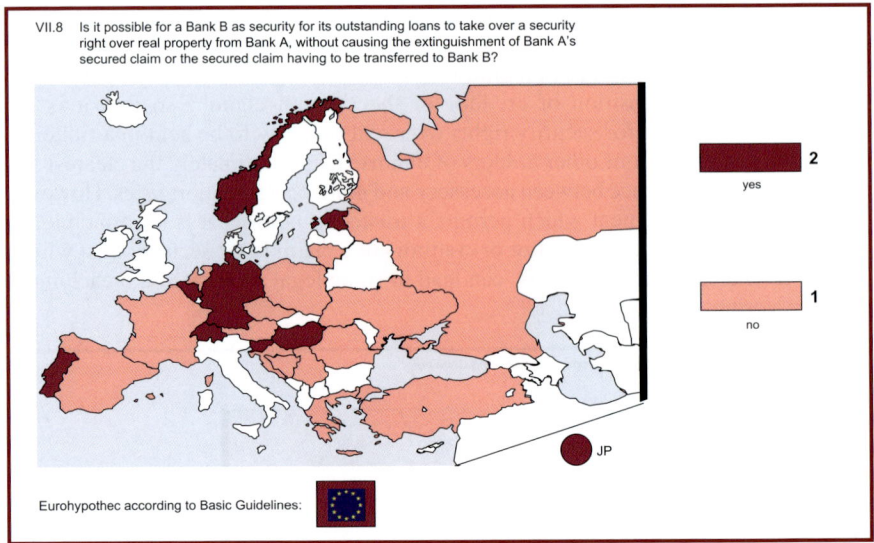

9.   Is it possible to use a security right over real property established for Bank A to (additionally) secure Bank B's claims (without having to transfer the security right over real property or the claims) (bridging finance)?

In this case – e.g. within the context of bridging finance – one creditor's claim under a loan is secured by a security right over real property that was created to secure another claim for another creditor. Only mortgages that are non-accessory as regards competence can provide a solution in this case.

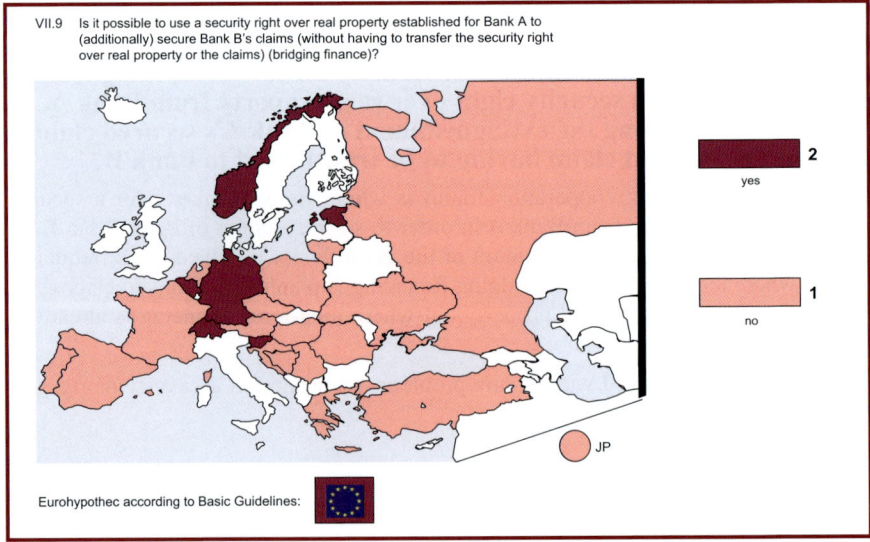

10. Can the claims of several creditors against the same debtor be secured by registering a security right over real property for a fiduciary who himself does not have a claim against the debtor? (fiduciary security right over real property – disregarding whether the fiduciary relationship would be protected in insolvency)

The security right over real property held in a fiduciary capacity is an important special case in practice that has already, in principle, been examined in Question 7.

In the case of syndicated financing in particular, security rights over real property are frequently held by a fiduciary[110] who has no share in the financing himself. This enables the later addition of additional lenders and any change of financing institution to be handled easily and flexibly. The fiduciary is the creditor of the security right over real property, yet he represents only the interests of the banks who actually have a claim secured by this fiduciary security right over real property. This function too can only be fulfilled by security rights over real property that are non-accessory as regards competence.

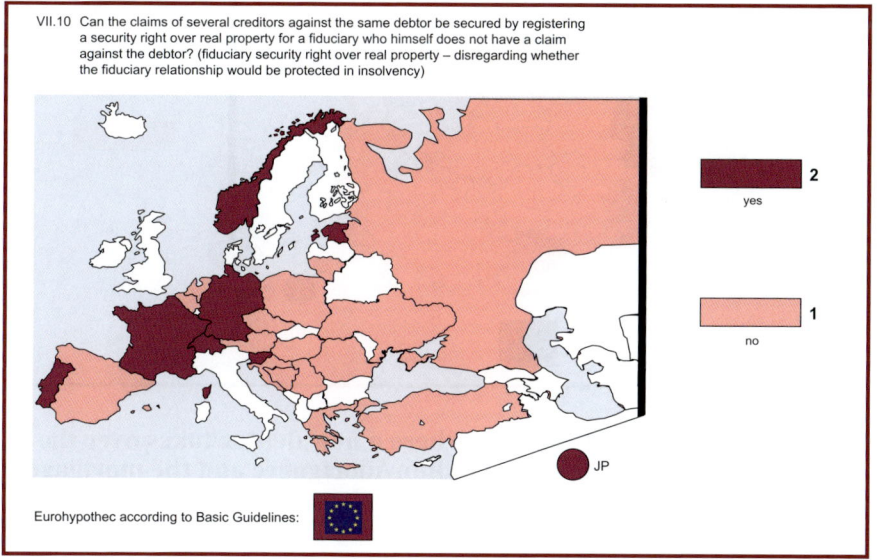

VII.10 Can the claims of several creditors against the same debtor be secured by registering a security right over real property for a fiduciary who himself does not have a claim against the debtor? (fiduciary security right over real property – disregarding whether the fiduciary relationship would be protected in insolvency)

2 yes

1 no

Eurohypothec according to Basic Guidelines:

---

110 This question is examined here irrespective of the additional, very complex question as to whether the fiduciary gives the banks an insolvency-proof legal position in the insolvency of the fiduciary.

11. If the security right over real property has been registered for one creditor, is it possible in an efficient way to do a later syndication of the loan with all creditors/syndication partners secured on the security right over real property directly?

For the support of its member institutions the vdp has carried out research over many years into which countries allow mortgages to be subsequently syndicated in an efficient way, i.e. with reasonable expenditure of time and expense, particularly in relation to large-scale commercial financing.[111] Such secondary syndication involves a large loan being extended by one bank which then sells and assigns the resulting payment claim in part shares to other banks. The result of this research shows that financing techniques of this sort can only be done efficiently in a few countries.

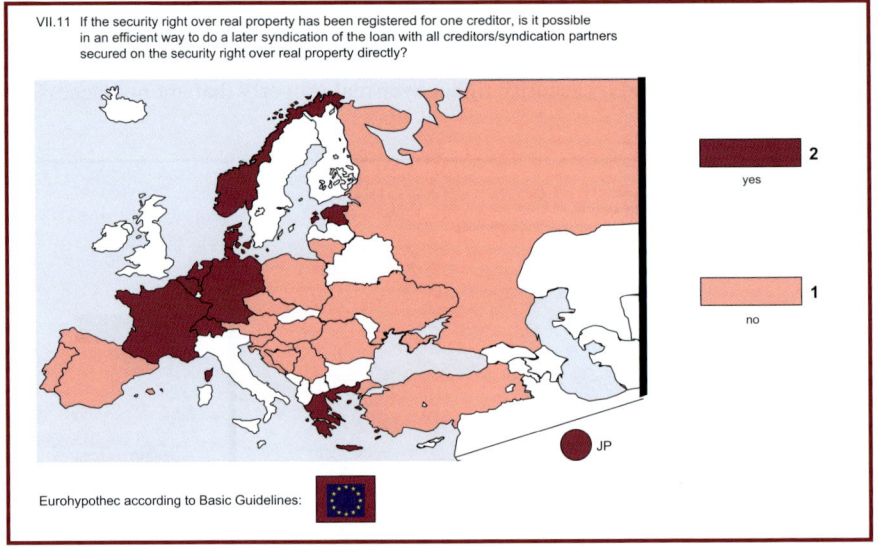

12. Is a conversion of the loan where a new debtor takes over the loan (with consent of the creditor/mortgagee and the mortgagor) possible without consequences for the existence of the security right over real property?

Changes may also occur in the person of the debtor of the secured claim. This is dealt with in Questions 12 and 13.

In all countries under investigation here security rights over real property can deal with the case of debt assumption without loss of their identity if the creditor and the owner of the encumbered property cooperate. This situation occurs frequently in practice, primarily where a property encumbered with a security right over real property is sold and the purchaser is prepared to take over the encumbrance. The accessoriness of the mortgage is ultimately not a problem here, however, as the secured claim persists and only passes to another debtor by way of debt assumption.

---

111 Cf. in more detail *Stöcker*, Die grundpfandrechtliche Sicherung grenzüberschreitender Immo-bilienfinanzierungen [*The mortgage security in cross-border property financing*], WM 2006, p. 1941 et seq. (1943 et seq.).

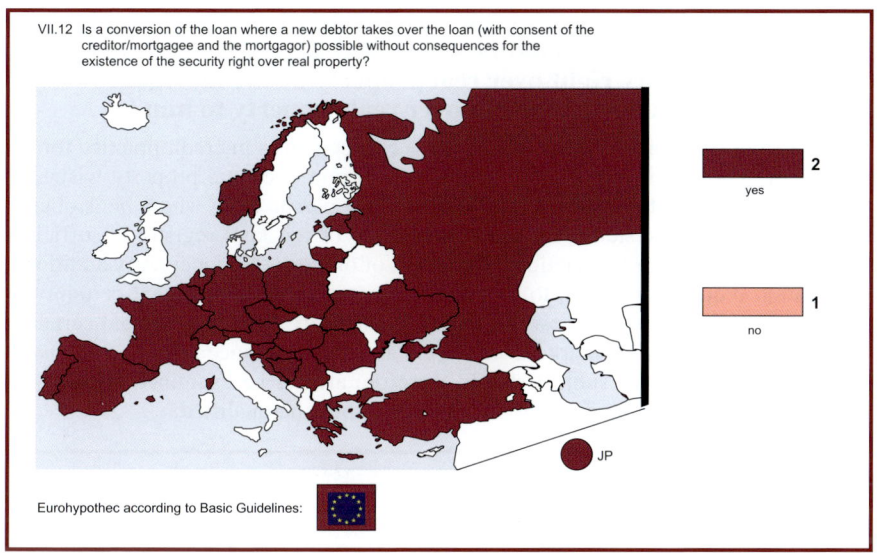

VII.12   Is a conversion of the loan where a new debtor takes over the loan (with consent of the creditor/mortgagee and the mortgagor) possible without consequences for the existence of the security right over real property?

13. Is it possible to use an existing security right over real property as security for a new loan given to the purchaser when a property is transferred to a new owner?

In this situation the secured claim does not persist but instead is extinguished. The purchaser does not want to take over the old loan but to redeem it in payment of the purchase price with a new loan. Security rights over real property with accessoriness of extinguishment cannot secure a new claim against the new owner. In Austria, e.g. is the continuation of the maximum amount hypothec permitted in the form of so-called debt redemption [Forderungseinlösung], if the old claim is taken over by the purchaser at least for a short moment. For non-accessory mortgages this case also presents no problems.

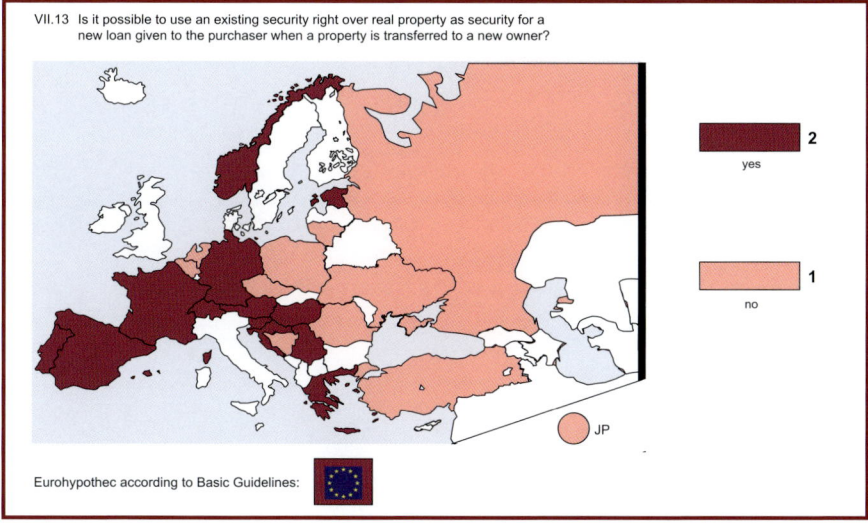

VII.13   Is it possible to use an existing security right over real property as security for a new loan given to the purchaser when a property is transferred to a new owner?

14. How can an acquirer of a security right over real property make sure that it would be effective if the owner provides him with a security right over real property or the mortgagee transfers the security right over real property to him?

The questions examined in chapter C.II. have consequences in credit practice for the method of approach if the acquirer of a security right over real property wishes to satisfy himself reliably about the entitlement of the person from whom he is obtaining his right. Legal systems, in which inspection of the land register is sufficient have the advantage, for transactional purposes, of obvious efficiency. Any additional verification requirement leads to greater expense and to reduced legal certainty. It should not go unrecognised, however, that it is precisely this reduced legal certainty that represents a lucrative market for lawyers and title insurance companies. Fundamental assertions on the subject should therefore always be examined critically to see who is making them and, if applicable, they must be qualified.

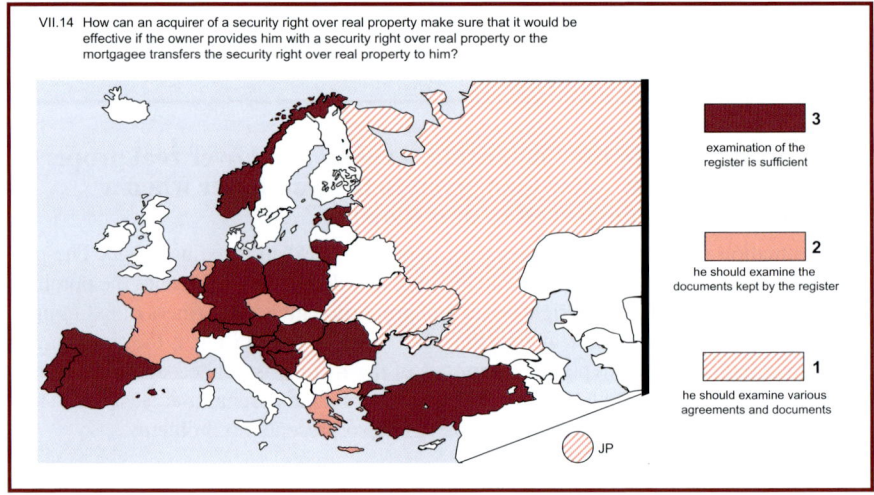

VII.14 How can an acquirer of a security right over real property make sure that it would be effective if the owner provides him with a security right over real property or the mortgagee transfers the security right over real property to him?

3 — examination of the register is sufficient

2 — he should examine the documents kept by the register

1 — he should examine various agreements and documents

D. Assessment system for legal framework conditions for security rights over real property in Continental Europe

Below we look at why a legally orientated assessment system for security rights over real property is necessary and what such a system might look like. In addition it is worthwhile considering how the findings could be used for future legal development in Europe.

I. Qualitative conclusion about current security rights over real property

In the first place we demonstrate why a need for the assessment of the legal quality of mortgages exists and how this could be achieved on a transnational basis.

1. Demand because of risk weighting under the requirements of banking law

Stable credit institutions are an essential prerequisite for a functioning national economy and for a modern national economic system. Both the individual state and the international community therefore have a great interest in the stability of the banking system. Consequently, individual states and supranational organisations develop statutory regulations or other sets of rules that are intended to ensure the stability of the banking industry. An important cornerstone is a system of banking supervision with a risk-sensitive focus. Particularly important in this regard is the fixing of limits up to which banks are permitted to undertake risks. In relation to loans, the risk profile is dependent, among other things, on the type and soundness of the loan collateral, and in relation to property loans, particularly on the quality of security rights over real property.

In 1974, a group of central banks and supervisory authorities of the G10 countries[112] established the Basel Committee[113] in order to develop common minimum requirements for the supervision of credit institutions with international operations and thereby promote stability in international financial markets. This committee does not have any legislative competence. However, its recommendations have a great influence on national legislatures in many countries in the world.

In 1988 the Basel Committee adopted the so-called Basel Capital Accord known as **Basel I**. This was largely incorporated into EU law and then implemented by the Member States in their national law. Basel I established the principle that banks must hold capital that covers at least 8% of their risk-weighted assets. Risk categories of 0, 20, 50 and 100% were defined. For residential mortgage lending a weighting of 50% applied and for commercial property lending, a weighting of 100%. The risk categories under Basel I were somewhat too broad and frequently did not match the true economic risks.

---

112 At that time the following countries belonged to the G10: Belgium, Federal Republic of Germany, France, Great Britain, Italy, Japan, Canada, the Netherlands, Sweden and the USA. In the meantime the following 3 countries have been added: Luxembourg, Switzerland and Spain.
113 This name is based on the fact that the committee's office is located in Basel.

Basel II brought in substantial changes and improvements and now offers two methods for risk assessment. As with Basel I, the **modified standardised approach** provides broad risk weight categories. This weighting is assigned either by statute or by the external credit ratings of the borrower by a credit rating agency. External rating procedures with a mere focus on the borrower alone are in principle not suitable for mortgage lending. Firstly, an assessment of the real estate collateral (in particular a valuation of the underlying property) would have to be carried out. Secondly, private residential construction financing has been allocated to the retail segment, for which external ratings are not available. Consequently, the required property-related external ratings are not available. Therefore, only the risk weight categories laid down by statute can be used for mortgage lending. For mortgage lending on residential properties a weighting of 35% is stipulated, i.e. the related capital requirement is reduced to 2.8 % of the loan amount. Mortgage lending on offices and multi-use buildings can, under certain circumstances, be weighted at 50%.

The **internal ratings-based approach**[114] determines the risk weighting through a combination of the following factors: probability of default (PD), loss given default (LGD), maturity (M) and exposure at default (EAD). With the **basic ratings-based approach**, the LGD ratios, among others, are stipulated by the supervisory authorities. With the **advanced ratings approach** they are determined by the individual credit institution itself. Where the credit institution is determining the LGD ratio the anticipated value of the security in the event that it has to be realised is the material issue.[115] The ratio expresses the relationship between the bank's loss after realisation of the real security and the loan amounts in default[116].

Of key importance for banks in Europe is how Basel II has been implemented in European law and then in national law. The relevant EU Capital Requirements Directive[117] specifies in Annex VI Number 48. c) and Number 54. c), in each case in conjunction with Annex VIII Part 2 Number 8[118] that a reduction of capital requirements on the basis of real estate collateral is only possible if the mortgage is enforceable and this enforceability has been legally verified. In addition the credit institution must be in a position to be able to realise the value of the mortgage within a reasonable period of time.[119] These requirements apply both in relation to the standardised approach and the internal ratings-based approach.

For banks that operate in several countries, and all the more so for international banking groups, this means that loan collateral must undergo a risk analysis that they use to mitigate risk and thereby reduce capital backing. In order to bring real estate collateral into one uniform risk assessment system, an evaluation system that could be used to assess loan collateral on a transnational basis would seem to be desirable.

---

114   The internal ratings-based approach is frequently also referred to as the IRB Approach.
115   Cf. in this regard the report by *Trotz*, I&F 2004, p. 78 et seq.
116   Default is defined as payment arrears of more than 90 days.
117   Directive 2006/48/EC of the European Parliament and of the Council of 14 June 2006 relating to the taking up and pursuit of the business of credit institutions, Official Journal of the European Union of 30.6.2006, L 177/1 et seq.
118   Capital Requirements Directive, Annex VIII Part 2 Number 8: "For the recognition of real estate collateral the following conditions shall be met: a) Legal certainty – The mortgage or charge shall be enforceable in all jurisdictions that are relevant at the time of the conclusion of the credit agreement, and the mortgage or charge shall be properly filed on a timely basis. The arrangements shall reflect a perfected lien (i.e. all legal requirements for establishing the pledge shall have been fulfilled). The protection agreement and the process underpinning it shall enable the credit institution to realise the value of the protection within a reasonable time frame. b) Monitoring of property values…"
119   On the implementation of these requirements in German bank supervision law cf. *Marburger*, I&F 2007, p. 128 et seq.; *Glos/Sester*, BKR 2008, p. 315 et seq. (319 et seq.).

As far as we are aware, an assessment system for mortgages has not yet been publicly discussed. Solely, 2005 the rating agency Moody's issued what was merely an overview in which it estimated the recovery rates for several European countries ("key jurisdictions"), largely on the basis of a short analysis of the legal framework and rather less on the basis of statistical data, such data being then (and now) not sufficiently available.[120] The resulting classification is very simplified but it does, however, at least show the usefulness of a qualitative comparative law analysis, particularly if statistical data is lacking. These findings should be taken into account in further deliberations concerning a legal assessment system.

Against this background, it was important for HypRating[121], having offered to their customers recovery rates for Germany since 2002[122], to find solutions for foreign countries. Although HypRating was able to appraise recovery rates for several countries based on statistical data, a long time will be necessary to draft a full picture over recovery rates in all relevant countries. This is why HypRating has made the findings of the Round Table the base of their considerations to assess recovery rates founded on comparative law.

2.   EBRD

At the end of 2007 the European Bank for Reconstruction and Development (EBRD) published a study on "Mortgages in transition economies" in which the efficiency of mortgage systems in Central and Eastern Europe was examined. An endeavour of this kind is, in principle, to be welcomed. The EBRD study shows the urgent need for evaluative conclusions about mortgages in Europe.

However, the way in which the EBRD carried out its inquiries is causing fundamental concerns, both in relation to its methodology and also in relation to the information on the individual countries. The Polish Mortgage Credit Foundation examined this study in detail and then wrote a critical statement which it has now published.[123]

The experts participating in the Round Table drafted a short response in English on the basis of this at Workshop V. In this both the classification method and the approach of the EBRD study are challenged. This position has been published in the first edition of this book.[124] Discussion with EBRD has already been initiated.

3.   White Paper

The White Paper on Mortgage Credit aims to increase the efficiency of mortgage markets. To this end it also deals with the duration of land registration and compulsory enforcement proceedings.[125] Protection of the owner or consumer in enforcement proceedings is not taken into consideration. This is all the more astonishing as the White Paper in other respects prioritises consumer protection issues. In the meantime, based on the White Paper, in 2008 the EU Commission has begun to prepare a

---

120 Cf. *Moody's* European Country Tiering for CMBS Recovery Rate Assumptions: Focus on Key Jurisdictions.
121 Hyp Real Estate Rating Services GmbH is a subsidiary of Verband deutscher Pfandbriefbanken e.V.
122 See *Lux*, LGD-Grading, in: Verband deutscher Pfandbriefbanken; Immobilien-Banking 2009 – 2010,; p. 51 et seq., and specially. p. 57 et seq.
123 *Drewicz-Tułodziecka/Mortgage Credit Foundation*, The expert opinion and position of the Mortgage Credit Foundation on the EBRD Report, Warsaw 2008
124 *Stöcker/Stürner* (ed.), Flexibilität, Sicherheit und Effizienz der Grundpfandrechte in Europa, Volume III, Berlin 2008 (vdp's publications series, Volume 37), p. 109 et seq.
125 *European Commission*, White Paper on the Integration of EU Mortgage Credit Markets, Brussels, 18.12.2007, 4.2.

Recommendation on real estate valuation, enforcement proceedings and registration. Motivated by the impression of the financial crisis, the EU Commission postponed the publication of its recommendation, thus changing its course increasingly considering aspects of debtor protection. In this context the EU Commission now is working on a report on measures to hinder enforcement proceedings. This again one-eyed perspective, putting now emphasis on debtors' interest only, does not seem to be suitable in order to comply with the complex legal issues of debtor and owner protection with mortgage loans.

II.   Round Table and assessment system

This chapter is designed to give an outline of how the demand for an assessment of the legal quality of security rights over real property could be considered on a transnational basis.

1.   How can an assessment system for security right over real property be established?

The various slides contain many questions on many countries. In order to reach a comparative law conclusion, in the sense of an assessment, it would be beneficial to generate a rating score per country at the end of the assessment process.

To achieve this, the legal conclusions of the slides would have to be brought into a points system. For this purpose the various answers from the individual slides would have to be weighted[126], but also, however, the individual questions in relation to each other.

The weighting of the questions would be geared to the significance of a question for the overall assessment, so according to how important the individual question is based on a balanced consideration of the various interests that have to be taken into account (bank risk, cost of credit, consumer and owner protection etc.). The weighting of the answers to one question would depend on how good or bad the outcome of the individual answers are; this would in turn also have to be judged on the basis of various interests.

Questions and answers that are judged to be neutral or of the same value could be given a weighting of 0 or receive the same number of points. They should not, however, be removed from the series of slides as they could be extremely important for understanding the legal interconnections.

In the final stage the weighted scores per country could be added together to produce the rating score and this could then be compared with the rating scores of the other countries.

Processes of this type to quantify quality are presently very common in many areas for establishing rankings. If the process is carried out with the maximum care and diversified weighting, useful conclusions are reasonably possible. Such findings should not, however, be rendered in absolute terms; the quantification of quality has too many fundamental weaknesses for that. When making decisions about taking on financing, it is above all advisable to avoid a rigid schematic approach without pragmatic reconsideration of the details of the individual case.

---

126 By way of clarification: the numbers stated in the present slides do not represent rating scores; they are only used to allocate the answer variants to the individual countries in the process of answering the questions.

2.   Importance of business model and business structure

Abstract theoretical judgments about the "mortgage law" of a country are problematic for the purpose of risk assessment by banks as all legal systems permit many versions of security by mortgage and most of them also have available several types of security right over real property. Any simplification thus inevitably leads to a gross distortion.

A more targeted approach is to examine the security quality of mortgages in terms of the specific security quality of business models and specific business structures, because the particular features of these have consequences for the contract and collateral structure. These business models may be different with every bank. Using these business models, the slides are then chosen that are actually relevant in the individual case, and this applies likewise for the individual answers to the various slides.

This institution-specific approach corresponds to the objectives of Basel II which aims to achieve high quality supervision that is specifically geared to the specific business structures of a bank. An assessment system for mortgages conforming to this directional approach is much more telling for the risk situation of security rights over real property that are actually used by a bank than an abstract, theoretical cross-section appraisal of many countries that by its nature must remain imprecise and superficial.

Example: in relation to commercial property financing via SPVs

- preferential rights for employees are not relevant, but are very relevant in relation to direct company financing and in particular in relation to working capital finance;

- preferential rights for persons entitled to alimonies can be disregarded, but not in relation to residential financing.

Thus, in relation to the business model for commercial property financing via SPVs, preferential rights of these types may also be left out of consideration in countries that in principle recognise such rights in enforcement and insolvency.

3.   Different perspectives

Alongside the evaluation of mortgages from the point of view of banks, meaning the mortgage creditors, other perspectives should, however, also be taken into consideration, namely the perspective of the debtor/owner whose protection against unjustified enforcement proceedings merits attention and the perspective of the legislature, which has to create a balanced overall system and to do this has to set priorities.

Evaluation of the legal quality of security rights over real property from these different perspectives sometimes leads on questioning to different priorities than if matters are considered solely from the point of view of a bank. But even for a bank the questions differ in significance depending on whether it only examines the prospects of realising a mortgage that already exists or whether it also wishes to evaluate the extent to which a security right over real property can and is to be used to secure a credit structure that is capable of being established in the market. For an overall complete assessment, political stability of the legal system may be of much significance, too.

In its advisory role the vdp has for a long time recommended that a balanced overall system should be the objective because it is only in this way that a stable legal framework can be established in the long-term. Regulations that strongly and unilaterally favour the mortgagee run the risk of being corrected sooner or later by case law or legislation. They are, at the end of the day, also unsuitable for safeguarding long-term market opportunities.

4.   Findings of the Round Table in cooperation with HypRating

The attachment gives detailed description of the findings of the Round Table in the 2 workshops of March and November 2009.

On the one hand, the Round Table could agree on weighting ratios to each question and answer, thereby evaluating each question and answer from 4 different perspectives:

- perspective of a bank, who has to exploit a security right over real property (bank/enforcement),

- perspective of a bank, using a security right over real property to secure loans (bank/usability),

- perspective of an owner facing enforcement of his real property (owner) and

- perspective of a legislator, who wants to consider diverging interests of all parties adequately (legislator).

On the other hand, findings are published, which are derived from the combination of those weighting ratios with the individual country information. For this, in a first step all 89 questions are considered for calculation. This results in the following categories of findings:

- Complete findings – perspective of enforcement

- Complete findings – perspective of usability

- Complete findings – perspective of the owner

- Complete findings – perspective of the legislator

- Complete findings – total addition of all scores

In a second step, only the questions of chapter VI. and VII. are considered in order to limit the analysis to problems of enforcement and insolvency law; issues of flexibility of the security rights over real property are not taken into consideration in this version of the findings in order to prevent possible criticism that the complete results would favour non-accessory security rights over real property inadequately. This leads to the following categories of findings:

- Partial findings enforcement and insolvency – perspective of enforcement

- Partial findings enforcement and insolvency – perspective of usability

- Partial findings enforcement and insolvency – perspective of the owner

- Partial findings enforcement and insolvency – perspective of the legislator

- Partial findings enforcement and insolvency – total addition of all scores

The publication of all these details is designed to make method and performance of the analysis more comprehensible. However, it would be beyond the limits of this book to give a detailed full description of the intense discussions of the Round Table and the reflections that resulted in the particular assessment of each ratio.

The technical calculation of the results was done by HypRating. It turned out that HypRating can use the findings of the Round Table very well, because this assessment system grants a high grade of transparency and is updated regularly. Moreover, its extension to further countries is possible.

III. Guidelines for statutory improvements

To conclude this report it remains to be considered how the findings of the Round Table from the slides could be used for further legal development in Europe.

1.   Model security right over real property for the modernisation of national laws

When it comes to legislative proposals, any modern legislature is well advised to make use of legislative ideas from other countries, or at least to compare its views with those of other legal systems. The importance of comparative law in modern legislation is particularly clear in relation to the far-reaching legal reforms in Central and Eastern Europe where the civil law systems have been put and to some extent are still being put under scrutiny. Only a few comparative law studies on security rights over real property are available. Any report that analyses the legal quality of security rights over real property in several countries is therefore of interest.

The earlier attempt to develop a model security right over real property[127] could be further developed using the detailed conclusions of the slides presented here. In structuring the legal framework for their mortgages national legislatures could more readily identify the priorities to be decided on a national level and obtain specific information about prioritisation in other countries.

2.   Harmonisation?

Whether there is an economic need for the harmonisation of mortgages in Europe has apparently as yet never been the subject of an evidence-based examination.[128]

It is remarkable that economists have not as yet taken up this fascinating topic or in any event have not tackled it with full academic rigour. There are admittedly some economic studies that "calculate" which costs are generated by the general legal differences in Europe. Kircher[129] refers to some model calculations that are, however, based on many hypothetical factors. Similar, reasonably in-depth analyses of the special case of security rights over real property have not been published as yet. Among authors, legal writers cannot be reproached for this. It would be much more desirable if instead this subject were tackled by economists, possibly in cooperation with legal writers.

---

127   See presently under 3.
128   Cf. *Stöcker*, Die Eurohypothek – Struktur einer ökonomischen Analyse [*The Eurohypothek – structure of an economic analysis*], Immobilien & Finanzierung 2005, p. 766 et seq.
129   p. 379 et seq.

However, it is also possible to base the necessity for a Eurohypothec on legal arguments.[130] The workshops that the vdp held in 2004/2005 in Berlin on the subject of the Eurohypothec[131], did admittedly reveal that a harmonisation of security rights over real property is not necessary if a single bank gives a customer a loan that is secured by a security right over real property on one property and nothing changes throughout the whole term of the mortgage. But this simple structure is becoming ever oftener the exception. Property investments are and remain by their nature long-term investments because the capital required for their financing can only be recouped over long time periods. The cycles of financial changes, which are also reflected in the financing structures, are, however, becoming ever shorter both in the commercial and the private sectors.

Today mortgage-backed loans are altered, redeemed, syndicated at the outset or later, assigned, securitised, secured on several properties, split and partially sold. Funding, optimisation of capital allocation, risk management and diversification measures make it increasingly necessary today to transfer large portfolios of mortgage loans.

As soon as the secured loan claim is affected by any sort of change to the financing, the question immediately arises as to what legal consequences will result for the security right over real property. If the nature of the change is that the secured claim is being replaced by a new claim (novation), in the case of an accessory mortgage the effect of this is that the old security right over real property expires and a new security right over real property has to be created to secure the new claim. This triggers costs and charges, possible loss of ranking and frequently requires a considerable expenditure of time.

Many national legal systems offer solutions for some of these legal problems, though frequently only for special structures.[132] A general trend towards the weakening of strict accessoriness[133] is apparent, but this is very inconsistent for individual case groups which are catered for differently in each case. All these solutions are already difficult enough to structure on a national level but well nigh unmanageable in transnational cases.[134] A uniform security right over real property should therefore

---

130 *Kircher*, p. 387; *Kiesgen*, p. 27 et seq. refers to the additional transaction costs that arise as a result of legal differences.

131 Cf. presently under 3.a).

132 Multiple special provisions were created in France for the transfer of mortgages but these only apply in respect of the special cases therein regulated; Cf. *Kircher*, p. 241 et seq.; *Stöcker*, Die Eurohypothek [*The Eurohypothec*], p. 108 et seq. Special provisions of this type were enacted in several European countries in order to make the securitisation of mortgage loans easier, e.g. along with France, also in Belgium, Italy and Spain, i.e. precisely where the transfer of mortgages for refinancing purposes under the general provisions can only be done at considerable expense.

133 On this trend towards non-accessoriness cf. above *Stürner*, Das Grundpfandrecht zwischen Akzessorietät und Abstraktheit und die europäische Zukunft [*The security right over real property between accessoriness and abstraction and the European future*], Festschrift für Rolf Serick, Heidelberg 1992, p. 377 et seq.; now *Baur/Stürner*, Sachenrecht [*Law of Property*] 18th ed. 2009, section 64 marginal notes 14, 43, 60, 76 et seq. and 85.

134 This becomes clear from the following practical example: the French law of "obligations foncières" provides that mortgages can be transferred without complying with the general civil law provisions from the parent bank (originator) to the highly specialised mortgage bank subsidiary which then issues French covered bonds on this basis. This can, however, only apply in respect of French mortgages as the French legislature cannot amend foreign mortgage and land register law with in rem effect. A foreign mortgage loan portfolio cannot therefore be refinanced via *obligations foncières* in a similarly efficient way. This is different to the German refinancing register that only regulates an appropriation under insolvency law but does not affect an appropriation under property law; cf. *Stöcker*, Bankrechts-Handbuch [*Banking Law Handbook*], section 86a, marginal note 102 et seq.

not be tailored to certain individual financing structures but, as a general security instrument, it should have a sufficiently flexible structure to enable it to be used for all financial usages and to be drawn upon for future credit structures too.

3.   Eurohypothec

One of the proposals for facilitating cross-border credit business is for a security instrument for property lending to be created that is applicable uniformly in all EU Member States in addition to existing national security rights over real property and flexible and efficient enough to be used for all property financing transactions. The idea of making modern legal instruments available for cross-border business across Europe by virtue of the differing European legal traditions is not in principle a new one, including in the area of property law. Even if one were to consider the notion of an optional, uniform EU mortgage to be premature, studies on a device of this sort make sense even if, for the time being, only one model emerges from which the national legislatures of Member States can take their cue. The most important milestones on the way to realising the idea of a Eurohypothec are presented below.

a)   Previously published proposals and studies

As long ago as 1966 the so-called **Segré Report** by the former EEC Commission proposed the introduction in all Member States of a flexible security right – similar to the German *Grundschuld* – in order to promote integration of European capital markets.[135] The research work on this was commenced but then abandoned as it was thought in the meantime that faster progress would be made with the plan of reciprocal recognition of financing techniques. This turned out not to be correct, however, in relation to the law of property.

In 1987 the International Union of Latin Notaries proposed the creation of a standard European **"Eurohypothec"** based on the example of the Swiss *Schuldbrief* that was to be available in addition to the types of security rights over real property already in existence.[136]

Academics in several European countries and, in recent years, ever increasing numbers of practitioners have given their attention to this subject. The vdp has played a leading part in this work, including its consultancy role begun in 1992 in the Central and Eastern European countries involved in reforms to formulate a model mortgage law for reform of the mortgage loan business. To this end the vdp assembled a working group of academics, notaries and banking lawyers who drew up and published the "**Guidelines** for a Non-Accessory Security Right over Real Property for Central Europe".[137]

---

135 On these proposals in the Segré Report cf. *Kircher*, p. 418 et seq. and p. 442 et seq.; *Kiesgen*, p. 38; *Stöcker*, Die Eurohypothek [*The Eurohypothec*], 216 et seq.
136 On the proposal by the UINL cf. in particular *Wehrens*, ÖNotZ 1988, p. 181 et seq.; *Wehrens*, WM 1992, p. 557 et seq.; *Wehrens*, Real Security Regarding Immovable Objects – Reflection on a Euro-Mortgage, in: Towards a European Civil Code, The Hague/London/Boston 1998, p. 551 et seq.; *Kircher*, p. 481 – 506; *Kiesgen*, p. 40 et seq.; *Stöcker*, Die Eurohypothek [*The Eurohypothec*], p. 228 et seq.; *Wachter*, Die Eurohypothek – Grenzüberschreitende Kreditsicherung an Grundstücken im Europäischen Binnenmarkt [*The Eurohypothec – cross-border loan security over real property in the European single market*], WM 1999, p. 49 et seq.
137 *Wolfsteiner/Stöcker*, A non-accessory security right over real property for Central Europe, ZBB 1998, p. 264 et seq., and DNotZ 1999, p. 451 et seq. (the English translation appeared in Notarius International 2003, p. 116 et seq.). The text is also reproduced in *Staudinger/Wolfsteiner* (2002), preliminary note 241 et seq. on section 1191 et seq.

In 2004 these guidelines in turn became the basis for the work of the pan-European group of experts initiated in Spain known as **"The Eurohypothec"**.[138] It reworked the vdp's guidelines and produced them in English.

At the end of 2004, the **"Forum Group on Mortgage Credit"**[139] set up by the EU Commission included the creation of a Eurohypothec in its recommendations.[140] This brought the idea of the Eurohypothec to the attention of the EU Commission.

At the instigation of "The Eurohypothec" expert group, the vdp invited the Eurohypothec experts, members of the Forum Group's "Collateral" Sub-Committee, experts from the North European initiative on cross-border land registry networking (EULIS)[141], experts from the pan-European study of property law at the European University Institute in Florence[142] and other experts to workshops lasting several days which were held in Berlin. Between November 2004 and April 2005 these experts jointly produced the **"Basic Guidelines for a Eurohypothec"**, which were published in May 2005 by the Polish Mortgage Credit Foundation.[143] The challenge was, on the one hand, to design a flexible loan security right that meets all the modern requirements demanded of financing structures and, on the other hand, to structure its functionality in such a way that it can be integrated into all European legal systems. Although it has not yet been possible for all the details to be worked out, this set of rules provides concrete proposals for the requisite legal structures and for identifying the interfaces to the national legal systems.

The greatest success to date of all the efforts made at the Brussels level has been the inclusion of the idea of the Eurohypothec in the EU Commission's **Green Paper** on Mortgage Credit in the EU that was published on 19.7.2005.[144] In the Green Paper the EU Commission takes note of the Eurohypothec project and announces that it is going to examine the proposals that have been drawn up. The economic analysis

---

138 Cf. the website of this expert group: www.eurohypothec.com. This contains an abundance of references on the subject of the Eurohypothec. The final report of this expert group has been published: *Muniz Espada/Nasarre Aznar/Sánchez Jordán*, Un modelo para una Eurohipoteca – Desde el Informe Segré hasta hoy, Madrid 2008.

139 In March 2003 the EU Commission set up the Forum Group on Mortgage Credit consisting of 25 national experts. The purpose of Forum Group was to identify barriers impeding cross-border mortgage credit in the EU and to come up with proposals for the further integration of the single market for mortgage credit. The Forum Group's report was published at the end of 2004: *European Communities*, The Integration of the EU Mortgage Credit Markets – Report by the Forum Group on Mortgage Credit, Brussels 2004.

140 *EC*, Report by Forum Group, p. 30, (116): "The Forum Group discussed other ways to facilitate transfers of mortgages, focussing on the Euromortgage and the European Security Trust." It is further stated, ibid. (117): "The Forum Group considered the Euromortgage to be an alternative tool which could be introduced by Member States, without substantial changes to their existing legal systems, as it would operate under the rule of lex rei sitae. Such a pan-European non-accessory mortgage instrument could avoid burdensome and costly inquiries in other Member States concerning local regulations and the quality of the national mortgage instruments; reduce additional and differing formalities and authentication; offer mortgage collateral as security for more than one mortgage credit; enable easy transfer of the mortgage as well as the property; meet the requirements for cross-collateralisation on a cross-border basis; meet the requirements for securitisation and mortgage portfolio management; and enable the creation of bank syndicates for mortgage finance."

141 Cf. the website of EULIS: www.eulis.org. See also *Tiemer* in EMF, Mortgage Info, Computerisation of land registers and of registration of land and mortgage collateral in Europe, Brussels October 2007, p. 1 et seq., on the status of development in Germany ibid. *Luckow*, p. 4 et seq.

142 Cf. the website http://www.iue.it/LAW/ResearchTeaching/EuropeanPrivateLaw/ProjectReal-PropertyLaw.shtml.

143 *Drewicz-Tułodziecka/Mortgage Credit Foundation*, Basic Guidelines for a Eurohypothec, Outcome of the Eurohypothec workshop November 2004/April 2005, Warsaw 2005. See more on this presently under b).

144 *EU Commission*, Green Paper – Mortgage Credit in the EU, Brussels, 17.6.2005, (47) and (48).

of the proposals by the Forum Group on Mortgage Credit commissioned by the EU Commission mentioned the concept of the Eurohypothec in positive terms.[145] Furthermore, the Eurohypothec was the subject of the EU Commission's public hearing of experts on the Green Paper on 7.12.2005 in Brussels.

While the workshops organised by the vdp concerned themselves with designing the content of a Eurohypothec, the discussions going on at that time in Brussels concentrated on the issue of whether a Eurohypothec is wanted at all and whether it could be introduced by way of the so-called 26th regime.[146] The idea behind the 26th regime was to introduce a Eurohypothec by means of an EU directive without any national adjustment measures being necessary. This plan fuelled a flurry of activity in Brussels that was certainly in part influenced by a lack of the requisite knowledge of the law of mortgages on a comparative basis. For the idea of the Eurohypothec this was not very helpful as sometimes unrealistic assumptions were made. Consumer policy issues of contract law are also frequently mixed up with mortgage law. Closer consideration of the matter shows that an adjustment to the national interfaces is very much necessary, in particular to land register, enforcement and insolvency law. As people became aware of the relatively high expense associated with this, the euphoria in Brussels visibly evaporated. Discussions are therefore again concentrating on the previous topic of consumer loans, but on cost grounds these are a less realistic scenario on a pan-European basis.

At present the previous proposals for the Eurohypothec are not being followed up in concrete form in Brussels. In particular, the EU Commission did not include the Eurohypothec in its **White Paper** on Mortgage Credit published on 19.12.2007.[147] However, the Eurohypothec is mentioned in Annex 3: "Impact assessment of specific issues" (ibid, p. 169) as the one of the possibilities for facilitating the cross-border transfer of mortgage portfolios. The fact that the EU Commission has not made any concrete statements on the idea of a Eurohypothec should not necessarily be viewed negatively because this hesitation will permit the in-depth consideration of the issues at an academic level that is still necessary without any politically motivated time pressure.

There was, however, a new, indirect impetus for further work. At the start of 2006 the EU Commission set up an expert group to deal with the cross-border funding of mortgage credit, the Mortgage Funding Expert Group. This expert group identified the legal obstacles preventing the transfer of mortgage collateral portfolios as the most important and pressing problem in relation to the creation of a single EU market for mortgage collateral and recommended facilitating cross-border portfolio transactions involving loans secured by mortgage.[148] The legal mechanisms for achieving this are not spelled out but it is clear that a Eurohypothec would be very beneficial in this regard.

On a national level, the discussions about a Eurohypothec have already contributed to **modernisation measures**, e.g. in the context of the reform of the mortgage law in France in 2006 and the mortgage law amendment in Spain in 2007. In relation to the work on far-reaching amendments of the civil law systems in Poland, Serbia and Hungary too, the experts have gone back to the thinking that was developed in the course of discussions about a Eurohypothec.

---

145 *London Economics*, The Costs and Benefits of Integration of EU Mortgage Markets, Report for European Commission, DG – Internal Market and Services, August 2005, p. 69.
146 By reason of the EU membership of Romania and Bulgaria one must consequently now speak of the 28th regime.
147 Commission of the European Union, White Paper, Brussels, 18.12.2007. The White Paper was published on http://ec.europa.eu/internal_market/finservices-retail/home-loans/integration_de.htm.
148 The report of the EU Mortgage Funding Expert Group was published on http://ec.europa.eu/internal_market/finservices-retail/home-loans/integration_de.htm.

At the present time **academics** in several countries are examining the flexibility of their national mortgage types and are also drawing on the "Basic Guidelines for a Eurohypothec" in this regard as a benchmark. Studies of this type should be increasingly initiated and supported. They are urgently necessary for the further work required on a Eurohypothec in order to prepare for its integration into national legal systems and to demonstrate in detail that a non-accessory Eurohypothec is compatible with the general fundamental principles of civil law which, in most of the Member States, include the principle that the act of disposal by which a right in rem is transferred is dependent on a valid *causa* (unity principle or, in the case of the separation of the planning and the execution, the causality principle).[149] In addition, such studies also provide valuable expertise that can be put to immediate practical use in relation to present day national security rights over real property.

Academic events also serve as forums for academic exchange. In 2007/2008 several conferences on property law in the Netherlands, Portugal and Spain dealt with the topic of the Eurohypothec in conjunction with the issue of the extension of the so-called "Common Frame of Reference" for contract law to property law.

b)   Basic Guidelines for a Eurohypothec

Between November 2004 and April 2005 a panel of experts produced the "Basic Guidelines for a Eurohypothec", which were published in May 2005 by the Polish Mortgage Credit Foundation.[150] What was planned was a flexible security right over real property that was not dependent for its existence on a claim to be secured, capable of multiple use and easy to transfer. The key part of these Basic Guidelines is reproduced below in English, as it was published in 2005 (pages 13 – 19 of the original version by the Polish Mortgage Credit Foundation):

"2.   PRINCIPLES

2.1.   Eurohypothec

The Eurohypothec is a non-accessory land charge entitling the holder of the Eurohypothec to the payment of a certain sum of money out of the property right. Regularly it is used in combination with a security agreement.

2.2.   Security Agreement

The security agreement stipulates under which the holder of the Eurohypothec may keep and enforce the Eurohypothec.

The security agreement is not the same as the loan contract. However, it may be included in the same document as the loan contract.

2.3.   Lex Rei Sitae

The law of the Member State where the property is located (lex rei sitae) is applicable to the Eurohypothec, including the competent land register, the certificate of the Eurohypothec, and to any related security agreement.

3.   CREATION

3.1.   Owner's Consent

Only the land owner can create a Eurohypothec. The land owner and the debtor of the secured claim may be two different persons.

---

149 *Baur/Stürner*, Sachenrecht [*Law of Property*], 18th ed. 2009, section 64 marginal note 7 et seq., 81, and above in C.III.

150 *Drewicz-Tułodziecka/Mortgage Credit Foundation*, Basic Guidelines for a Eurohypothec, Outcome of the Eurohypothec workshop November 2004/April 2005, Warsaw 2005.

National law may require an agreement between the owner and the future holder of the Eurohypothec as a substantive requirement for the creation of the Eurohypothec.

3.2. Registration and Formal Requirements

Within the framework of registration (number 7) the following principles apply to the Eurohypothec:

Opposability *(third party effect): The Eurohypothec must be registered in the competent national register as defined by national law.*

Only when registered, the Eurohypothec is opposable against third parties.

Formal Requirements: *Formal requirements as regards the declarations of the parties and registration are the same as for other real estate charges (mortgages) under national law.*

Contents of Registration: *Registration should contain the following points:*

- *the amount and currency of money payable[151],*

- *the name of the holder of the Eurohypothec,*

- *whether it is a certificated right (letter right) or a non-certificated right (non-letter right) (if the national law provides for both versions),*

- *whether or not the Eurohypothec is enforceable (if it is not yet enforceable by law),*

- *in the case of a multi-parcel (joint) Eurohypothec, the other land charged.*

3.3. Certificated Right and Non-Certificated Right

National law may provide that the Eurohypothec be structured either as a certificated right (letter right) or as a non-certificated right (registered only right or non-letter right), according to the parties' choice.

The land register should state whether it is a certificated right or a non-certificated right, if the national law provides for both possibilities.

3.4. Payment

Capital Amount: *The holder of the Eurohypothec is entitled to payment of the capital as registered. It must be a claim for payment of money.*

The currency of any EU Member State may be used for the Eurohypothec; national law may provide that it also be created in another currency.

Interest: *The Eurohypothec does not yield interest.[152]*

Secured Claim: *The creation, transfer and existence of the Eurohypothec and the exercise of the rights therein is not dependent on the existence of the secured claims.[153]*

However, if the Eurohypothec is used for security purposes, the owner can object if the holder of the Eurohypothec exercises rights under the Eurohypothec which are not given to him under the terms of the security agreement.

---

151 This currency and amount may differ from the amount payable according to the contractual agreement.

152 Some members propose that the national law may provide for the Eurohypothec to yield interest, which may differ from the interest rate agreed upon in the loan contract. The interest rate (or in the case of a flexible interest rate, the maximum rate) must be registered in the land register.

153 The *causa* of the Eurohypothec may lie in the security agreement or in a separate duty to create a Eurohypothec which might be included in the same document as the loan contract (see part C.II.2).

3.5. Object

Land: *A Eurohypothec may be charged on land situated in any Member State of the European Union.*

Other Charged Objects: *The lex rei sitae determines to what extent land, but also buildings owned independently of the land or any another land charge or Eurohypothec, may be charged with an Eurohypothec. (In the case of a land charge, it will be called a sub-Eurohypothec).*

Multi-Parcel (Joint) or Transnational Eurohypothecs: *National law must provide for the possibility of several pieces of land situated within the same Member State to be charged under a single Eurohypothec (joint or multi-parcel Eurohypothecs).*

Several Eurohypothecs in different Member States may secure one or more claims (credit agreements) at the same time through a single security agreement (transnational Eurohypothecs).

Scope of the Eurohypothec: *The scope of the Eurohypothec is the same as for other land charges under national law, insofar as they cover the property and the fruits and profits of the property, in particular rents, appurtenances and also claims under insurance contracts for losses to the property, buildings and specified items.*[154]

3.6. Holder

Owner's Eurohypothec: *National law may provide that the Eurohypothec can also be created in favour of the present owner himself. Then the owner stays holder of the Eurohypothec even after ownership of the land changes.*

Register Representative: *All natural persons and/or legal entities may hold a Eurohypothec. In the case of the creation or transfer of a Eurohypothec in favour of a legal entity with no legal personality (e.g. in the form of a trust or some other fiduciary capacity), the national law may require that the registration be valid only where there is registration of a register representative who will give full information and who is entitled to make any declaration on behalf the actual ownership of the Eurohypothec.*

4. SECURITY AGREEMENT

4.1. Definitions and applicable law

'Security agreement' means a contractual agreement under which the owner provides a Eurohypothec by way of security in favour of the (future) holder of the Eurohypothec.

'Secured claim' means the obligations which are secured by a Security Agreement and which give rise to a right to cash settlement. They may consist of or include:

- *present or future, actual, contingent or prospective obligations (including such obligations arising under a master agreement or similar arrangement);*

- *obligations owed to the future holder of the Eurohypothec by a person other than the collateral provider; or*

- *obligations of a specified class or kind arising from time to time.*

The Eurohypothec can be used to secure cross-border loans but also, depending on the wishes of the parties, loans that only affect one country.

The security agreement is not subject to legal provisions for loan contracts. The applicable substantive law for the security agreement is the law of the Member State where the property is located (lex rei sitae).[155]

---

154 Some members would prefer harmonisation of the scope of the Eurohypothec.
155 Some members would prefer free choice of the applicable law for security agreements, in particular where commercial real estate loans are concerned.

4.2.   Form and Content

Any acquisition of a Eurohypothec as security, by a person other than the owner of the charged property, requires a security agreement.

Form

The security agreement must take the form required by national law. Oral agreements are invalid.

The owner is entitled to obtain a written copy of the security agreement. However, it does not have to be entered in the land register.

Minimum Provisions

A Security Agreement must contain the following minimum provisions:

- *the names of the parties and the date of agreement,*
- *the Eurohypothec; it is possible to use one security agreement for several created Eurohypothecs or for multi-parcel Eurohypothecs,*
- *the claims to be secured,*
- *the conditions for redemption of the Eurohypothec by the security provider,*
- *the conditions of the enforcement procedure of the Eurohypothec, within the limits of the laws of the jurisdictions concerned.*

Forbidden Clauses

The security agreement may not stipulate the following:

- *restrictions on the sale of the property as a whole,*
- *a clause of voie parée.[156]*

Without the consent of the holder of the Eurohypothec in the form foreseen by the national law, the owner of the charged property may not create any charges on the property which could affect the Eurohypothec. This does not apply to charges inferior in rank.

4.3.   Redemption and Owner's Rights

If there is no valid security agreement or if all secured claims have been repaid, the security provider has the right to demand redemption of the Eurohypothec or parts of it. He has the right to decide the means of redemption, whether it be extinguishment, transfer of the Eurohypothec to the security provider, or at his discretion to a third party. The holder of the Eurohypothec must contribute therefore, if necessary, at his own expense.

The security provider is allowed to assign the right to redemption to a third party.

In the case of a certificated Eurohypothec, the right to redemption includes the right to receive the certificate.

In the case of over-collateralisation, the security provider may, at his own expense, ask for partial adaptation of the collateral by reducing the amount of the Eurohypothec or via partial redemption.

In the event of enforcement, the holder of the different Eurohypothecs may be entitled under the security agreement to choose over which properties he wishes to carry out enforcement. As regards individual properties, the enforcement proceedings may be carried out separately or jointly.[157]

---

156 Forfeiture clause.
157 Some members propose that a joint procedure should follow the same rules in all Member States.

If the holder of the Eurohypothec breaks the security agreement, the owner of the land is entitled to compensation for the damage suffered under the lex rei sitae. National law must provide effective compensation.

5.   TRANSFER

5.1.   Non-Certificated Right

The assignment of a non-certificated right is opposable to third parties only upon registration.

Registration of the assignment requires the consent of the previously registered owner of the Eurohypothec. National law may require an agreement between the previous and the new owner of the Eurohypothec as a substantive requirement for the assignment of the Eurohypothec.

5.2.   Certificated Right

The assignment of a certificated right is governed by the law of the state where the land is situated.

The assignment is effective only if the Eurohypothec certificate has been handed over to the new holder of the Eurohypothec.

5.3.   Formal Requirements

Formal requirements as to the parties' declarations of assignment, registration and transfer of the certificate must be the same as for other mortgages under national law.

5.4.   Good Faith

Whoever, according to national law, acquires in good faith, is protected,

- *as if the registered person were the true mortgagee,*

- *in case of a certificated right also, as if the holder of the certificated right were the true holder of the Eurohypothec, provided he can prove his right by an unbroken chain of assignments in authentic instruments.*

This does not affect the owner's objections (5.6.).

5.5.   Independence of Secured Claim

The transfer of the Eurohypothec cannot be made dependent on the condition of transfer of the secured claim.

5.6.   Owner's Objections

National law may provide

- *either that the security agreement in its latest version is binding for any future holder of the Eurohypothec and any third party as long as the security provider is not the holder of the Eurohypothec.*

- *or, alternatively, that the previous Eurohypothec holder is liable for all damages incurred by the owner, if he assigns the Eurohypothec without binding the assignee to the security agreement.*

If the holder of the Eurohypothec transfers it to a third party, the holder must inform the third party about the security agreement. If there is no further agreement, the holder can fulfil this obligation by handing over the original documents to the third party.

The owner's rights to redemption are not subject to any time limitation or prescription as long as the Eurohypothec is registered.

6.   EXTINGUISHMENT

6.1.   Cancellation in the Register

The Eurohypothec is extinguished when it is deleted from the national competent register with the consent of the holder of the Eurohypothec and the owner. The Eurohypothec is not extinguished by the payment of the secured claims.

6.2.   Passage of Time

The capital of the Eurohypothec is not subject to any time limit or prescription.[158]

6.3.   Owner's Rights under the Security Agreement

If the secured claims have been paid in full, the owner can demand cancellation of the Eurohypothec or its assignment to himself or to some other person of his choice.

The security agreement may state other cases in which the owner can demand cancellation or assignment of the Eurohypothec.

6.4.   Exclusion of Unknown Holder

In the case where the holder of a Eurohypothec is permanently unknown or unattainable, or where the Eurohypothec certificate has been lost, the process foreseen under national law to cancel real charges will be applied."

c)   Structure of a Eurohypothec

In terms of functionality a Eurohypothec should be designed as collateral security and not as an isolated security right over real property. The notion of an isolated security right over real property would encounter very strong resistance, particularly in countries belonging to the Roman legal family. In order to be able to put across the concept of appropriation for a specific purpose via a security agreement more easily, the talk these days in relation to the claim-securing land charge [Sicherungsgrundschuld] and the Eurohypothec is sometimes less of non-accessoriness than of "contractual accessoriness".[159] The structural flexibility of the mortgage is achieved by the statutory accessoriness[160] being transformed by means of a legally required security agreement into contractual accessoriness.[161]

The linking of a security right over real property with an unconditional promise of payment that is separate from the loan claim, which is customary in the Scandinavian countries and Switzerland, would also probably be hard to implement as a statutorily regulated model across Europe, at any rate where the creator of this form of security is a consumer. The issue of whether different regulations could be put in place for commercial property owners should, however, be the subject of closer examination.

---

158 However, if the Eurohypothec yields interest, prescriptions or other time limits may apply to the interest.

159 *Baur/Stürner*, Sachenrecht [*Law of Property*], 18th ed. 2009, section 64, margin note 85 and section 36 marginal note 77a. The use of the term "contractual accessoriness" for the Eurohypothec was devised in 2005 in a talk given by the German notary Michael Becker (Dresden) and the French notary Maître Jerôme Chevrier in a fringe meeting at a notaries' conference in Paris on the Eurohypothec. The linguistic change from "non-accessory" to "contractually accessory" has already contributed to a better understanding of the fundamental structure of a Eurohypothec and of the central legal instrument, the security agreement, and has reduced much of the doctrinal opposition, particularly in countries belonging to the Roman legal family.

160 In the European discussions the terms "accessoriété légale" and "statutory accessoriness" were used.

161 This is described as "accessoriété conventionelle obligatoire" and "compulsory contractual accessoriness".

Parallel debt structures[162] that are used with increasing frequency in international commercial lending practice suggest a structure of this kind.[163]

The practical use to which a security right over real property can be put depends very much on its structural flexibility. The stronger the structural link between the secured claim and the security right over real property, the less flexible the arrangement of the credit relationship can be. With strictly accessory mortgages, changes relating to the secured claim, or a change of creditor and, as a result, transferability are heavily restricted and are only possible with a high expenditure of time and effort and the possible loss of ranking, or may even not be possible at all.[164] The proposals of authors who suggest an accessory Eurohypothec should therefore not be followed;[165] Kiesgen,[166] Kircher[167] and Stürner[168] have all come out very strongly against such proposals. Mortgages in Europe do exhibit very differing degrees of accessoriness and are accordingly not uniformly flexible for use in securing loans. Despite this diversity it can, however, be said that ultimately all mortgages are more or less accessory as regards enforcement.

In discussions about the Eurohypothec, accessoriness of scope and of competence are sometimes demanded in order to prevent double payment under the secured claim and under the security right over real property. This is, however, to confuse issues regarding the accessoriness of a mortgage with the issue of the good faith acquisition of a security right over real property without a secured claim, which can be permitted by statute in the case of both accessory and non-accessory mortgages and is structurally possible. The protective effect that is sought for the debtor and owner is sufficiently addressed if the accessoriness of enforcement can also be asserted in relation to public reliance on the land register. This has recently become the case in Germany in the case of the *Grundschuld*, but not, however, in the case of the accessory mortgage (*Hypothek*).[169] If a Eurohypothec were to be structured with full accessoriness of scope and of competence, many advantages of the flexibility that a Eurohypothec should display would again be lost.

It therefore remains to be said that in relation both to a Eurohypothec and also to national security rights over real property, accessoriness of scope and of extinguishment should be dispensed with, and likewise also accessoriness of competence. Any deficiencies in the protection of the debtor/owner can be compensated by strict accessoriness of enforcement. The creditor side should be permitted to receive no more in the enforcement process than corresponds to the outstanding claim, but this should be the subject matter of the accessoriness of enforcement and not of the accessoriness of scope.

---

162 On parallel debt cf. above under C.III.1.c).

163 But in this case too it must be borne in mind that the structuring of a Eurohypothec based on real rights makes no distinction on the basis of whether the owner of the encumbered property is a company or a consumer.

164 See *Baur/Stürner*, Sachenrecht [*Law of Property*], section 36 marginal note 79a; *Kircher*, p. 389; *Stöcker*, Die Eurohypothek [*The Eurohypothec*], Berlin 1992, p. 191 et seq.

165 These include, in particular, Wachter, Die Eurohypothek – Grenzüberschreitende Kreditsicherung an Grundstücken im Europäischen Binnenmarkt [*The Eurohypothec – cross-border loan security over real property in the European single market*], WM 1999, p. 49 et seq., and *Habersack*, Die Akzessorietät – Strukturprinzip der europäischen Zivilrechte und eines künftigen europäischen Grundpfandrechts [*Accessoriness- structural principle of European civil law and of a future European mortgage*], JZ 1997, p. 857 et seq.; see further recently *Sparkes*, European Land Law, Oxford 2007, p. 398 et seq., 401.

166 p. 55 et seq.

167 p. 556 et seq.

168 *Baur/Stürner*, Sachenrecht [*Law of Property*], section 64 marginal note 85.

169 Cf. section 6 RisikobegrenzungsG [*Law on risk limitation*] of 12.8.2008, Federal Law Gazette I 2008, 1666 et seq., inserted into the BGB by section 1192 subsection 1a.

E. Attachments

1. Spread sheet: Weighting Ratios

Weighting of questions and answers according to the questionnaire of the Round Table "Flexibility, security and efficiency of security rights over real property in Europe" (as of February 16, 2010)

Objective and focus:

Objective of the analysis is the calculation of a country ranking of legal structures with regard to security rights over real property. Commercial as well as residential properties are considered.

(1) Perspective of a bank regarding enforcement

The focus here is, whether national law influences successful exploitation of property positively or negatively in default of a debtor. Relevant issues are for example aspects of time, costs or legal uncertainty based on competing other claims. If questionable the perspective of a bank, having a first ranking security right, is considered.

(2) Perspective of a bank regarding usability/flexibility

When securing complex and innovative credit structures by security rights over real property it is important that this security right can be used in a flexible way. The focus is on considerations how legal structures of security rights over real property influence product strategies, acquisition processing etc.

(3) Perspective of the owner

For the owner it is most important that he can defend himself against unjustified attempts of enforcement. This issue therefore is a question of consumer protection, too.

(4) Perspective of a legislator

For legislators it is important to bring all involved interests into a fair and transparent equity.

assessment scale for questions 0 – 5, in special cases up to 10, and for answers 0 – 10

I.	Types of security rights over real property	(1) bank/ enforce-ment	(2) bank/ usability	(3) owner	(4) legislator	specification	(1) bank/ enforce-ment	(2) bank/ usability	(3) owner	(4) legislator
I.1	How many types of security rights over real property are there?	0	0	0	0	(2) several types and forms of security rights				
						(1) only 1 type				
I.2	Are mortgages embodied in a security paper (certificated rights) or are they only entered in the register?	0	2	1	1	(3) both certificated security rights and register-only security rights		6	6	6
						(2) exclusively certificated security rights		5	5	5
						(1) exclusively register-only security rights		4	4	4
I.3	Can mortgages be established on several properties in such a way that the mortgagee can choose from which property to be satisfied?	4	3	3	3	(4) yes, one security right can be established on several properties	10	10	5	7
						(3) yes, several security rights can be established securing the same debt	10	7	1	2
						(2) the amount of the debt must be divided on the properties	1	1	4	2
						(1) no	0	0	0	0
I.5	Is the duration of the security right over real property limit-ed by law?	3	2	1	2	(3) no	7	6	6	6
						(2) automatic conversion into a normal hypothec	2	2	2	2
						(1) yes, with a statutory limit	0	0	0	0

II. Public disclosure requirements and protection of trust	(1) bank/enforce-ment	(2) bank/usability	(3) owner	(4) legislator	specification	(1) bank/enforce-ment	(2) bank/usability	(3) owner	(4) legislator
II.1 Who keeps the land register?	2	2	3	3	(3) courts	6	6	6	6
					(2) an independent public authority	6	6	6	6
					(1) a public authority subject to instructions	3	3	3	3
II.2 Which rights are registered?	1	1	1	2	(2) proprietorship, security rights and other limited rights over real property	6	6	6	8
					(1) proprietorship and other limited rights over real property, particular register for security rights	2	2	2	2
II.3 Are contracts and disposals over real property concluded before a notary?	3	1	3	3	(5) yes, mandatory by law	8	6	7	7
					(4) yes, not mandatory for all types of transactions, but common in practice (e.g. for the purpose of third party protection)	7	5	7	6
					(3) use of notary not mandatory, but common in practice	6	5	6	5
					(2) notaries do exist, but are usually not involved in property transactions	3	3	3	3
					(1) not before notaries but usually with the assistance of specialised advocates or professional third parties	5	5	5	5

No.	Question					Answer option				
II.4	What is the connection between the land register and the cadastre?	0	0	1	1	(3) joint administration of land register and cadastre			5	6
						(2) completely separate, but the land register refers to the cadastre			5	6
						(1) there is no cadastre			2	3
II.5	Are buildings part of real property (apart from rights equivalent to real property) or are they legally separate and registered separately?	2	3	3	4	(4) part of the real property (superficies solo cedit)	10	10	7	10
						(3) not part of the property, but the real property and the buildings can only be mortgaged jointly	6	5	5	5
						(2) very often still legally separate, but consolidation is possible	2	2	3	2
						(1) always legally separate	0	0	0	0
II.6	Can requests for registration be indicated even before registration of a mortgage?	1	4	4	4	(5) yes, with the effect that the rank is reserved against anybody	10	10	8	10
						(4) yes, with the effect that the rank is reserved against anybody, but for a limited period of time	8	7	7	8
						(3) yes, by a mention in the margin of the register with the effect that the rank is reserved in the registration procedure	7	7	6	7
						(2) no, but the register can be blocked for a certain period ("freeze")	5	3	5	5
						(1) no	0	0	0	0

No.	Question / Option	Y1	Y2	Y3	Y4	W1	W2	W3	W4
II.7	How is the grantor's consent to registration verified?	1	2	3	3				
	(5) exclusively by documents authenticated by a notary					6	4	8	7
	(4) a notarial certification of the signature is enough, however, documents authenticated by a notary are commonly used in practice					6	4	8	7
	(3) by a signature certified by a notary, court or advocate								
	(2) by the assistance of a notary or use of bank documents					4	6	5	5
	(1) by documents in writing					3	6	4	3
II.8	What is the basic structure of the register?	2	3	3	5				
	(2) registration of rights					9	9	9	9
	(1) collection of documents from which rights appear					3	3	3	3
II.9	Can anyone inspect the list of current rights in the land register (excluding the actual registered documents)?	0	3	3	3				
	(2) unrestricted					8	4	4	6
	(1) restricted to certain persons					2	6	6	4
II.10	How is the register technically designed?	0	4	4	4				
	(4) complete electronic procedures (e-conveyancing) without interference of a neutral keeper of the registry					7	7	7	0
	(3) supra-regional electronic database								
	(2) electronic access, but regionally limited					3	3	3	3
	(1) register kept on paper only					1	1	1	1
II.11	Is electronic access from other countries via EULIS (European Union Land Information Service) possible?	0	2	1	2				
	(5) free cross-border access to the register over the internet					10	5	5	5
	(4) yes					9	5	7	7
	(3) in preparation					3	5	5	5
	(2) under consideration					1	4	1	1
	(1) for the time being not planned					0	3	0	0

II.12	Is between the parties the validity of conveyance of real property dependent on registration?	2	2	3	4	(2) yes	7	7	7	7	7
						(1) no	3	3	3	3	3
II.13	Is the validity of the establishment of a mortgage dependent on registration?	2	3	3	4	(2) yes	7	7	7	7	7
						(1) no	2	2	2	2	2
II.14	If registration of a mortgage is applied for with all necessary documentation, how long does registration usually last?	0	5	5	5	(6) up until 3 days	10	10	10	10	10
						(5) up until 2 weeks	8	8	8	8	8
						(4) up until 2 months	5	5	5	5	5
						(3) up until 6 months	3	3	3	3	3
						(2) up until a year	1	1	1	1	1
						(1) longer	0	0	0	0	0
II.15	Is the validity of the transfer of a security right over real property, which is not connected to a mortgage certificate, dependent on registration?	2	3	2	3	(3) yes	7	7	7	7	7
						(2) no	3	3	3	3	3
						(1) only security right certificates	7	7	7	7	7
II.16	Is the reliance of the acquirer of a mortgage on the contents of the register legally protected?	3	5	3	5	(4) the register is always regarded as correct in favour of the acquirer	10	10	10	10	10
						(3) the register is assumed to be correct, but this assumption can be proven wrong within a certain period	6	6	6	6	6
						(2) the register is assumed to be correct, but this assumption can be proven wrong	3	3	3	3	3
						(1) there is no protection of reliance in the register	0	0	0	0	0

	Effects of accessoriness	(1) bank/ enforce-ment	(2) bank/ usability	(3) owner	(4) legislator	specification	(1) bank/ enforce-ment	(2) bank/ usability	(3) owner	(4) legislator
II.17	Is the creation of a mortgage effective if done by a mortgagor who is registered as owner but is not the true owner?	1	5	3	5	(2) possible (legal relations are protected)	8	8	7	8
						(1) in principle not possible (true owner is protected)	2	2	3	2
II.18	Is the transfer of a security right over real property effective if done by a registered mortgagee who is not the true mortgagee?	1	5	3	5	(3) possible = protection of the acquirer	8	8	7	8
						(2) in principle not possible = protection of the true mortgagee	2	2	3	2
						(1) only the possession of the security right certificate is decisive	7	7	6	7
II.19	Is good faith acquisition of a security right over real property dependent on the expiration of a time limit?	2	3	2	3	(4) no	9	9	8	9
						(3) to some extent	5	5	5	5
						(2) yes	2	2	2	2
						(1) good faith acquisition not possible	1	1	1	1
II.20	Does an acquirer of property who is in good faith regarding the fact that there is no security right over real property acquire the property unencumbered? (extinction of a contractual security right over real property)	1	3	5	4	(2) yes (legal relations are protected)	6	6	7	7
						(1) no (true owner is protected)	4	4	3	3

III.	Effects of accessoriness	(1) bank/ enforce-ment	(2) bank/ usability	(3) owner	(4) legislator	specification	(1) bank/ enforce-ment	(2) bank/ usability	(3) owner	(4) legislator
III.1	If a security right over real property has been created, is it effective even if there is not yet a secured claim? (accessoriness of origin)	0	3	1	4	(3) neither a claim nor a legal foundation for it is necessary		8	7	7
						(2) a legal foundation for the claim to be secured is necessary		5	5	5
						(1) legal foundation as well as a (conditional) claim are necessary		2	3	3

ID	Question					Answer options				
III.2	Is it possible to register a higher amount for the security right over real property than the size of the secured claim? (accessoriness of scope)	0	4	3	4	(2) yes		8	8	8
						(1) no		2	2	2
III.3	Is the creditor of the secured claim by operation of law always the mortgagee? (accessoriness of competence)	0	4	2	4	(2) no		9	6	8
						(1) yes		1	4	2
III.4	Can the security right over real property only be enforced if the secured claim can be enforced? (accessoriness of enforcement)	1	1	5	5	(2) yes	7	7	10	10
						(1) no	3	3	0	0
III.5	Does the extinguishment of the secured claim lead to the extinguishment of the security right over real property by operation of law? (accessoriness of extinguishment)	2	3	4	3	(2) no	6	7	8	8
						(2) not if further claims may arise from the legal foundation	5	5	5	5
						(1) yes	4	3	2	2
III.6	Is the security right over real property linked to the secured claim by a security agreement on the scope of the secured claims?	1	2	4	4	(4) yes, mandatory by law	6	7	9	9
						(3) yes, customary practice	5	7	7	7
						(2) yes, seen as tacitly agreed	4	4	3	3
						(1) not necessary due to legal accessoriness	6	0	1	1

		(1) bank/ enforce-ment	(2) bank/ usability	(3) owner	(4) legislator	specification	(1) bank/ enforce-ment	(2) bank/ usability	(3) owner	(4) legislator
III.7	How can subordinate (junior) mortgagees or unsecured creditors acquire the position of the free parts of the first ranking mortgage?	0	2	1	4	(4) the owner's right to those parts of the security right not (no more) needed for the secured claim can be assigned or seized/ garnished		4	6	9
						(3) it is only possible to register subordinate rights which then (economically) advance in ranking		5	5	6
						(2) it is not possible to be secured on the real property, but to participate in the proceeds		6	4	4
						(1) only by agreement		7	1	1
IV.	Protection of the owner	(1) bank/ enforce-ment	(2) bank/ usability	(3) owner	(4) legislator	specification	(1) bank/ enforce-ment	(2) bank/ usability	(3) owner	(4) legislator
IV.1	Can the owner object that there is no secured claim due if the acquirer of the security right over real property is in good faith?	1	2	5	4	(2) yes (owner protected)	3	3	10	8
						(1) no (mortgagee protected)	7	7	0	2
IV.2	Is it possible for the owner to have the registered amount of the security right over real property reduced when it is clear that only a part of the set maximum amount of the security right over real property will be used?	0	2	4	4	(3) yes, the mortgagee is obliged to consent	3	3	10	9
						(2) only if agreed when establishing the security right		5	5	5
						(1) no, only if everything has been repaid		7	0	1

IV.3	Is there statutory regulation or court practice (case law) protecting the owner of a real property who has established a security right over real property to secure another person's debt? (protection of a third party mortgagor)	0	3	4	4	(2) yes (1) no			3 7	8 2	6 4

V.	Enforcement	(1) bank/ enforcement	(2) bank/ usability	(3) owner	(4) legislator	specification	(1) bank/ enforcement	(2) bank/ usability	(3) owner	(4) legislator
V.1	How is an executory title for enforcement of the mortgage obtained?	5	2	3	5	(7) enforcement without title if agreed	10	6	1	6
						(6) there is always an executory title because security rights are always created by a notarial act and notarial acts are always enforceable	10	6	3	7
						(5) banks are authorized to grant themselves executory titles; executory titles can also be created by a notarial act	9	6	1	4
						(4) there is usually an executory title because security rights are usually created in a notarial act and equipped with an executory title	6	4	3	6
						(3) executory titles can be created by notarial act	5	3	5	5
						(2) execution is granted in special quick court procedure	4	2	6	6
						(1) executory title must be obtained in a full court procedure	0	1	9	0

ID	Question					Option				
V.2	Is a statement that the copy of the executory title can be used for enforcement necessary (executory clause), and if so, how can it be obtained?	4	0	2	3	(4) statement of enforceability not necessary	8		2	6
						(3) the notary or the court will attach the statement of enforceability	6		4	5
						(2) notarial titles do not need an executory clause	8		2	6
						(1) the executory title must be granted by court in a special procedure	1		8	3
V.3	How can the owner assert his rights against enforcement (e.g. that the debt does not exist or has been repaid)? (substantive or procedural objections)	3	0	5	5	(4) only in a separately initiated proceeding	9		0	6
						(3) in a separate proceeding or in the ongoing proceeding	4		6	7
						(2) only in the ongoing proceeding	6		4	6
						(1) the court will always examine on its own initiative whether the conditions for enforcement are fulfilled	0		10	2
V.4	When disputed, who has to prove that the secured debt has come into existence and/or is due? (no change of mortgagee)	3	2	5	5	(4) always the owner	10	10	0	4
						(3) only for the originally secured claim the owner (but different with a security agreement covering unspecified future claims)	5	6	7	5
						(2) the owner – with confirmation of disbursement in a set form or before a notary	8	4	2	6
						(1) always the mortgagee	0	0	10	7

Ref	Question	Answer options									
V.5	When the burden of proof is with the owner, must the mortgagee cooperate by submitting documents?	(3) no	3	0	3	3	10			10	0	3
		(2) yes					0			0	10	7
		(1) the owner has never the burden of proof					0			0	10	7
V.6	Can subordinate mortgagees separately initiate enforcement of the mortgage?	(2) yes	2	2	2	2	3	7		7	7	7
		(1) only if agreed with the first-ranking mortgage					7	3		3	3	3
V.7	During enforcement proceedings, can subordinate mortgagees obtain the position of the first-ranking mortgage without his consent or the consent of the owner by paying him out?	(2) yes	0	1	0	3	6	6		6	6	6
		(1) no					4	4		4	4	4
V.8	Which other options for enforcement are provided by law?	(3) by private sale, also in public auction	4	0	2	2	6			4		6
		(2) by public auction through a publicly commissioned authority					4			6		4
		(1) both options					7			4		7
V.9	During enforcement, can the yields of the property be seized before the sale of the property?	(3) yes, through a particular form of enforcement or if the claim for yields had been assigned or pledged	4	2	2	3	8	8	8	4	4	8
		(2) yes, through a particular form of enforcement, if it had been expressly agreed					6	6	6	6	6	6
		(1) only, if the claim for yields had been assigned or pledged					2	2	2	4	4	2
V.10	Can the owner be entirely deprived of control of the property before a forced sale?	(2) yes, by a particular form of enforcement (e.g. forced administration)	2	0	2	2	8	2		2	2	7
		(1) no, only particular measures for particular breaches					2			8	8	3

ID	Question	Answer							
V.11	What are the effects of the decision to transfer the real property in forced sale proceedings on the rights over the property?	(4) all security rights on the property are extinguished completely; some other limited rights only partly affected	1	0	2		7		7
		(3) all security rights on the property are extinguished, but not servitudes of other properties (appurtenant easements)					6		6
		(2) security rights are extinguished, if they are in the same ranking as the security right for which an enforcement was initiated or in a posterior ranking					7		7
		(1) different effects depending on the way of proceedings chosen					2		2
V.12	Can subordinate mortgagees initiate enforcement and cause the extinction of better ranking (senior) rights even if the bid is not sufficient to cover the better ranking rights?	(2) no	4	2	0	3	10	10	10
		(1) yes					0	0	0
V.13	How does the decision to transfer the real property in a forced sale affect those claims not covered by the proceeds of the forced sale?	(2) they persist and can be enforced as unsecured claims	3	0	3	3	10	0	8
		(1) they are extinguished					0	10	2
V.14	Is it possible to use the security right over real property of a mortgagee initiating enforcement to finance the acquisition of the property in forced sale proceedings by the new owner?	(2) yes	2	1	0	1	8	8	8
		(1) no					2	2	2

		Col 1	Col 2	Col 3	Col 4
V.15	Under what circumstances is it possible for the owner to have enforcement proceedings that are substantively and procedurally lawful temporarily or permanently suspended?	4	0	4	3
	(3) only with the consent of the mortgagee	10		2	7
	(2) only in exceptional cases (extreme personal affection)	8		6	6
	(1) generally for reasons of social protection	0		8	3
V.16	If the enforcement proceedings are suspended at the request of the owner, without the consent of the mortgagee, is the suspension permanent or temporary?	4	0	4	3
	(4) always with a time limit	10		2	7
	(3) with or without a time limit; if unlimited the resumption of the proceeding is possible after a certain time	5		5	5
	(2) without a time limit, but resumption is possible	2		7	3
	(1) suspension of enforcement only with the consent of the mortgagee	10		2	7
V.17	Does a valuation of the property take place within the enforcement proceedings?	3	0	3	3
	(5) no, value is irrelevant	8		0	3
	(4) only in special cases (e.g. with a private sale)	4		3	6
	(3) mandatory before the forced sale	1		8	6
	(2) only retrospectively if the owner or the debtor demands it	3		7	4
	(1) usually not, as the value has been set by the parties when establishing the security right	7		3	3

ID	Question					Answer			
V.18	Is the forced sale concluded even if the price achieved for the property is below a certain threshold value?	3	0	3	3	(4) yes, value is irrelevant	8	2	4
						(3) yes, but only if the property is taken over and the claim is extinguished	6	5	6
						(2) if a certain part of the property value is not reached the proceeding is prolonged but not suspended	6	5	6
						(1) no	2	8	4
V.19	Can a mortgage be enforced by the mortgagee using a right to take over the property? (lex commissoria)	4	0	2	4	(5) this is customary	10	2	3
						(4) possible in principle but rarely practiced	8	3	4
						(3) only after unsuccessful attempts for forced sale	6	5	7
						(2) possible if agreed in advance	7	4	4
						(1) no	0	8	3
V.20	When the mortgagee takes over the property, must compensation be paid if the value of the property exceeds the debt?	1	0	5	4	(3) no right for takeover	0	10	10
						(2) yes	0	10	10
						(1) no	10	0	0
V.21	Can the mortgagee himself take part in a forced sale auction and acquire the property?	5	0	4	4	(3) yes, but a possible remainder of the debt ceases to exist (constructive settlement)	7	10	10
						(2) yes, the secured claim is compensated only up to the amount of the auction price	10	7	7
						(1) no	0	0	0

						Answer			
V.22	Which unregistered claims have priority over registered mortgages?	10	5	0	10	(5) only costs of the proceedings and irrefutable costs of administration	10	10	10
						(4) + property-related taxes, public burdens and maintenance costs	8	8	8
						(3) + salary claims of employees within limits and/or alimonies	5	5	5
						(2) + all salary claims against the owner	2	2	2
						(1) + all tax claims	0	0	0
V.23	Can contractors and tradesmen who have contributed to the construction or renovation of the property secure priority over the property for their claims?	3	1	0	3	(4) they are secured on the property without registration, with ranking according to the time of their performance	0	0	0
						(3) they have a right to have a security right registered; the ranking is decided by the time of their performance	2	2	2
						(2) they have a right to have a security right registered; the ranking is decided by the time of registration	8	8	10
						(1) they can only establish security by agreeing upon a contractual security right	10	10	8

		(1) bank/ enforce-ment	(2) bank/ usability	(3) owner	(4) legislator	specification	(1) bank/ enforce-ment	(2) bank/ usability	(3) owner	(4) legislator
V.24	To what extent can the creditor claim interest and costs from the proceeds of enforcement (excluding the cost of the proceeding)?	4	1	0	4	(5) contractually agreed frame for interest and costs which also can be used for other claims	8	8		8
						(4) statutory fixed claim for interest and costs which also can be used for other claims	6	6		7
						(3) no separate frame for interest and costs but coverage by an increased maximum amount of the security right	6	5		6
						(2) interest according to the loan agreement	6	4		3
						(1) interest according to the loan agreement within certain limits	3	2		4
V.25	How long do enforcement proceedings last in practice from initiation until distribution of the proceeds in non-complex cases where the owner does not object?	5	0	3	5	(4) less than 6 months	10	10	10	10
						(3) less than a year	7	7	7	7
						(2) one to two years	3	3	3	3
						(1) more than two years	0	0	0	0
V.26	How long do enforcement proceedings last in practice from initiation until distribution of the proceeds in non-complex cases if the owner uses judicial remedies?	5	0	3	5	(4) less than 6 months	10	10	8	10
						(3) less than a year	7	7	3	7
						(2) one to two years	3	3	1	3
						(1) more than two years	0	0	0	0

VI.	Insolvency	(1) bank/ enforce-ment	(2) bank/ usability	(3) owner	(4) legislator

ID	Question					Answer option		
VI.1	Who may initiate realisation of the property after the opening of insolvency proceedings over the owner's estate?	3	0	0	3	(3) only the mortgagee	8	6
						(2) the mortgagee or the insolvency office holder	5	5
						(1) only the insolvency office holder	2	4
VI.2	To what extent can the mortgagee influence the realisation of the encumbered property when the owner is subject to insolvency liquidation proceedings?	3	0	0	3	(3) separate enforcement procedure for the security right or remedies of influence on the selection of the insolvency office holder and on his measures	10	8
						(2) for the mortgaged properties there is a separate class of distribution where the consent of the mortgagees is needed	5	5
						(1) influence only by means of the general supervision of the insolvency courts; the administrator of the bankruptcy estate acts to a large extent independently	0	2
VI.3	To what extent can the mortgagee influence the realisation of the encumbered property when the owner is under reorganisation or composition proceedings?	4	0	0	3	(2) shortening of payments to the mortgagees only with their consent	10	10
						(1) shortening of payments to the mortgagees without their consent is possible	0	0
VI.4	Can the forced sale of the mortgage property be affected in the interest of the insolvency estate or of other creditors?	5	1	0	4	(4) such interests are not considered	10	7
						(3) delay for a limited period of time	6	6
						(2) possible due to commercial or social interests in general	2	5
						(1) unlimited delay of enforcement possible	0	4

ID	Question				Answer options			
VI.5	If the enforcement procedure is delayed in the interest of the insolvency estate, must the insolvency estate compensate the mortgagee's loss?	3	0	2	(3) delay not possible	10		7
					(2) yes	10		7
					(1) no	0		3
VI.6	When does the insolvency take effect? (disregarding possible rescissions)	2	2	2	(3) not until the opening of insolvency proceedings	8	8	8
					(2) the opening of insolvency proceedings; there are, however, preliminary constraints or retroactive time periods	4	4	4
					(1) retroactive or partly retroactive	2	2	2
VI.7	What legal status must a mortgage have achieved in order to be effective in insolvency proceedings?	10	5	10	(4) the establishment of the security right must have been agreed inter partes	10	10	5
					(3) the request for registration or request for a priority notice must have been filed	8	8	10
					(2) the request for registration must have been filed	7	7	8
					(1) registration must have been completed	0	0	2
VI.8	How is the revenue from the forced sale distributed?	3	0	3	(3) the mortgagee receives payment directly from the enforcement proceedings	10		8
					(2) the received payment is forwarded to the mortgagee separately	7		6
					(1) the outcome is transferred to the insolvency estate, where the mortgagee has a privileged position	0		2

ID	Question					Answer option			
VI.9	Which unregistered claims have priority over mortgages?	10	5	0	10	(5) only the cost of the insolvency procedure and irrefutable administration costs	10	10	10
						(4) + property-related taxes, public burdens and maintenance costs	8	8	8
						(3) + salary claims of employees within limits and/or alimonies	5	5	5
						(2) + all salary claims against the owner	2	2	2
						(1) + all tax claims	0	0	0
VI.10	Are parts of the proceeds from the forced sale of the property used to cover ordinary insolvency claims?	5	0	0	5	(4) in principle not	10	10	6
						(3) up to 5%	4		7
						(2) up to 10%	2		5
						(1) more than 10%	0		3
VI.11	Does the mortgagee receive payment for interest and costs from the proceeds of the forced sale of the property?	5	1	0	4	(2) yes, in principle fully covered	7	7	7
						(1) costs and interests within certain limits	3	3	3
VI.12	Until which point in time must interest covered under the mortgage be due in order to be paid from the proceeds of the forced sale?	3	0	0	3	(4) until the distribution of the proceeds	10		10
						(3) until the forced sale of the encumbered property	8		8
						(2) until the opening of insolvency procedures	3		3
						(1) until an act of insolvency applies (petition of insolvency is possible)	0		0

		(1) bank/ enforce-ment	(2) bank/ usability	(3) owner	(4) legislator	specification	(1) bank/ enforce-ment	(2) bank/ usability	(3) owner	(4) legislator
VI.13	What is the effect of insolvency proceedings against consumers (private individuals)?	1	0	5	5	(3) the consumer is released from all debts after a certain period of time (and after all encumbrances have been realised)	3		10	7
						(2) the debt remains even after the completion of insolvency proceedings	7		0	3
						(1) insolvency proceedings against consumers are not possible	7		0	3
VI.14	Do consumers in insolvency proceedings enjoy stronger protection in relation to mortgages compared to debtors/owners in insolvency proceedings generally?	3	0	5	4	(4) no	10		2	8
						(3) yes, through deferment	4		6	4
						(2) yes, through remission (including deferment)	0		8	3
						(1) there are no insolvency proceedings against consumers	10		2	3
VII.	**Utilisation in practice**	(1) bank/ enforce-ment	(2) bank/ usability	(3) owner	(4) legislator	specification	(1) bank/ enforce-ment	(2) bank/ usability	(3) owner	(4) legislator
VII.1	Is it possible to structure a security right over real property in such a way that the amount of an existing secured claim can be increased without changing the security right over real property itself?	0	5	5	5	(2) yes		8	10	8
						(1) no		2	0	2

VII.2	Is it possible to replace the existing secured claim with another claim against the current debtor – without affecting or changing the security right over real property? (the new claim immediately replacing the old one – novation, subrogation)	0	5	5	5	(3) yes (2) yes, when the legal relationship between the parties still exists (1) no		10 5 0	10 5 0	10 5 0
VII.3	Is it possible to secure new claims under the security right over real property once the original claims have been extinguished completely?	2	3	4	3	(3) yes (2) yes, when the legal relationship between the parties still exists (1) no	10 5 0	10 5 0	10 5 0	10 5 0
VII.4	Is it possible to secure a revolving credit line without further action and without necessitating alterations to the security right over real property itself?	0	3	3	3	(2) yes (1) no	10 0	10 0	10 0	10 0
VII.5	Is it possible (without alterations to the security right over real property) to secure a long-term loan where the interest rate is only set for a part of the term and must subsequently be agreed again for shorter or longer periods? (sectioned loans)	1	5	5	5	(2) yes (1) no	10 0	10 0	10 0	10 0

No.	Question					Answer			
VII.6	Can the security right over real property be transferred from Bank A to Bank B and then secure new claims? (change of secured claim and creditor through transfer of the security right over real property)	0	4	5	5	(4) yes	10	10	10
						(3) yes, when also the existing secured claim is transferred form bank A to bank B (novation/ subrogation)	6	6	6
						(2) yes, if all secured claims and the relationship to the customer are transferred	2	2	2
						(1) no	0	0	0
VII.7	Can the security right over real property and secured claim be held by different persons?	0	5	4	5	(2) yes	10	10	10
						(1) no	0	0	0
VII.8	Is it possible for a Bank B as security for its outstanding loans to take over a security right over real property from Bank A, without causing the extinguishment of Bank A's secured claim or the secured claim having to be transferred to Bank B?	0	3	5	4	(2) yes	8	8	8
							2	2	2
VII.9	Is it possible to use a security right over real property established for Bank A to (additionally) secure Bank B's claims (without having to transfer the security right over real property or the claims) (bridging finance)?	0	3	5	4	(2) yes	8	8	8
						(1) no	2	2	2

Corrigendum
Band 44 vdp-Schriftenreihe

On page 146 the last part of the *Spread sheet: Weighting Ratios* is missing. This part (questions VII.10-14) is therefore printed on the following pages (146a / 146b).

VII.	Utilisation in practice	(1) bank/ enforcement	(2) bank/ usability	(3) owner	(4) legislator	specification	(1) bank/ enforcement	(2) bank/ usability	(3) owner	(4) legislator
VII.10	Can the claims of several creditors against the same debtor be secured by registering a security right over real property for a fiduciary who himself does not have a claim against the debtor? (fiduciary security right over real property – disregarding whether the fiduciary relationship would be protected in insolvency)	0	5	3	3	(2) yes		10	10	10
						(1) no		0	0	0
VII.11	If the security right over real property has been registered for one creditor, is it possible in an efficient way to do a later syndication of the loan with all creditors/syndication partners secured on the security right over real property directly?	0	5	2	3	(2) yes		10	8	10
						(1) no		0	2	0

No.	Question					Answer				
VII.12	Is a conversion of the loan where a new debtor takes over the loan (with consent of the creditor/mortgagee and the mortgagor) possible without consequences for the existence of the security right over real property?	2	2	3	2	(2) yes	10	10	10	10
						(1) no	0	0	0	0
VII.13	Is it possible to use an existing security right over real property as security for a new loan given to the purchaser when a property is transferred to a new owner?	0	2	3	2	(2) yes		10	10	10
						(1) no		0	0	0
VII.14	How can an acquirer of a security right over real property make sure that it would be effective if the owner provides him with a security right over real property or the mortgagee transfers the security right over real property to him?	0	4	2	4	(3) examination of the register is sufficient		9	9	9
						(2) he should examine the documents kept by the register		3	3	3
						(1) he should examine various agreements and documents		0	0	0

2.   Bar Graphs

- Complete findings – perspective of enforcement
- Complete findings – perspective of usability
- Complete findings – perspective of the owner
- Complete findings – perspective of the legislator
- Complete findings – total addition of all scores
- Partial findings enforcement and insolvency – perspective of enforcement
- Partial findings enforcement and insolvency – perspective of usability
- Partial findings enforcement and insolvency – perspective of the owner
- Partial findings enforcement and insolvency – perspective of the legislator
- Partial findings enforcement and insolvency – total addition of all scores

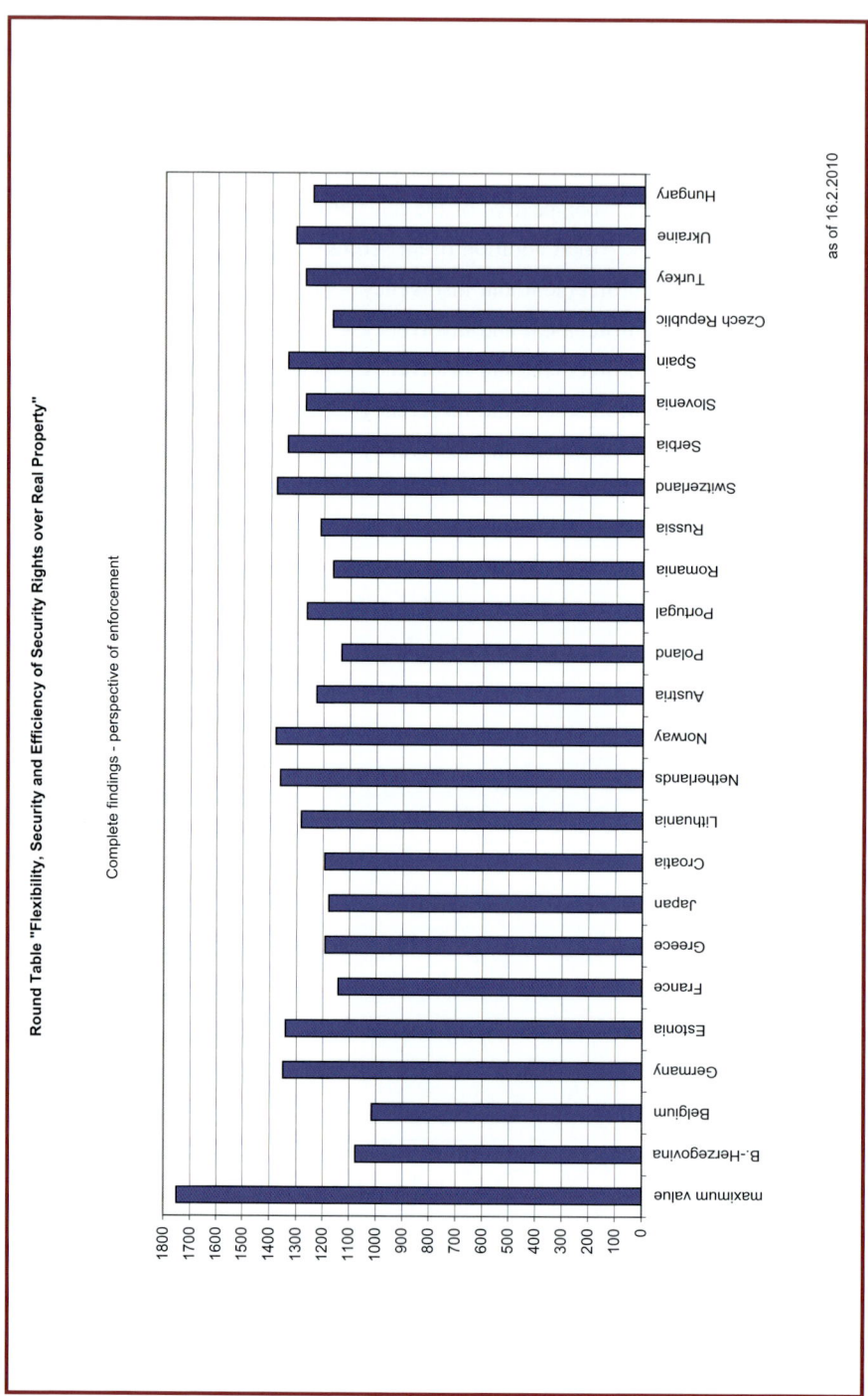

Round Table "Flexibility, Security and Efficiency of Security Rights over Real Property"

Complete findings - perspective of enforcement

as of 16.2.2010

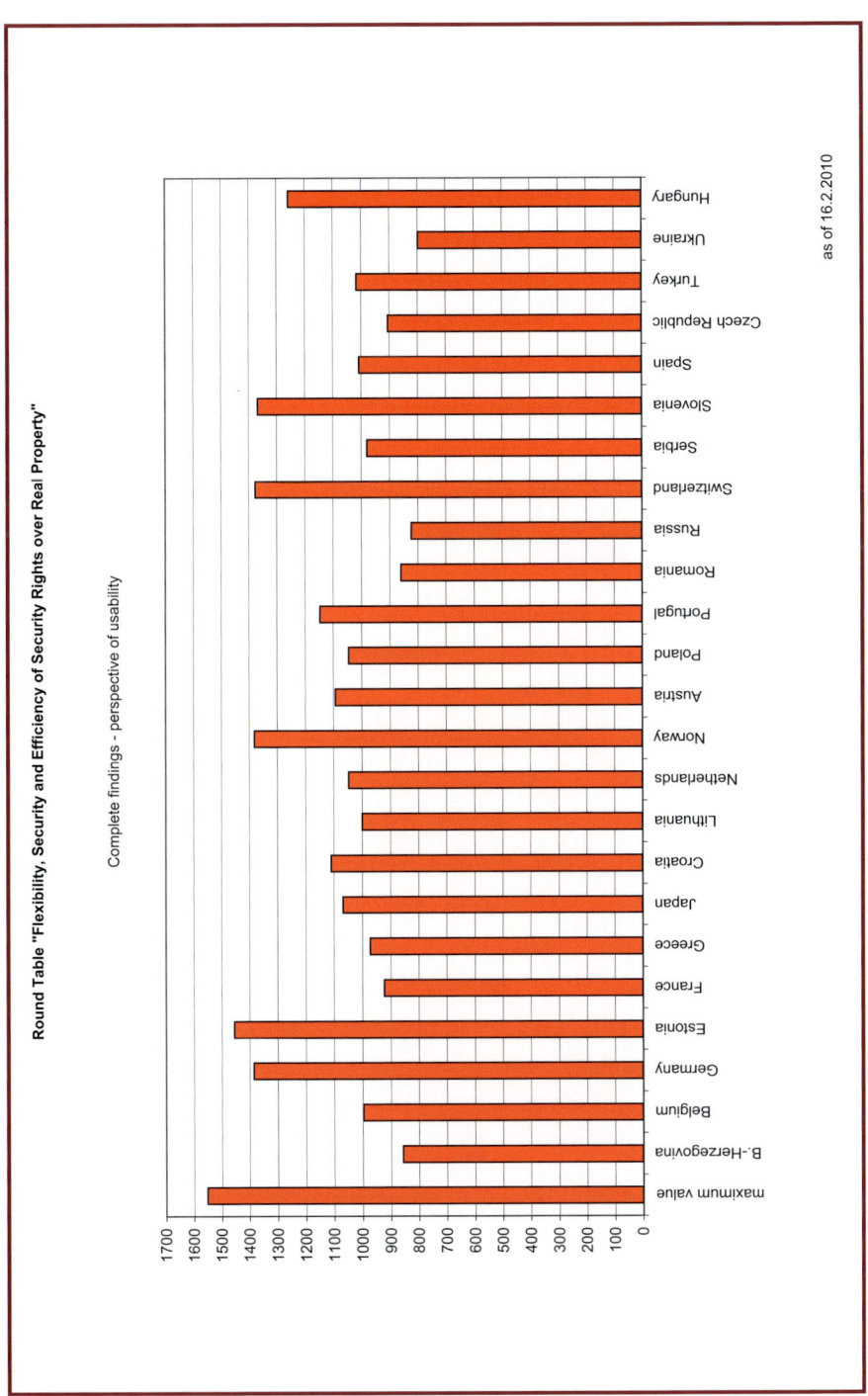

Round Table "Flexibility, Security and Efficiency of Security Rights over Real Property"

Complete findings - perspective of usability

as of 16.2.2010

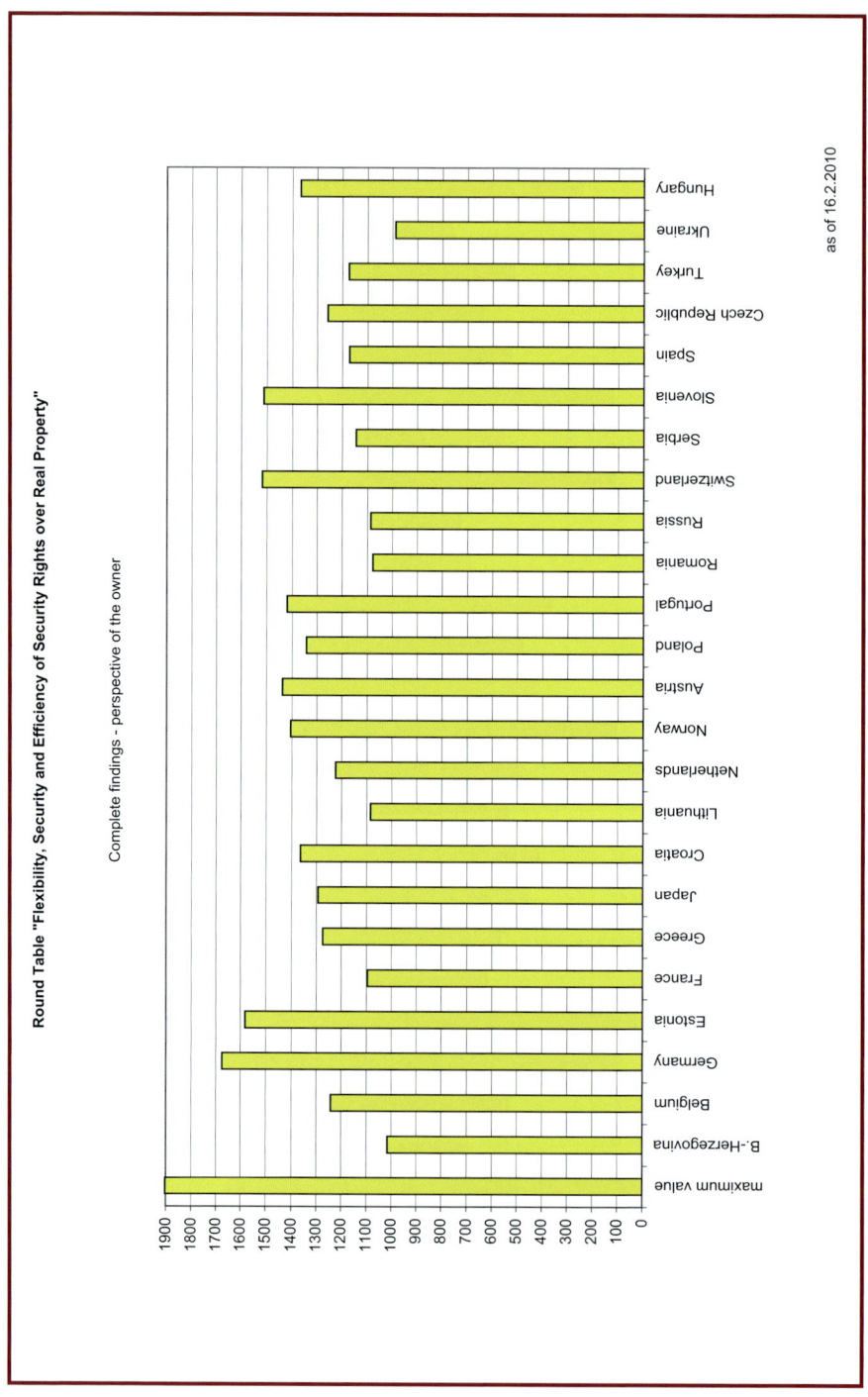

Round Table "Flexibility, Security and Efficiency of Security Rights over Real Property"

Complete findings - perspective of the owner

as of 16.2.2010

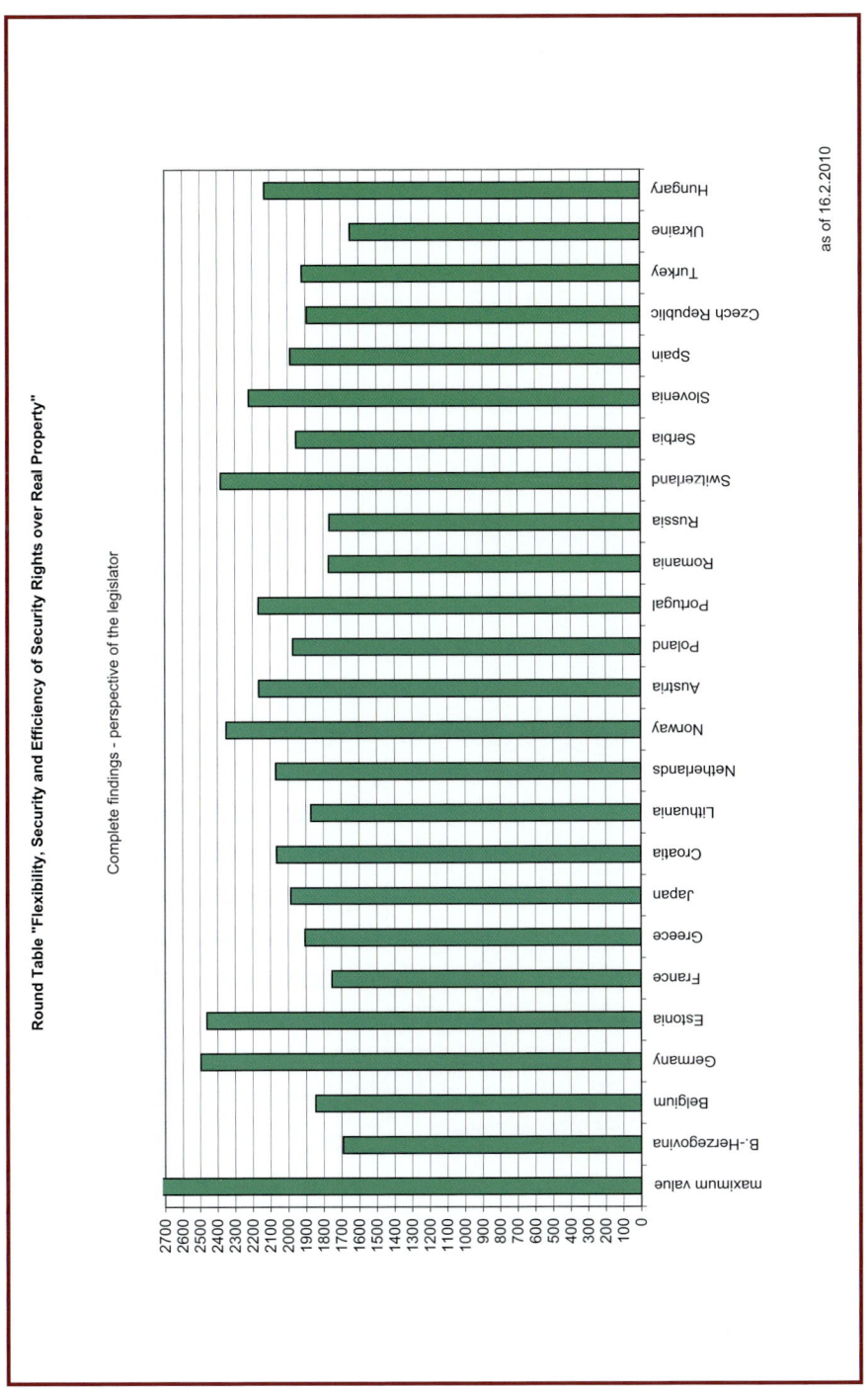

Round Table "Flexibility, Security and Efficiency of Security Rights over Real Property"

Complete findings - perspective of the legislator

as of 16.2.2010

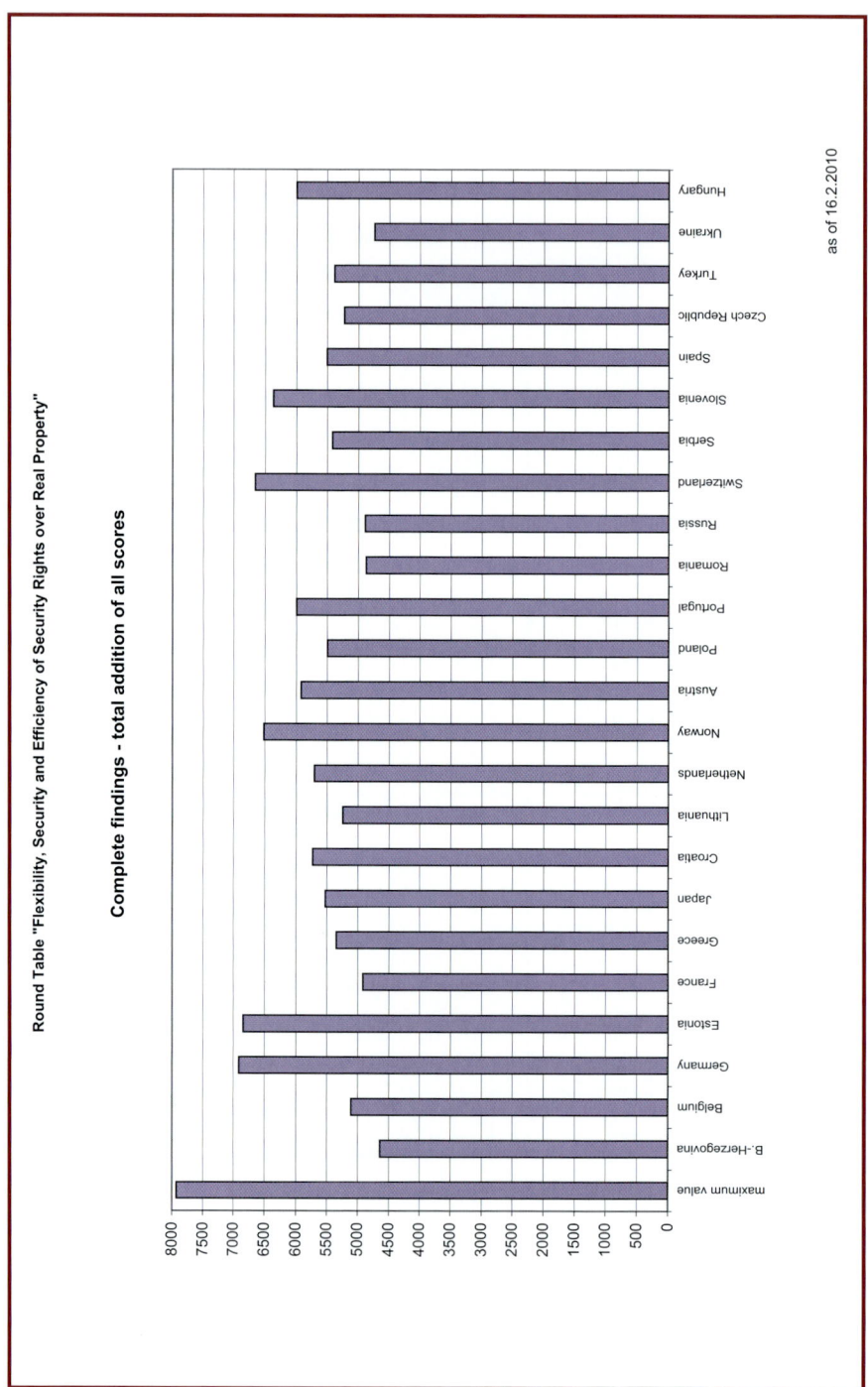

Round Table "Flexibility, Security and Efficiency of Security Rights over Real Property"

Complete findings - total addition of all scores

as of 16.2.2010

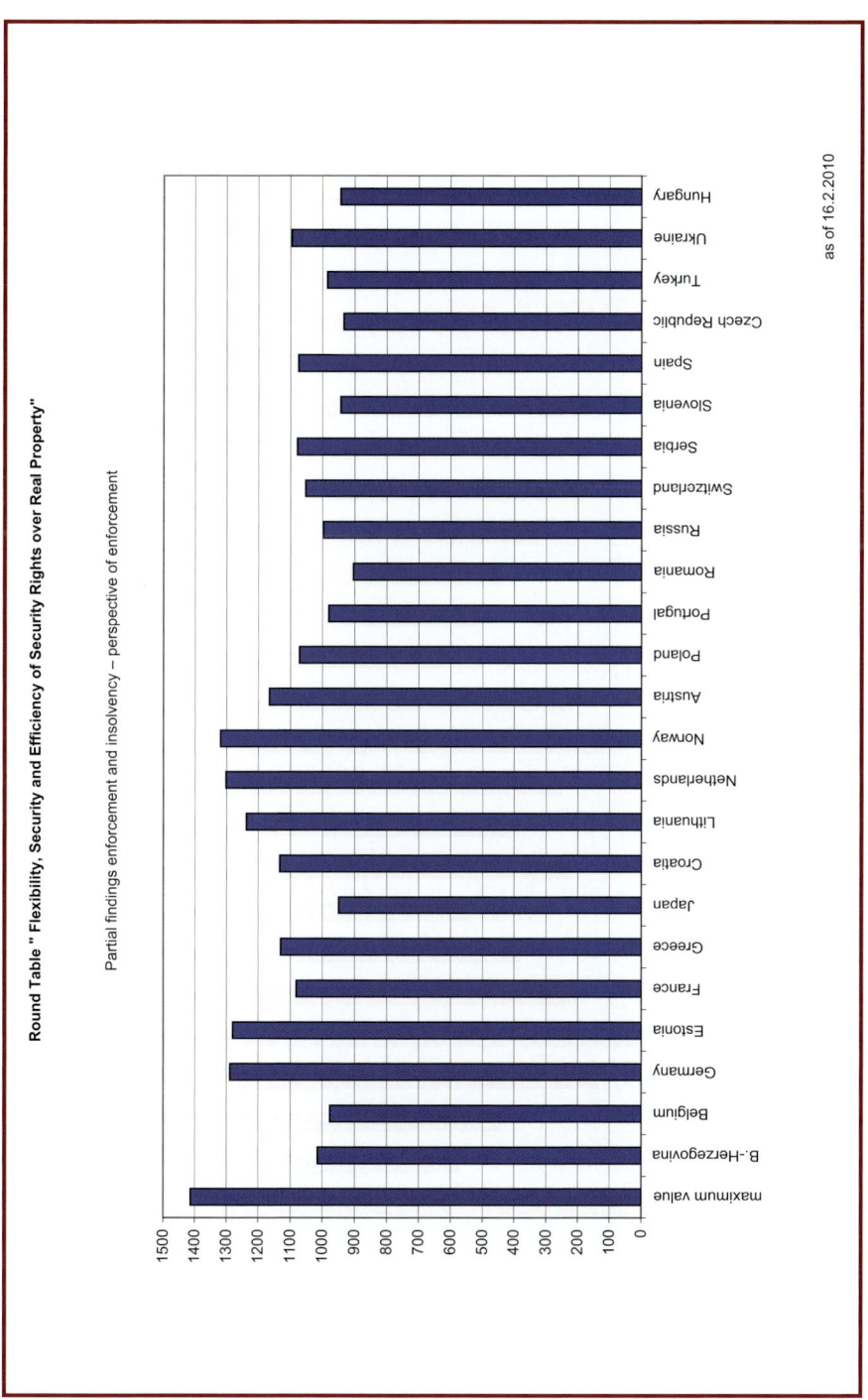

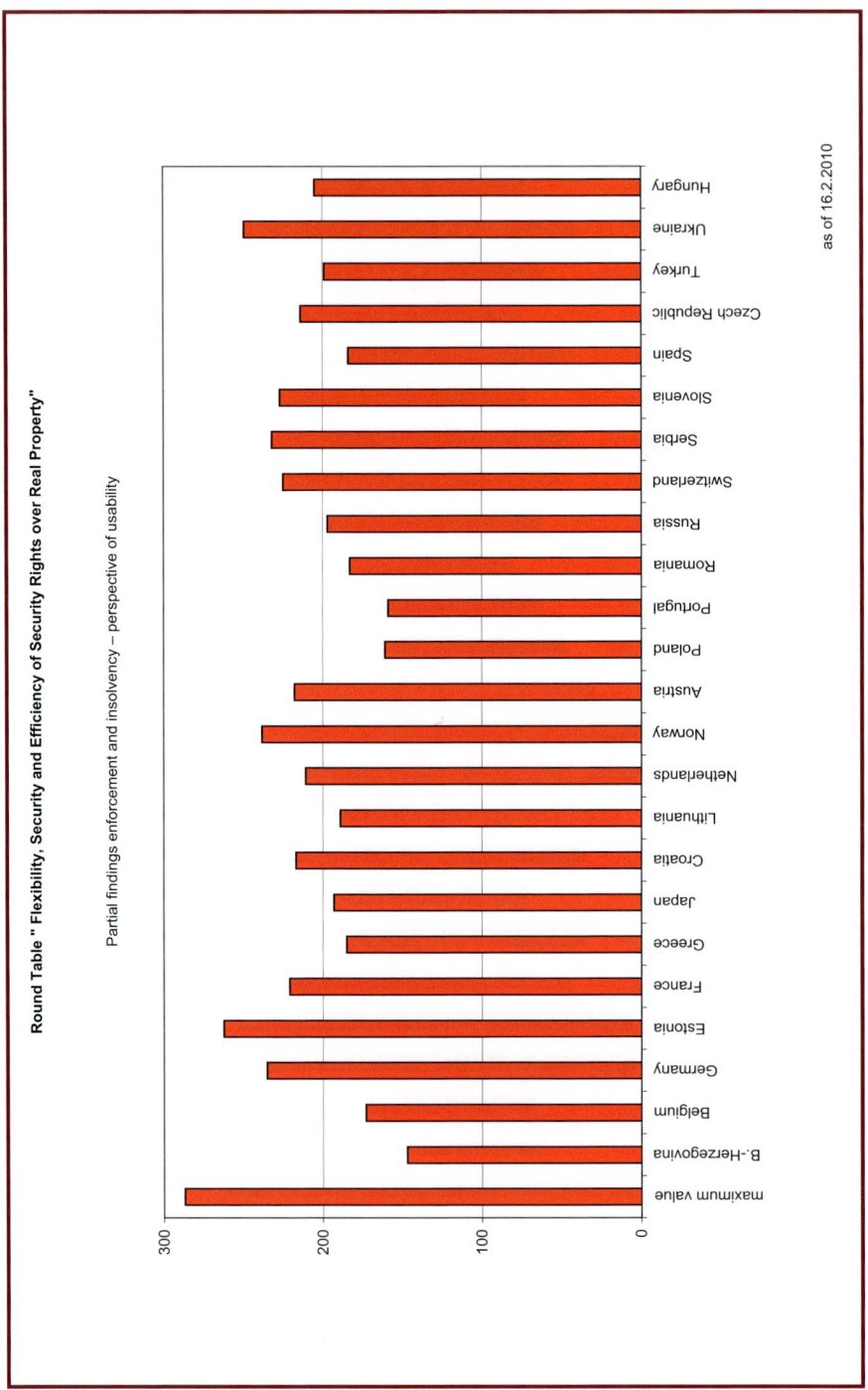

Round Table " Flexibility, Security and Efficiency of Security Rights over Real Property"

Partial findings enforcement and insolvency – perspective of usability

as of 16.2.2010

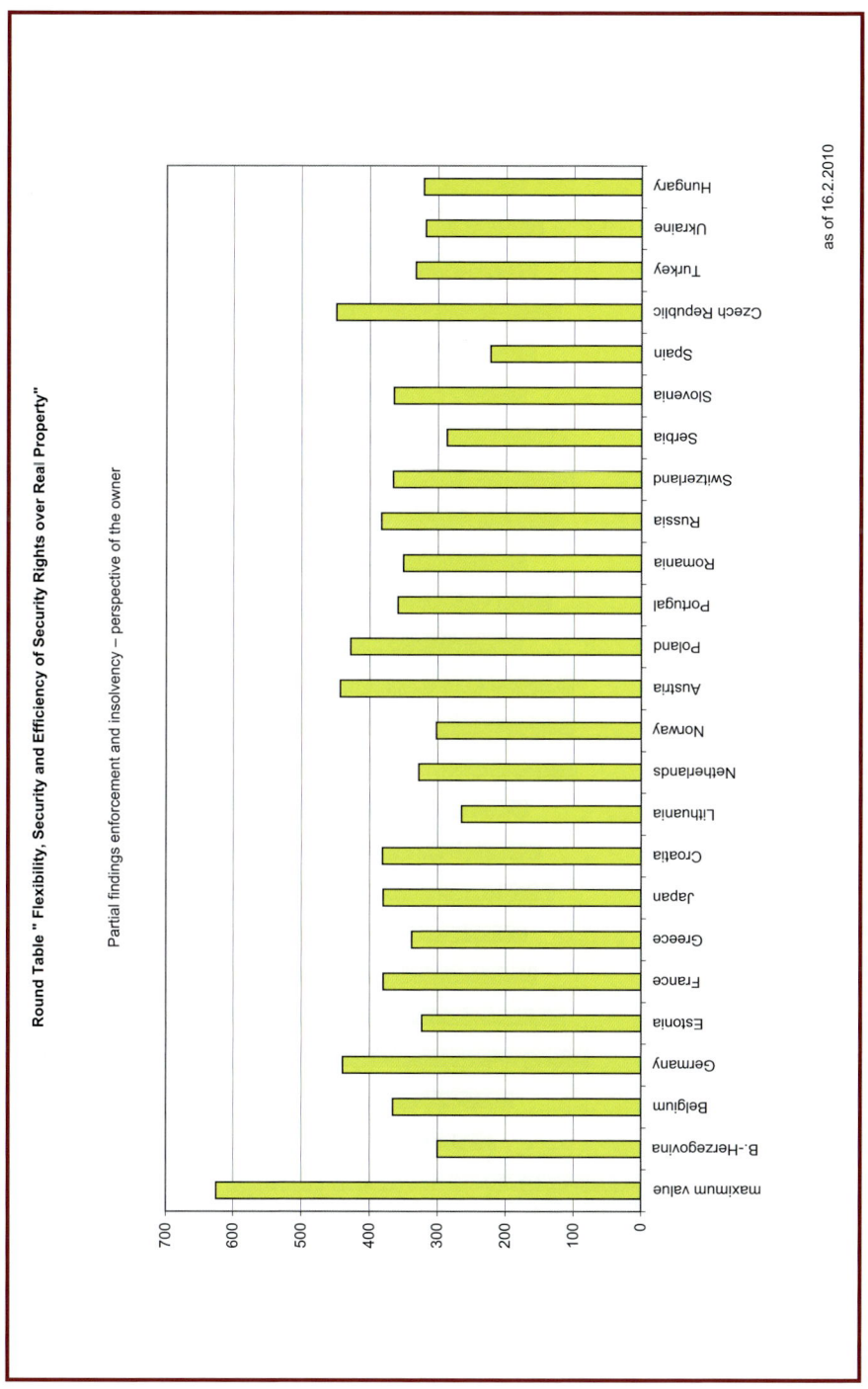

Round Table " Flexibility, Security and Efficiency of Security Rights over Real Property"

Partial findings enforcement and insolvency – perspective of the owner

as of 16.2.2010

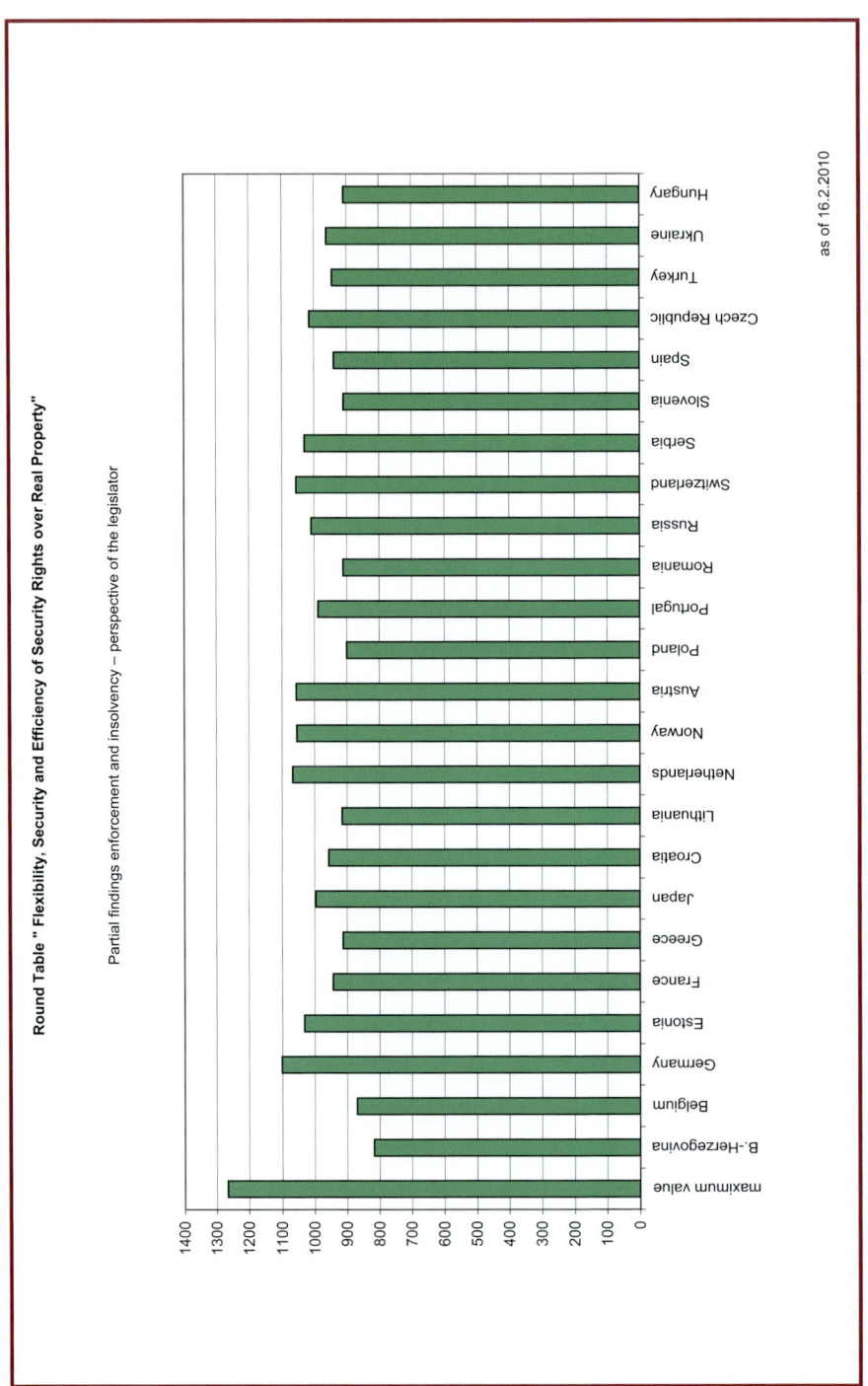

Round Table " Flexibility, Security and Efficiency of Security Rights over Real Property"

Partial findings enforcement and insolvency – perspective of the legislator

as of 16.2.2010

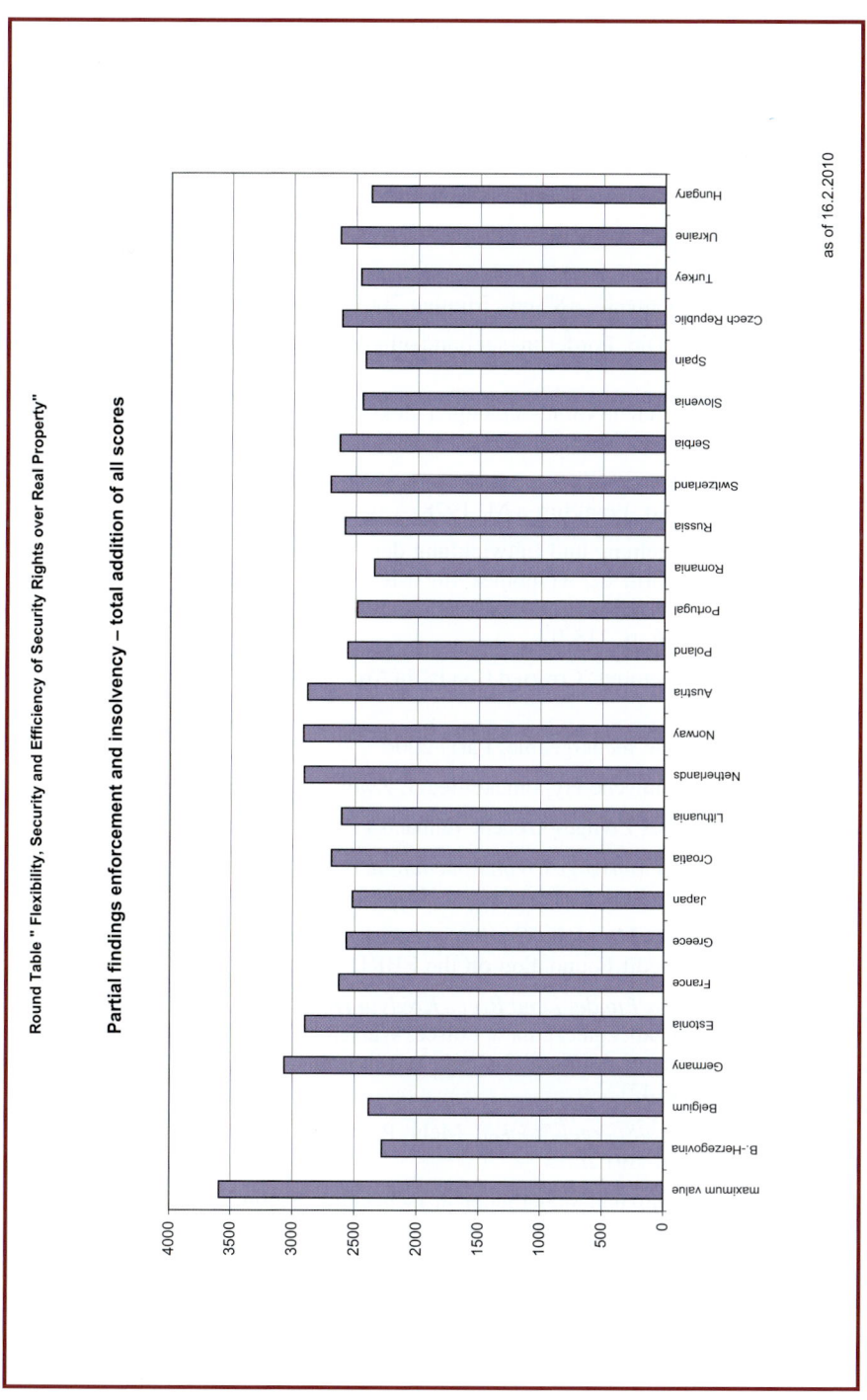

Round Table " Flexibility, Security and Efficiency of Security Rights over Real Property"

Partial findings enforcement and insolvency – total addition of all scores

as of 16.2.2010

Bibliography

Abbey/Richards, Blackstone's Guide to the Land Registration Act 2002, Oxford 2002

Aynès/Crocq, Les sûretés – La publicité foncière, Paris, 4th edition 2009

v. Bar (Publisher), Sachenrecht in Europa, Vol. 1, Osnabrück 2000; Vol. 4, Osnabrück 2002

Baur/Stürner, Sachenrecht, 18th ed., Munich 2009 (to be published shortly)

Becker-Eberhard, Die Forderungsgebundenheit der Sicherungsrechte, Bielefeld 1993

Biederer, Die rechtlichen Voraussetzungen elektronischer Grundstückstransaktionen in rechtsvergleichender Sicht, Berlin 2006 (vdp's publication series, Volume 22)

Buchholz, Abstraktionsprinzip und Immobiliarrecht – Zur Geschichte der Auflassung und der Grundschuld, Frankfurt a.M. 1978

Buchholz, Zur Entstehung und Entwicklung der "abstrakten Hypothek": die Grundschuld als Sonderform der Hypothek im ostelbischen Raum, in: Coing/Wilhelm, Wissenschaft und Kodifikation des Privatrechts im 19. Jahrhundert, Volume III, Frankfurt a.M. 1976, p. 218 ff.

Cristiá/Stöcker, Structured "Covered Bonds" in Argentina, Immobilien & Finanzierung 2007, p. 318 ff.

Dagot, L'hypothèque rechargeable, Paris 2006

Dernburg, Das preußische Hypothekenrecht, Zweite Abtheilung, Leipzig 1891

Dürr, Schweizerisches Zivilgesetzbuch, Teilband IV 2b, Das Grundpfand, Zürich 2009

Drewicz-Tułodziecka/Mortgage Credit Foundation, Basic Guidelines for a Eurohypothec, Outcome of the Eurohypothec workshop November 2004/April 2005, Warsaw 2005

Drewicz-Tułodziecka/Mortgage Credit Foundation, The expert opinion and position of the Mortgage Credit Foundation on the EBRD Report, Warsaw 2008

Drewicz-Tułodziecka/Fundacja na Rzecz Kredytu Hipotecznego, Nieruchomość jako przedmiot obrotu i zabezpieczenia w Polsce, Warschau 2008 (in German translation: Immobilien, Grundeigentum und Sicherheiten in Polen, Berlin 2009, vdp's publication series, Volume 42)

Drewicz-Tułodziecka/Soergel/Stöcker, Mehr Rechtssicherheit für die Hypothek in Polen, WM 2002, p. 891 ff.

Ebner, Grundeigentum und Sicherheiten in Tschechien, Berlin 2006 (vdp's publication series, Volume 21)

Kommission der Europäischen Gemeinschaften, Grünbuch – Hypothekarkredite in der EU, Brussels, 17.6.2005

Kommission der Europäischen Gemeinschaften, Weissbuch über die Integration der EU–Hypothekarkreditmärkte, Brussels, 18.12.2007

Europäischer Hypothekenverband, Efficiency of mortgage collateral in the European Union, Brussels 2002/2007

European Bank for Reconstruction and Development (EBRD), Mortgages in transition economies, London 2007

European Communities, The Integration of the EU Mortgage Credit Markets – Report by the Forum Group on Mortgage Credit, Brussels 2004

European Mortgage Federation (EMF), Mortgage Info October 2007, Computerisation of land registers and of registration of land and mortgage collateral in Europe

European Mortgage Federation (EMF), Efficiency of mortgage collateral in the European Union, Brussels 2002/2007

Frank/Wachter, Handbuch Immobilienrecht in Europa, Cologne 2004

Glos/Sester, Rechtliche Anforderungen an die Berücksichtigung von Kreditsicherheiten im Rahmen der SolvV, BKR 2008, p. 315 ff.

Gourio, L'hypothèque rechargeable, Revue de droit bancaire et financier, septembre-octobre 2006, p. 39 ff.

Großfeld/Heppe, The 2008 Bankruptcy of Literacy – A Legal Analysis of the Subprime Mortgage Fiasco (Part 1), DAJV-Newsletter 2009, p. 175 ff.

Habersack, Die Akzessorietät – Strukturprinzip der europäischen Zivilrechte und eines künftigen europäischen Grundpfandrechts, JZ 1997, p. 857 ff.

Habersack, Die Vollstreckungsunterwerfung des Kreditnehmers im Lichte des Risikobegrenzungsgesetzes, Neue Juristische Wochenschrift 2008, p. 3173 ff.

Heun, Der Staat und die Finanzkrise, Juristenzeitung 2010, p. 53 ff.

Hofmann, Mortgage and Change. Gestaltungsmöglichkeiten im englischen Kreditsicherungsrecht, Berlin 2002

Hurndall, England and Wales, 3.2.1 in: Property in Europe – Law and Practice, edit Anthony Hurndall, London 1998

Hypothekenverband bei der EG, Der Hypothekarkredit in der Europäischen Gemeinschaft, Bonn 1990

Hypothekenverband bei der EG, Vergleichende Studie der Grundstückspfändungsverfahren, Brussels 1979

Jaschinska, Polnische und deutsche Grundpfandrechte im Vergleich (Diss.), Berlin 2004

Jungmann, Grundpfandgläubiger und Unternehmensinsolvenz (Deutschland – England – Schottland), Cologne 2004

Kiesgen, Ein Binnenmarkt für den Hypothekarkredit – Der Vorschlag zur Einführung einer Eurohypothek unter besonderer Berücksichtigung des Sicherungsvertrages, Köln 2004 – mit einer Darstellung des deutschen, französischen und italienischen Hypothekenrechts

Kircher, Grundpfandrechte in Europa – Überlegungen zur Harmonisierung der Grundpfandrechte unter besonderer Berücksichtigung der deutschen, französischen und englischen Rechtsordnung, Berlin 2004

Knack/Keefer, Does Social Capital Have an Economic Payoff?, the Quarterly Journal of Economies, Harvard 1997, p. 1251 ff.

Köndgen/Stöcker, Die Eurohypothek – Akzessorietät als Gretchenfrage?, ZBB 2005, p. 112 ff. (114)

Kucherenko/Lassen: Ukraine, in: Stöcker, Flexibilität der Grundpfandrechte in Europa – Volume II, Berlin 2007 (vdp's publication series, Volume 32), p. 193 ff.

Langenbucher, Kredithandel nach dem Risikobegrenzungsgesetz, Neue Juristische Wochenschrift 2008, p. 3169 ff.

Lassen, Die Hypothek nach russischem Recht als Kreditsicherungsmittel, Berlin 2007 (vdp's publication series, Volume 30)

Lassen, Das neue russische Katastergesetz, Forum – Zeitschrift des Bundes der Öffentlich bestellten Vermessungsingenieure e. V. (BDVI Forum) 2009, p. 146 ff.

Lassen, Reformen im russischen Recht: Stärkung der Pfandgläubiger, WiRO 2009, p. 321 ff.

Lassen: Russland, in: Stöcker, Flexibilität der Grundpfandrechte in Europa – Band II, Berlin 2007 (vdp's publication series, Volume 32), p. 81 ff.

Legeais, Sûretés et garanties du crédit, Paris, 7th edition 2009

London Economics, The Costs and Benefits of Integration of EU Mortgage Markets, Report for European Commission, DG – Internal Market and Services, August 2005

Luckow, Germany, in EMF, Mortgage Info, Computerisation of land registers and of registration of land and mortgage collateral in Europe, Brussels October 2007

Lutter, Bankenkrise und Organhaftung, Zeitschrift für Wirtschaftsrecht 2009, p. 197 ff.

Lux, LGD-Grading – ein Baustein für die Risikosteuerung im Immobilien-finanzierungsgeschäft, in: Verband deutscher Pfandbriefbanken; Immobilien-Banking 2009 – 2010,; p. 51 ff.

Marburger, Gewichtung von Hypothekarkrediten nach neuer Solvabilitätsverordnung, Immobilien & Finanzierung 2007, p. 128 ff.

Marthinussen, Forholdet mellom panterett og pantekrav (Das Verhältnis zwischen Pfandrecht und Pfandforderung), Bergen 2009

Medicus, Die Akzessorietät im Zivilrecht, JuS 1971, p. 497 ff.

Moody's Investors Service, Moody's European Country Tiering for CMBS Recovery Rate Assumptions: Focus on Key Jurisdictions, London, 28 January, 2005

Muniz Espada/Nasarre Aznar/Sánchez Jordán, Un modelo para una Eurohipoteca – Desde el Informe Segré hasta hoy, Madrid 2008

Murray, Real Estate Conveyancing in 5 European Union Member States: A Comparative Study, Cambridge August 2007

Murray, There is no free lunch – Rechtsvergleichende Studie zu Immobilientrans-aktionen, notar 5/2008, p. 4 ff.

Nietsch, Grundschulderwerb nach dem Risikobegrenzungsgesetz – Der Ausschluss des gutgläubigen einredefreien Erwerbs nach § 1192 Ia BGB, Neue Juristische Wochenschrift 2009, p. 3606 ff.

Picherer, Sicherungsinstrumente bei Konsortialfinanzierungen von Hypotheken-banken, Frankfurt a.M. 2002 (vdp's publication series, Volume 14)

Ploeger/van Loenen, EULIS – At the Beginning of the Road to Harmonization of Land Registry in Europe, European Rev. of Private Law 2004, p. 379 ff.

Rink, Die Sicherheit von Grundpfandrechten in Deutschland und England (Diss.), Freiburg 2006

Schulz-Trieglaff, Grundschuld und Floating Charge zur Absicherung von Unterneh-menskrediten, Frankfurt/M. 1997

Shiller, The Subprime Solution: How Today's Global Financial Crisis Happened, And What To Do About It, Princeton 2008

Soergel/Stöcker, EU-Osterweiterung und dogmatische Fragen des Immobiliarsachen-rechts – Kausalität, Akzessorietät und Sicherungszweck, ZBB 2002, 412-420

Sparkes, European Land Law, Oxford, 2007

Sparkes, Real Property Law and Procedure in the European Union, Annotated Draft Questionnaire, Report from England and Wales, project is co-directed by the European University Institute (EUI) and the Deutsches Notarinstitut (DNotI), Würzburg/Ger-many (2004/2005)

Stadler, Gestaltungsfreiheit und Verkehrsschutz durch Abstraktion – eine rechtsver-gleichende Studie zur abstrakten und kausalen Gestaltung rechtsgeschäftlicher Zu-wendungen anhand des deutschen, schweizerischen, österreichischen, französischen und US-amerikanischen Rechts, Tübingen 1996

Städtler, Grundpfandrechte in der Insolvenz, Tübingen 1998

Staudinger/Wolfsteiner, Kommentar zum Bürgerlichen Gesetzbuch, Buch 3, Sachen-recht, §§ 1113 – 1203, Berlin 2002

Steven, Immobiliarsicherheiten im englischen und deutschen Recht, Frankfurt/M. 2002

Stöcker, § 86a: Grundzüge des Pfandbriefrechts, in: Schimansky/Bunte/Lwowski, Bankrechts-Handbuch, München 2007

Stöcker (ed.), Flexibilität der Grundpfandrechte in Europa, Band I, Berlin 2006 (vdp's publication series, Volume 23)

Stöcker (ed.), Flexibilität der Grundpfandrechte in Europa, Band II, Berlin 2007 (vdp's publication series, Volume 32)

Stöcker, Die Eurohypothek – Struktur einer ökonomischen Analyse, Immobilien & Finanzierung 2005, p. 766 ff.

Stöcker, Die Eurohypothek, Internationale Juristenvereinigung Osnabrück, Jahresheft 2007, p. 71 ff.

Stöcker, Die Eurohypothek – Zur Bedeutung eines einheitlichen nicht-akzessorischen Grundpfandrechts für den Aufbau eines "Europäischen Binnenmarktes für den Hypothekarkredit" mit einer Darstellung der Verwendung der Grundschuld durch die deutsche Hypothekarkreditpraxis sowie des französischen, spanischen und schweizerischen Hypothekenrechts, Berlin 1992 (zitiert: Stöcker, Die Eurohypothek)

Stöcker, Die grundpfandrechtliche Sicherung grenzüberschreitender Immobilienfi-nanzierungen, Die Eurohypothek – ein Sicherungsinstrument mit Realisierungs-chancen, WM 2006, p. 1941 ff.[170]

Stöcker/Stürner, Flexibilität, Sicherheit und Effizienz der Grundpfandrechte in Europa, Band III, Berlin 2008 (vdp's publications series, Volume 37). This book was published in an English translation: Stöcker/Stürner, Flexibility, Security and Efficiency of Security Rights Over Real Property in Europe, Volume III, Berlin 2009 (vdp's publication series, Volume 39)

Stöcker, Immobilienfinanzierung in Japan und deutsche Pfandbriefe, ZJapanR/J. Japan.L Nr. 28 (2009), p. 205 ff.

Stürner, Das Grundpfandrecht zwischen Akzessorietät und Abstraktheit und die eu-ropäische Zukunft, Festschrift für Rolf Serick, Heidelberg 1992, p. 377 ff.

Stürner, Der Schutz des Eigentümers bei rechtsgeschäftlicher Übertragung von Grundp-fandrechten und die jüngste Reform des Rechts der Grundschuld, in Festschrift für Dieter Medicus zum 80. Geburtstag, p. 513 ff., Köln 2009

Stürner/Kern, Grundsatzfragen des US-Hypothekenrechts, in Schwenzer/Hager (Hrsg.) Festschrift für Peter Schlechtriem, 2003, p. 923 ff.

Stürner/Kern, Deutsche Hypothekenpfandbriefe und U.S.-amerikanische Deckungs-werte, 2007

Stürner/Stadler, Hypothekenpfandbriefe und Deckungswerte in der Schweiz, Berlin 2007 (vdp's publication series, Volume 31)

Tiemer, Introduction, in EMF, Mortgage Info, Computerisation of land registers and of registration of land and mortgage collateral in Europe, Brussels October 2007, p. 1 f.

Trotz, Aspekte der Bewertung: Rating, Securitisation und Standardisierung, Immo-bilien & Finanzierung 2004, p. 78 f.

vdp, Annual Report 2007

Wachter, Die Eurohypothek – Grenzüberschreitende Kreditsicherung an Grundstücken im Europäischen Binnenmarkt, WM 1999, p. 49 ff.

Wehrens, Der Schweizer Schuldbrief und die deutsche Briefgrundschuld, Ein Rechts-vergleich als Basis einer zukünftigen Eurohypothek, Österreichische Notarzeitung (ÖNotZ) 1988, p. 181 ff.

Wehrens, Real Security Regarding Immovable Objects – Reflection on a Euro-Mortgage, in: Towards a European Civil Code, The Hague/London/Boston 1998, p. 551 ff.

Wehrens, Überlegungen zu einer Eurohypothek, WM 1992, p. 557 ff.

Wolfsteiner/Stöcker, Nicht-akzessorisches Grundpfand für Mitteleuropa, ZBB 1998, p. 264 ff., und DNotZ 1999, p. 451 ff. (in English translation – A non-accessory Security Right over Real Property for Central Europe – appeared in Notarius International 2003, p. 116 ff.).

Zevenbergen, Registration of property rights; a systems approach – Similar tasks, but different roles, Notarius International 2003, p. 125 ff.a

Zywicki/Adamson, The Law and Economics of Subprime Lending, University of Colorado Law Review, Vol. 80, No. 1, Winter 2009, p. 1 ff.

---

170 This contribution has also been published in English translation: Stöcker, Real estate liens as security for cross-border property finance, The Eurohypothec – a security instrument with real prospects, Revista Crítica de Derecho Inmobiliario, Madrid 2007, p. 2255 et seq.

In der Schriftenreihe des Verbandes deutscher Pfandbriefbanken erschienen bisher:

Bühler/Hies/Zimmermann:
Liquidität für den deutschen Pfandbrief
Fritz Knapp Verlag, 1996
ISBN 3 7819 0575 6
Band 1

Hies:
**Refinanzierung deutscher Hypotheken-
banken – Gegenwart und Zukunft**
Fritz Knapp Verlag, 1996
ISBN 3 7819 0578 0
Band 2

Dübel/Pfeiffer:
**Risikogewichtete Eigenkapital-
anforderungen und die Risiken des
gewerblichen Hypothekarkredites
in Europa**
Fritz Knapp Verlag, 1996
ISBN 3 7819 0585 3
(auch in Englisch)
Band 3

Gluch:
**Gewerbliche Bauinvestitionen in
ausgewählten EU-Staaten Entwicklung
und Strukturen seit 1980**
Fritz Knapp Verlag, 1997
ISBN 3 7819 0595 0
Band 4

Stöcker:
**Die Hypothekenbanken und der
Pfandbrief in den mitteleuropäischen
Reformländern**
Fritz Knapp Verlag, 1998
ISBN 3 7819 0627 2
Band 5

Verband deutscher
Hypothekenbanken (Hrsg.):
**Die Steuerreform aus immobilien-
wirtschaftlicher Sicht – Materialien**
Fritz Knapp Verlag, 1998
ISBN 3 7819 0629 9
Band 6

Stürner:
**Die Sicherung der Pfandbrief-
und Obligationengläubiger vor einer
Insolvenz der Hypothekenbank –
Geltendes Recht und Reformvorschläge**
Fritz Knapp Verlag, 1998
ISBN 3 7189 0633 7
Band 7

Köndgen/Dübel/Lea:
**Die vorzeitige Rückzahlung von
Festzinskrediten. Eine rechtsvergleichende
und ökonomische Analyse**
Fritz Knapp Verlag, 2000
ISBN 3 7819 061 5
Band 8

Stürner/Stadler:
**Deutsche Pfandbriefe und
Deckungswerte in den Niederlanden
Ein Gutachten**
Fritz Knapp Verlag, 2000
ISBN 3 7819 0655 8
Band 9

Stürner/Schumacher/Bruns:
**Der deutsche Pfandbrief und
englische Deckungswerte**
Fritz Knapp Verlag, 2000
ISBN 3 7819 0656 6
Band 10

Verband deutscher
Hypothekenbanken (Hrsg.):
**Struktur und Entwicklung der
Eigenheim- und Gewerbefinanzierung
der deutschen Hypothekenbanken**
Fritz Knapp Verlag, 2000
ISBN 3 7819 0663 9
Band 11

Birg:
Trends der Bevölkerungsentwicklung
Fritz Knapp Verlag, 2000
ISBN 3 7819 0668 X
Band 12

Rüchardt:
Der Beleihungswert
Fritz Knapp Verlag 2001
ISBN 2 8314 0715 0
(auch in Englisch)
Band 13

Picherer:
**Sicherungsinstrumente bei Konsortial-
finanzierungen von Hypothekenbanken**
Fritz Knapp Verlag, 2002
ISBN 3 8314 0718 5
Band 14

Stürner/Stadler:
Pfandbriefe und Beleihung in Spanien
Fritz Knapp Verlag, 2002
ISBN 3 8314 0734 7
Band 15

Schätzl:
**Strukturwandel im Gewerbe-
immobilienmarkt**
Fritz Knapp Verlag, 2002
ISBN 3 8324 0729 0
Band 16

Schmidt:
**Absicherung von Darlehen
durch Grundpfandrechte**
Fritz Knapp Verlag, 2004
ISBN 3 8314 0761 4
Band 17

Stöcker:
Realkredit und Pfandbriefsicherheit
Fritz Knapp Verlag, 2004
ISBN 3 8314 0769 X
Band 18

Stürner:
**Deutsche öffentliche Pfandbriefe
und Deckungswerte aus Darlehen
an US-amerikanische öffentliche
Körperschaften**
Fritz Knapp Verlag, 2005
ISBN 3 8314 0787 8
Band 19

Dübel/Köndgen:
**Die vorzeitige Rückzahlung von Festzins-
krediten in Europa – Zwei Gutachten**
Fritz Knapp Verlag, 2006
ISBN 3-8314-0796-7
Band 20

Ebner:
**Grundeigentum und Sicherheiten
in Tschechien**
Hrsg.: vdp, in Zusammenarbeit mit dem Center
of Legal Comptence (CLC), Wien 2006
ISBN 3-9811273-0-7
Band 21

Biederer:
**Die rechtlichen Voraussetzungen
elektronischer Grundstückstransaktionen
in rechtsvergleichender Sicht**
Hrsg.: vdp, 2006
ISBN 3-9811273-1-5
Band 22

Stöcker:
**Flexibilität der Grundpfandrechte
in Europa Band I**
Hrsg.: vdp, 2006
ISBN 3-9811273-2-3
Band 23

Stürner/Kern:
**Deutsche öffentliche Pfandbriefe und
japanische Deckungswerte**
Hrsg.: vdp, 2006
ISBN 3-9811273-3-1
Band 24

**Rechtsfragen der Immobilienfinanzierung
in England und Wales**
Hrsg.: vdp, 2006
ISBN 978-3-9811273-4-8
Band 25

Voigtländer/Hofer:
**Mietwohnungsmarkt und Wohneigentum –
Zwei Gutachten**
Hrsg.: vdp, 2006
ISBN: 978-3-9811273-5-5
Band 26

Ebner/Illa:
**Grundeigentum und Sicherheiten
in Ungarn**
Hrsg.: vdp in Zusammenarbeit mit dem
Center of Legal Competence (CLC),
Wien, 2007
ISBN: 978-3-9811273-6-2
Band 27

Stürner/Kern:
**Deutsche Hypothekenpfandbriefe und
U.S.-amerikanische Deckungswerte**
Hrsg.: vdp, 2007
ISBN: 978-3-9811273-8-6
Band 28

Sacalschi:
**Grundeigentum und Sicherheiten
in Rumänien**
Hrsg.: vdp in Zusammenarbeit mit dem
Center of Legal Competence (CLC),
Wien, 2007
ISBN: 978-3-9811273-9-3
Band 29

Lassen:
**Die Hypothek nach russischem Recht
als Kreditsicherungsmittel**
Hrsg.: vdp, 2007
ISBN: 978-3-9811816-0-9
Band 30

Stürner/Stadler:
**Hypothekenpfandbriefe und
Deckungswerte in der Schweiz**
Hrsg.: vdp, 2007
ISBN: 978-3-9811816-1-6
Band 31

Stöcker:
**Flexibilität der Grundpfandrechte
in Europa Band II**
Hrsg.: vdp, 2007
ISBN: 978-3-9811816-2-3
Band 32

Crimmann/Rüchardt:
**Der Beleihungswert
– Zwei Teile –**
Hrsg.: vdp, 2008
ISBN: 978-3-9811816-3-0
Band 33

Stessl:
**Real Property Rights in the
Slovak Republic**
Hrsg.: vdp in Zusammenarbeit mit dem
Center of Legal Competence (CLC), 2008
ISBN: 978-3-9811816-4-7
Band 34

Stoimenov/Ivanov:
**Grundeigentum und Sicherheiten
in Bulgarien**
Hrsg.: vdp in Zusammenarbeit mit dem
Center of Legal Competence (CLC), 2008
ISBN: 978-3-9811816-5-4
Band 35

Linkert:
**Insolvenzrechtliche Risiken bei
Asset-Backed Securities**
Berlin, 2008
ISBN: 978-3-9811816-6-1
Band 36

Stöcker/Stürner:
**Flexibilität, Sicherheit und Effizienz der
Grundpfandrechte in Europa Band III**
Berlin, 2008
ISBN: 978-3-9811816-7-8
Band 37

Rudolf/Saunders:
**Refinancing Real Estate Loans –
Lessons to be Learned from the
Subprime Crisis**
Berlin, 2009
ISBN: 978-3-9811816-8-5
Band 38

Stöcker/Stürner
**Flexibility, Security and
Efficiency of Security Rights over
Real Property in Europe Volume III**
Berlin, 2008
ISBN 978-3-9811816-9-2
Band 39

Crimmann/Rüchardt:
Mortgage Lending Value
Berlin, 2009
ISBN 978-3-9811816-3-0
Band 40

Dimitar Stoimenov/Boris Ivanov
**Die Durchsetzung von Forderungen
in der Zwangsvollstreckung und
Insolvenz in Bulgarien**
Hrsg.: vdp in Zusammenarbeit mit dem
Center of Legal Competence (CLC),
Berlin/Wien, 2009
ISBN 978-3-9812784-0-8
Band 41

Sammelband unter redaktioneller Leitung
von Agnieszka Drewicz-Tułodziecka:
**Immobilien, Grundeigentum und
Sicherheiten in Polen**
Hrsg.: vdp in Zusammenarbeit mit dem
Center of Legal Competence (CLC),
Berlin, 2010
ISBN 978-3-9812784-1-5
Band 42

Otmar M. Stöcker/Rolf Stürner
**Flexibilität, Sicherheit und Effizienz
der Grundpfandrechte in Europa
Band III**
Berlin, 2010
ISBN 978-3-9812784-2-2
Band 43